Gentrification of the City

EDITED BY

NEIL SMITH and
PETER WILLIAMS

Boston
UNWIN HYMAN
London   Sydney

**Allen & Unwin Inc., 8 Winchester Place, Winchester, Mass. 01890,
USA**

The US Company of
Unwin Hyman Ltd
15/17 Broadwick Street, London W1V 1FP, UK

Allen & Unwin (Australia) Ltd,
8 Napier Street, North Sydney, NSW 2060, Australia

First published in 1986
Reprinted 1988

Library of Congress Cataloguing in Publication Data

Main entry under title:
    Gentrification of the city.
Bibliography: p.
Includes index.
1. Gentrification – Addresses, essays, lectures.
2. Urban renewal – Addresses, essays, lectures.
I. Smith, Neil.   II. Williams, Peter, 1947–
HT170.G46 1986   307.2   85-22889
ISBN 0-04-301201-9
ISBN 0-04-301202-7 (pbk.)

British Library Cataloguing in Publication Data
Smith, Neil
    Gentrification of the city.
1. Social mobility   2. Social classes   3. Cities and towns
I. Title   II. Williams, Peter
305'.09173'2   HT609
ISBN 0-04-301201-9
ISBN 0-04-301202-7 Pbk

Set in 10 on 11 point Bembo by
Computape (Pickering) Ltd, North Yorkshire
and printed in Great Britain by
Billing and Son Ltd, London and Worcester

Preface

This book seeks to present alternatives to the mainstream discussions of gentrification. It does not present a single coherent vision of the causes, effects and experiences of gentrification, but a number of different views that do not always coincide. What the authors have in common is the attempt to escape a naive empiricism which has dominated much mainstream research, as well as the conviction that questions of social class lie at the heart of this issue. With one exception, the chapters are original, unpublished contributions.

In the several years it has taken to compile this collection, a number of people have helped us. We would like to thank the authors who have had little choice but to be patient when transoceanic editorial coordination was not always as efficient as it might have been. Our greatest debt is to Linda Cranor who criticized the work at every stage and who organized and typed the manuscript. Several people provided comments and advice on different parts of the manuscript, especially Liz Cocke, Hal Kendig, Helga Leitner, Pat Mullins and Alan Murie. Among the contributors, Chris Hamnett and Bob Beauregard offered useful editorial comments. Finally, Tetsuji Uchiyama drew the maps in Chapter 8 with great speed and skill. Our thanks to him and all who have contributed to the enterprise.

We are indebted to the editors of the *Urban Lawyer*, published by the American Bar Association, for permission to reprint in revised form the piece by LeGates and Hartman (Ch. 9). This originally appeared in the *Urban Lawyer* **31** (1982).

NEIL SMITH and PETER WILLIAMS

Cover background photograph courtesy of Professor M. H. Port, Queen Mary College.

Contents

vii

CONTENTS

List of tables

Contributors

Robert A. Beauregard is an associate professor in the Department of Urban Planning and Policy Development, Rutgers University. His teaching and research concerns economic restructuring, urban decline and redevelopment, urban economic development and planning theory. He co-authored *Revitalizing cities* with Briavel Holcomb and has written recently on gentrification, the occupation of planning, planning theory and the spatial restructuring of central business districts. Dr Beauregard is a member of Planners Network, an organization of progressive planners, and sits on its Executive Committee.

Roman A. Cybriwsky is Associate Professor of Geography and Urban Studies at Temple University and past Director of the urban studies program there. His PhD is from Pennsylvania State University and he has researched the gentrification in Philadelphia, especially in the Fairmont section where he lives. He is co-author of *Philadelphia: a study of conflict and social cleavages*, published by Ballinger. He is Chairperson of the Urban Geography Specialty Group of the Association of American Geographers, and has just completed a year at the Temple University in Japan.

Chris Hamnett is a lecturer in geography at the Open University, Milton Keynes (UK). He has held visiting positions at the University of Kent, London School of Economics and the University of British Columbia and he has recently been appointed to the Bannekar Visiting Research Professorship at the Center for Washington Area Studies, George Washington University. His principal interest is in the relationships between labour market, housing market and social change and he is currently directing an ESRC funded research project in London on this issue. He is currently research director of a government inquiry into the management problems of privately owned apartment blocks in Britain.

Chester Hartman is a Fellow at the Institute for Policy Studies in Washington, DC. He holds a PhD in City and Regional Planning from Harvard University and has taught there, as well as at Cornell, the University of North Carolina, Yale, and the University of California at Berkeley. He chairs the Planners Network, a national organization of progressive urban and rural planners. Among his books are: *The transformation of San Francisco* (Rowman and Allanheld 1984), *America's housing crisis: what is to be done?* (Routledge & Kegan Paul 1983), *Displacement: how to fight it* (National Housing Law Project 1982), and *Critical perspectives on housing,* co-edited with Rachel Bratt and Ann Meyerson (Temple Univ. Press 1985, in press).

Michael Jager has recently completed his PhD in sociology at La Trobe University, Melbourne. The chapter is part of his thesis. He has studied in Australia and France and is interested in French sociology and the middle strata of advanced societies.

Richard T. LeGates is Associate Professor of Urban Studies at San Francisco State University. He is a member of the California Bar and author of *City lights* (Oxford University Press 1981).

David Ley is Professor of Geography at the University of British Columbia in Vancouver. A graduate of Oxford and Pennsylvania State University, his empirical research has been concerned with a range of inner-city issues. He is author of *The Black inner city as frontier outpost* (1974) and *A social geography of the city* (1983), and co-editor of *Humanistic geography and ethnic pluralism* (1984). He is currently completing a three year study on inner-city change in the Canadian urban system.

Peter Marcuse is a Professor of Urban Planning at Columbia University. He has been Chairperson of the Los Angeles City Planning Commission, and is presently Chair of the Housing Committee of Community Board 9 of New York City. He is author of "The myth of the benevolent state", "Housing abandonment; does rent control make a difference?", "Housing in the history of city planning", and numerous other articles. His primary interests are in housing policy, city planning, and urban history. He is a member of the Planners Network and the American Institute of Certified Planners.

Bill Randolph is a Research Fellow at the Faculty of Social Science, the Open University, Milton Keynes (UK). He graduated from the London School of Economics, where he is now in the process of completing a doctoral thesis on housing market and labour market polarization in London. His main research interests include contemporary processes of residential restructuring: housing and employment linkages, and population movement.

Neil Smith is Assistant Professor of Geography at Columbia University. He has written numerous papers on gentrification and is the author of *Uneven Development: nature, capital and the production of space*. His current research includes work on deindustrialization and an historical analysis of the career of Isaiah Bowman, as well as empirical work on gentrification in New York City. He is on the Board of Directors of the Urban Geography Specialty Group of the Association of American Geographers.

John Western is Associate Professor of Geography at Syracuse University. After studying at Jesus College, Oxford, he gained a BA in geography in 1968. In 1972 the University of Western Ontario conferred his MA, after fieldwork on racial–ethnic patterns in the Louisiana bayou country. In 1978 he gained his PhD from the University of California, Los Angeles, following a two-year research scholarship at the University of Cape Town; *Outcast Cape Town* (Minneapolis: University of Minnesota Press and London: George Allen & Unwin and Cape Town: Human & Rousseau 1981) resulted. He has also taught at the Ohio State University in Columbus and Temple University in Philadelphia. His research interests revolve around ethnic and racial cleavages in both Third World and revitalizing North American cities.

Peter Williams is Assistant Director at the Institute of Housing, London. Previously he worked at the Australian National University and the University of Birmingham, England. He has undertaken research on housing markets in Britain and Australia and has published papers and monographs on housing, social theory, urban change and gentrification. He has edited *Conflict and development* (Allen & Unwin 1984), *Social process and the city* (Allen & Unwin 1983) and co-edited *Urban political economy and social theory* (Gower 1982). He is co-author of *Public housing and market rents in South Australia* (Australian Housing Research Council 1984) and *Salvation and despair: home ownership in the inner city* (Gower 1985). He is currently preparing books on home ownership (with A. Murie and R. Forrest) and urban geography, and co-editing a volume on class and space. He is on the editorial boards of *Environment and Planning A, Society and Space* and *Housing Studies*.

1

Alternatives to orthodoxy: invitation to a debate

NEIL SMITH and PETER WILLIAMS

On definitions

More than 20 years have passed since the term "gentrification" was first used. Originating in Britain, gentrification has become a popular concept in the United States, where its terminological debut in established dictionaries was an unheralded but nonetheless significant event. According to the *American Heritage* dictionary of 1982, gentrification is the "restoration of deteriorated urban property especially in working-class neighborhoods by the middle and upper classes." In similar vein, the *Oxford American* dictionary of two years earlier contains the following definition: "movement of middle class families into urban areas causing property values to increase and having secondary effect of driving out poorer families."

It is remarkable how quickly this quite specific definition of a new process has become institutionalized. The explanation probably lies in the speed with which gentrification has proceeded in the urban landscape, and its high visibility in the popular press as well as academic circles. Even more remarkable is the fact that in a society and in a period when class analysis is widely held to be an historical or geographical anomaly – a holdover from the 19th century or quaintly Old World – these dictionary definitions embrace a class analysis of gentrification without the least hint of squeamishness. The temptation to dilute the phraseology must have been considerable, but perhaps the most remarkable thing of all is that with the process itself developing rapidly, these highly innovative definitions may already be outdated.

As the terminology suggests, "gentrification" connotes a process which operates in the residential housing market. It refers to the rehabilitation of working-class and derelict housing and the consequent transformation of an area into a middle-class neighborhood.

1

Much of the early research focused on immediate empirical questions: Where is the process occurring? How widespread is it? Who are the gentrifiers (their age, race, income, life-style, occupation)? This empirical documentation marked a first phase of research into a newly emerging process. With few exceptions, the focus was on the gentrifying middle class, not the displaced working class, and on the gentrifying neighborhood, not the location and fate of displacees. Although often detached in tone, much of this early empirical work represented an uncritical celebration of the process and was at times indistinguishable from the fiscal boosterism which permeated treatments of gentrification in the popular and parochial press, especially in the United States. As such the emphasis was on effects rather than causes; the causes were generally taken for granted, but the effects were hailed by many as a timely answer to inner-city decay, and research was often oriented toward extrapolation of statistical trends and public-policy prescriptions. This empirical phase still dominates the North American literature (James 1977, Laska & Spain 1980, Schill & Nathan 1983, Gale 1984).

A second phase of research, with its origins in Britain, emerged in the late 1970s. This work emphasizes causation over effect, theoretical analysis over statistical documentation. This second phase of research tended to see gentrification not as a unique and isolated process but as integral to the broader spheres of the housing and urban land markets. Several authors attempted to explain the phenomenon in terms of public and private policies toward housing (Hamnett 1973, Williams 1976, 1978, Kendig 1979). This led, in turn, to further theoretical attempts to explain gentrification (Smith 1979a, Berry 1980b, Ley 1980) and to set it in the context of uneven development and the massive restructuring of urban space and urban land uses that is currently under way (Holcomb & Beauregard 1981, Smith 1982, Anderson et al. 1983). Sufficient of this work has been done to allow for the recent appearance of two comprehensive and critical reviews of theoretical work on gentrification (Hamnett 1984a, Rose 1984). If some of this latter work was necessarily theoretical to the virtual exclusion of empirical analysis, the pendulum is now swinging back, and the present volume presents essays that incorporate the theoretical work of recent years and attempt to deepen our understanding of the causes of the process.

If we look back at the attempted definitions of gentrification, it should be clear that we are concerned with a process much broader than merely residential rehabilitation. Even into the late 1970s, this particular definition of gentrification vis-à-vis redevelopment may have made some sense. But as the process has continued, it has

2

become increasingly apparent that residential rehabilitation is ⟨
one facet (if a highly publicized and highly visible one) of a m
profound economic, social, and spatial restructuring. In realit⟩,
residential gentrification is integrally linked to the redevelopment of
urban waterfronts for recreational and other functions, the decline
of remaining inner-city manufacturing facilities, the rise of hotel and
convention complexes and central-city office developments, as well
as the emergence of modern "trendy" retail and restaurant districts.
Underlying all of these changes in the urban landscape are specific
economic, social and political forces that are responsible for a major
reshaping of advanced capitalist societies: there is a restructured
industrial base, a shift to service employment and a consequent
transformation of the working class, and indeed of the class structure in general; and there are shifts in state intervention and political
ideology aimed at the privatization of consumption and service
provision. Gentrification is a visible spatial component of this social
transformation. A highly dynamic process, it is not amenable to
overly restrictive definitions; rather than risk constraining our
understanding of this developing process by imposing definitional
order, we should strive to consider the broad range of processes that
contribute to this restructuring, and to understand the links between
seemingly separate processes.

Invitation to a debate

Capital and class are recurrent themes that run throughout this
collection. All of the authors look to capital and class, albeit in
different ways, in an effort to understand the causes and effects of
gentrification. Although this implies a commonality of perspective
at a very general level, a perspective quite antithetical to the
empiricist tradition mentioned earlier, it should become obvious
very quickly to the reader that there are fundamental disagreements
and debates (both explicit and implicit) between the authors in this
collection. This we perceive as the best way forward in gentrification research today. If the barrenness of the empiricist tradition
quickly became obvious, the limitations of more abstract theoretical
analyses are also clear. What is necessary today, more than anything
else, is a statement and clarification of the theoretical issues in the
gentrification debate and an active engagement of contrasting
theoretical propositions with empirical data. This collection is
offered as a preliminary contribution to this process.

The debates and differences in the following pages are not so
simple and untangled that they can adequately be separated into a

list. Nonetheless, because only some causes of the debates are made explicit, we feel that it will be useful here to lay out some of the major themes of the discussions involved. Five issues are readily identifiable:

(a) Production-side versus consumption-side explanations.
(b) The question of the emergence of a "post-industrial" city.
(c) The relative importance of social structure *vis-à-vis* individual agency in the gentrification process.
(d) Is there a "new middle class" and what is its role?
(e) What are the costs of gentrification today and in the future?

It is apparent that these questions are closely related and that there are clear patterns of response to the issues taken as a whole. Someone who emphasizes consumption-side explanations, for example, is likely to take one position rather than another in some of the succeeding questions. But before looking at the larger pattern, let us first examine these questions in order.

Production-side versus consumption-side explanations

The explanations taken for granted in the empiricist tradition were for the most part consumption-side explanations (e.g. Laska & Spain 1980). They isolated a number of factors including life-style changes, preference patterns, and simple descriptions of demographic change. The implicit assumption behind these explanations was that of consumer sovereignty in the land and housing markets; the changing urban patterns were the expression of changed consumption choices among certain sections of the middle class. Against this, several authors have emphasized the role of institutional agents and of capital, rather than consumers, in sculpting the urban landscape. Gentrification, according to this perspective, results from the private and public investment of capital in certain land uses, its devaluation through use and disinvestment, and the resulting opportunity for profitable reinvestment that is thereby created.

Whereas the empiricist tradition has never seriously entertained explanations involving more than lip service to a simplistic consumption-side argument, others have developed a more sophisticated argument which retains a certain primacy for consumption, while fitting gentrification within a broader framework of social, demographic and cultural change. This usually involves an analysis of changes in family structure, the increased participation of women in the labor force, and the expansion of an educated middle class. Thus, in Chapter 3, Beauregard deals with a number of production-

4

and consumption-side factors but stresses that an explanation must begin with an account of how the gentrifiers come to exist as a social group. Smith, on the other hand, in Chapter 2, focuses in the first place upon how gentrifiable properties (relatively inexpensive properties on potentially expensive land) come to exist in specific geographical areas.

Elements of this discussion suffuse most of the other chapters, but perhaps the most important point here is that whatever the differing emphases, few are arguing an exclusively production-based or consumption-based argument. Smith does attempt to outline the significance of consumption-side forces, and production-side considerations are central to Beauregard's argument. Most of the other authors also attempt to balance these two perspectives. The ideas presented here are in no way final but should be seen as contributions to a debate in which the ground has moved very rapidly, even in the last five years.

The question of the emergence of a "post-industrial" city

The appearance of gentrification in the urban landscape has been linked by some theorists to the emergence of a so-called "post-industrial society." David Ley in particular has advanced this idea, attempting explicitly to view gentrification and contemporary urban restructuring as a hallmark of what Daniel Bell has dubbed post-industrial society (Bell 1973, Sternlieb & Hughes 1976, Ley 1980, 1982a). Bell attempted to extrapolate present changes in the social, economic and political structure of Western society into the future, and sought to encapsulate this historical development as the emergence of post-industrial society. The decline of industrial production and employment and the rapid growth of the so-called service sector along with information-oriented employment are only one aspect of this larger transformation, according to Bell. In the context of the city, Ley has argued that, with the development of post-industrial society, the rationale behind the allocation of urban land to different uses is altered. Priorities are reversed; whatever the importance of production-based land use allocation in the industrial city, it is consumption factors, taste and a certain esthetic, as well as political forces, which come to dominate today. Not only is gentrification the product of certain sets of consumption choices, but it represents an historically new phase in urban development and the primacy of consumption over production. It also represents, for Ley, the political victory of reform politicians over established interests and the construction of a "reform landscape."

Bell's work was motivated in part by a desire to provide an

alternative historical account of societal development to that offered by marxist theorists. This is equally true of proponents of the "post-industrial city" thesis. Thus the debate on this question is closely related to that about production-side and consumption-side explanations. Marxist writers have tended to stress the production-side explanations and the role of capital, privately as well as publicly mediated, in fashioning the urban landscape. Thus in pointing to the superficial misreading of real changes in advanced capitalist society, implicit in the "post-industrial" thesis, Walker and Greenberg (1982a,b) stress the functionality of reform movements and the new consumption ethic for capital. After Sayer (1982), they view the "post-industrial city" as a chaotic concept. This debate emerges in the present book with the chapter by Cybriwsky, Ley and Western (Ch. 6) and that by Jager (Ch. 5) presenting elements of the post-industrial city thesis. Chapter 2, along with Chapter 7 by Hamnett and Randolph, focus on the importance of capital investment in urban restructuring, and consider the changing forms taken by capital in the context of gentrification.

The relative importance of social structure and individual agency in the gentrification process

The arguments here feed directly into the now fashionable question of the relationship between "structure and agency." Drawing heavily on the work of Anthony Giddens, a number of social scientists in the early 1980s were concerned to explore societal questions in terms of "structure and agency" (Giddens 1981). Again, this trend emerged and became fashionable partly in reaction to marxist theories, but also in reaction to liberal political conceptions. Giddens attempted a complex and not always coherent blend of Marx, Weber and Durkheim, but the applications of his work have been rather more prosaic. If marxist theory seemed to depend too much on structural explanations of societal change, and was even on occasion equated with structuralism (Duncan & Ley 1982), liberal political theory was thought to depend too heavily on the action and behavior of human individuals. Simply put, the structure and agency paradigm assumes that although there are certainly social structures that guide and inhibit social action, it is individual human beings who perform social acts and thereby make and change the social structures.

The debate over structure and agency is only beginning. Whether it represents a viable new framework for research or an unsustainable attempt to integrate two irreconcilable traditions remains to be seen. In this volume we present three essays which employ elements of the structure and agency framework. Namely Chapters 3 and 4, by Beauregard and Williams respectively, seek to capture the complexities of the gentrification process as a set of varied responses to a changing social and economic environment. In some respects, the chapter by Cybriwsky, Ley, and Western puts these ideas into practice. The authors view gentrification as having larger societal causes, but focus very much on individual and group actors and attempt to blend these in a comparative study of neighborhoods in Philadelphia and Vancouver.

Is there a "new middle class" and what is its role?

Gentrification is widely identified with the supposed emergence of a new middle class, because the process seems to bring with it the concentration of trendy restaurants, boutiques, clubs and other recreation and retail facilities that are frequented by the "new young professionals." The question of a "new middle class" is widely debated in left-wing circles. The class structure of capitalist society has changed throughout the 20th century and this has led to numerous formulations on the new class structure (Walker 1979). If Barbara and John Ehrenreich (1979) argue that a new professional–managerial class has nudged the working class and the ruling class into far smaller niches, Eric Olin Wright (1979) prefers to talk about "contradictory class relations." The debate at this level is less over whether any change has taken place but rather about the character of the changing class structure and, in some cases, about the effects of these changes on traditional conceptions of class difference and class struggle. Thus Callinicos (1983) attempts to demonstrate that although there has certainly been a rapid growth of white-collar employment in service and administrative activities, most of these new employees are properly considered working class; though certainly not blue collar, they are still obligated to sell their labor power for a wage.

A number of the chapters touch on this issue, but perhaps the most explicit and innovative is the essay by Jager who attempts to read the rise of the new middle class and their societal niche from the architecture of their gentrified residences. This essay is an original interpretation of the class-based esthetics of gentrification and the way in which gentrification itself contributes to the social constitution of the new middle class. It has clear links with the arguments of Ley concerning a reform landscape, although Jager focuses on the architectural rather than metropolitan scale. This theme is also developed by Williams (Ch. 4) who seeks to understand gentrifi-

cation as a class-based process reflecting and reinforcing the reconstitution of class structure in advanced capitalist societies.

If the lines of this debate are not yet well established, its implications are nonetheless important. Where Callinicos sees a large but
transformed working class, André Gorz (1982) has bid "farewell to
the working class," seeing instead the origins of a "post-industrial
socialism." "Post-industrial socialism" is the subtitle to Gorz's
book, and this makes immediately clear the links between the
argument over the "new middle class" and the argument, referred
to earlier, concerning post-industrialism. The importance of this
debate is not just that we try to understand the class anatomy of
contemporary society, but that action geared toward profound
social change can only succeed if it is premised on an accurate
understanding of that society and the social forces capable of
creating change. In the context of gentrification, this debate has a
clear prescriptive relevance. Whether one encourages or opposes the
process depends among other things upon how one sees the class
configurations. If one opposes gentrification, against whom is
community activism oriented, and whom is it meant to mobilize?
The authors of this collection are mostly opposed to gentrification,
but there is little or no agreement on the strategy and tactics of
opposition. Although these questions have been raised in various of
the chapters that follow, they remain by and large open to debate.

What are the costs of displacement today and in the future?

Echoing the conservative wisdom about gentrification, Sternlieb
and Ford (1979: 97) assert that "the problems of displacement of less
advantaged citizens in a declining city are relatively small." This was
also the official position of the US Department of Housing and
Urban Development (1979; see also Hartman 1979; Sumka 1979),
but no matter how conservative or conventional, this assertion was
rarely backed up by data. The essential vision here is that gentrification is a small scale but welcome reversal of previous decay; in the
form of abandonment, this decay continues and is responsible for a
far greater amount of displacement.

Chapters 8 and 9 confront this orthodoxy concerning the significance, or rather insignificance, of gentrification and the displacement it involves. Peter Marcuse shows that far from being
separate processes, abandonment and gentrification are part of a
single economic transformation in the urban land market, and that
the result for working-class displacees is the same whether displacement is inspired by abandonment or by gentrification. He
offers tentative estimates on the annual extent of displacement in

New York City. LeGates and Hartman, in the following chapter, provide painstaking empirical evidence of the extent of gentrification-caused displacement in the United States. This chapter represents one of the most exhaustive surveys of information on the effects of gentrification upon the working class.

The final essay in the collection looks to the future and evaluates more directly how long term and extensive the process is likely to be. This exercise in cautious forecasting does not represent the quantitative extrapolation of present empirical data into an otherwise unchanging future. Rather we attempt to base our view of the future upon the qualitative analyses of forces, causes and actors that make up preceding chapters. Further, we attempt to situate gentrification and urban restructuring in the broader international and geographical context of economic crisis, a new international division of labor, deindustrialization, the changing function of the city, the role of the state, the changing political arena, and so forth. Finally, we take up explicitly the question of strategies and tactics in opposition to gentrification.

This brief survey of debates and disagreements is necessarily short and oversimplified. We want to emphasize the differences as a way of pressuring future research to confront some of these issues, but we have not attempted a comprehensive coverage of all the extant debate. Thus we have not mentioned at all the claim that gentrification represents a back-to-the-city movement from the suburbs. The data on this is now sufficiently substantial that the idea of a back-to-the-city movement survives only in the popular press. But beyond these debates, which should be more or less obvious to the reader, there is also a level of agreement about contemporary changes in the central and inner city, and it is to this that we now turn.

Society and space

Traditional 20th-century urban theory has generally maintained a strict separation between the spatial and social dimensions of urban process and form. This very distinction between process and form expresses the separation of social and spatial. An early exception to this norm came with the human-ecology tradition of Park, Burgess and others, according to which the patterns of human settlement in urban areas could be understood in terms of concepts and processes borrowed from biology and ecology. The theoretical justification for this naturalistic analogy was never clear, and however dubious this tradition seems in retrospect, its adherents were making some attempt at reconciling space and society (Park 1936).

In the 1950s and 1960s, another tradition emerged. In what came to be called spatial economics or regional science, a number of researchers attempted to "spatialize" neoclassical economic theory and thereby develop an analysis of the urban land market, the journey to work, the spatial structure of the housing market, and location theory in general (Isard 1956, Alonso 1960, Muth 1961, Kain 1962).[1] The limitations of this approach soon became apparent, however. In the first place, the basic theory is rigidly aspatial, and its application could produce only very general spatial insights. Society and space were brought into the same arena, with the emergence of regional science, but in so far as the basic neoclassical assumptions were not challenged the level of integration was minimal. Second, the social and political uprisings of the 1960s demonstrated vividly the narrowness of a purely economic location theory, at least on the urban scale. The 1960s highlighted the role of white flight, state-financed and planned urban renewal and housing policies, the destruction of black neighborhoods, and so forth.

Third, and most important, the neoclassical analysis is ahistorical, treating as eternal certain economic categories that applied only in the period of emerging industrial capitalism. Thus, to take just the most obvious illustration, Alonso's (1960) theory of the urban land market provides an explanation for the spatial structure not of London or Boston in the late 20th century, but of Manchester and Chicago in the 19th. It is a suitable explanation for the concentric ring model developed on the basis of empirical evidence by the Chicago School. As regards the advent of gentrification and the nascent reversal of this empirical pattern, the neoclassical tradition is stranded. Only by analytical contortions that would strain the credibility of the theory (see, for example, Schill & Nathan 1983) could this analysis of the urban land market possibly be made to explain the present restructuring of urban space (Smith 1982, Hamnett 1984a, Williams 1984a).

Frustration with the neoclassical approach in turn led to a more direct search for an integration of society and space (Harvey 1973). In association with the social uprisings of the 1960s also, the focus of this search was moved substantially to the left. Researchers surveyed vast literatures in search of some kind of theory of contemporary society, the idea being that only if we understood the way in which the society functions and develops would we be able to comprehend the way in which it creates its urban areas. If only a few completed the intellectual sojourn to Marx, many others were drawn in that direction. Marx's theory of capitalist society offered the possibility of a closer integration of space and society, allowing some researchers to examine gentrification as one aspect of the geography of capitalism.

The search for appropriate social theory did not necessitate a marxist destination. As we have seen from the above discussion, some authors favored the theory of post-industrial society, some preferred an institutional approach or urban managerialism, and still others have settled more recently on an agency–structure framework. Regardless of the complexion of the social theory, however, all of these researchers have tried to fashion a more sophisticated integration of space and society than was hitherto available. There is therefore unanimity in the view that – far from being an isolated phenomenon, however interesting it may be – gentrification is the expression in the urban landscape of deeper social processes and social change. Further, there is probably also unanimity in the view that gentrification, as an urban spatial process, contributes to the social determination and differentiation of class. The debates and disagreements apparent in this book begin from this foundation of agreement.

We have outlined the substance and direction of this book. Let us now briefly review its organization. We began with an introductory chapter reviewing the debates around gentrification and highlighting five main strands of argument; production versus consumption; the post-industrial city; structure and agency; the new middle class; and the impact and future of gentrification. In reviewing these arguments we located the contributions in this volume, thus exposing the tensions and conflicts which exist between the contributors. While we wished to expose these differences and engender debate which may resolve them, we would also stress their uniform rejection of simplistic empirical research.

The introductory chapter leads the reader into the body of the volume. The contributions have been arranged in an order which moves from chapters which, on balance, emphasize theoretical argument through to chapters which give greater weight to empirical evidence. There is no clear boundary, however, and each chapter contributes substantially to the debates, theoretical and empirical.

On balance the United States receives the closest attention but, as well as direct contributions on Australia, Britain and Canada, the scope of most of the chapters is international. This, plus the substantive attention to theory, means that the contributions are highly complementary, with issues raised in one chapter being taken up and developed in another. It should be stressed that each was written independently and there has been no attempt to edit out conflict and disagreement.

11

The volume ends with a further essay by the editors in which we seek to illustrate the path from the ideology of "the urban renaissance" to the reality of urban restructuring. This reflection on the future of gentrification is intended to emphasize the concern which all the authors demonstrate regarding the impact of this process. The theoretical and empirical arguments are certainly very important, not least because they have been so weakly developed, but so too are the questions of the social, economic, and political consequences of gentrification. In this final essay we aim to raise issues which bring politics back to the centre stage.

Note

1 Some of these essays from the neoclassical and human ecology tradition as well as the later marxist tradition are reprinted in a very useful volume edited by Robert Lake (1983).

Gentrification of the City

CONTRIBUTED ESSAYS

2

Gentrification, the frontier, and the restructuring of urban space

NEIL SMITH

In his seminal essay on "The significance of the frontier in American history," written in 1893, Frederick Jackson Turner (1958 edn) wrote:

> American development has exhibited not merely advance along a single line, but a return to primitive conditions on a continually advancing frontier line, and a new development for that area. American social development has been continually beginning over again on the frontier .... In this advance the frontier is the outer edge of the wave – the meeting point between savagery and civilization ... The wilderness has been interpenetrated by lines of civilization growing ever more numerous.

For Turner, the expansion of the frontier and the rolling back of wilderness and savagery were an attempt to make livable space out of an unruly and uncooperative nature. This involved not simply a process of spatial expansion and the progressive taming of the physical world. The development of the frontier certainly accomplished these things, but for Turner it was also the central experience which defined the uniqueness of the American national character. With each expansion of the outer edge by robust pioneers, not only were new lands added to the American estate but new blood was added to the veins of the American democratic ideal. Each new wave westward, in the conquest of nature, sent shock waves back east in the democratization of human nature.

During the 20th century the imagery of wilderness and frontier has been applied less to the plains, mountains and forests of the West, and more to the cities of the whole country, but especially of the East. As part of the experience of suburbanization, the 20th-

15

century American city came to be seen by the white middle class as an urban wilderness; it was, and for many still is, the habitat of disease and crime, danger and disorder (Warner 1972). Indeed these were the central fears expressed throughout the 1950s and 1960s by urban theorists who focused on urban "blight" and "decline," "social malaise" in the inner city, the "pathology" of urban life; in short, the "unheavenly city" (Banfield 1968). The city becomes a wilderness, or worse a jungle (Long 1971, Sternlieb 1971; see also Castells 1976a). More vividly than in the news media or social science theory, this is the recurrent theme in a whole genre of "urban jungle" Hollywood productions, from *West Side Story* and *King Kong* to *The Warriors*.

Anti-urbanism has been a dominant theme in American culture. In a pattern analogous to the original experience of wilderness, the last 20 years have seen a shift from fear to romanticism and a progression of urban imagery from wilderness to frontier. Cotton Mather and the Puritans of 17th-century New England feared the forest as an impenetrable evil, a dangerous wilderness, but with the continual taming of the forest and its transformation at the hands of human labor, the softer imagery of Turner's frontier was an obvious successor to Mather's forest of evil. There is an optimism and an expectation of expansion associated with "frontier;" wilderness gives way to frontier when the conquest is well under way. Thus in the 20th-century American city, the imagery of urban wilderness has been replaced by the imagery of urban frontier. This transformation can be traced to the origins of urban renewal (see especially Abrams 1965), but has become intensified in the last two decades, as the rehabilitation of single-family homes became fashionable in the wake of urban renewal. In the language of gentrification, the appeal to frontier imagery is exact: urban pioneers, urban homesteaders and urban cowboys are the new folk heroes of the urban frontier.

Just as Turner recognized the existence of Native Americans but included them as part of his savage wilderness, contemporary urban-frontier imagery implicitly treats the present inner-city population as a natural element of their physical surroundings. Thus the term "urban pioneer" is as arrogant as the original notion of the "pioneer" in that it conveys the impression of a city that is not yet socially inhabited; like the Native Americans, the contemporary urban working class is seen as less than social, simply a part of the physical environment. Turner was explicit about this when he called the frontier "the meeting point between savagery and civilization," and although today's frontier vocabulary of gentrification is rarely as explicit, it treats the inner-city population in much the same way (Stratton 1977).

16

The parallels go further. For Turner, the westward geographical progress of the frontier line is associated with the forging of the national spirit. An equally spiritual hope is expressed in the boosterism which presents gentrification as the leading edge of an American urban renaissance; in the most extreme scenario, the new urban pioneers are expected to do for the national spirit what the old ones did: to lead us into a new world where the problems of the old world are left behind. In the words of one Federal publication, gentrification's appeal to history involves the "psychological need to re-experience successes of the past because of the disappointments of recent years – Vietnam, Watergate, the energy crisis, pollution, inflation, high interest rates, and the like" (Advisory Council on Historic Preservation, 1980: 9). No one has yet seriously proposed that we view James Rouse (the American developer responsible for many of the highly visible downtown malls, plazas, markets and tourist arcades) as the John Wayne of gentrification, but the proposal would be quite in keeping with much of the contemporary imagery. In the end, and this is the important conclusion, the imagery of frontier serves to rationalize and legitimate a process of conquest, whether in the 18th- and 19th-century West or in the 20th-century inner city. The imagery relies on several myths but also has a partial basis in reality. Some of the mythology has already been hinted at, but before proceeding to examine the realistic basis of the imagery, I want to discuss one aspect of the frontier mythology not yet touched upon: nationalism.

The process of gentrification with which we are concerned here is quintessentially international. It is taking place throughout North America and much of western Europe, as well as Australia and New Zealand, that is, in cities throughout most of the Western advanced capitalist world. Yet nowhere is the process less understood than in the United States, where the American nationalism of the frontier ideology has encouraged a provincial understanding of gentrification. The original pre-20th-century frontier experience was not limited to the United States, but rather exported throughout the world; likewise, although it is nowhere as rooted as in the United States, the frontier ideology does emerge elsewhere in connection with gentrification. The international influence of the earlier American frontier experience is repeated with the 20th-century urban scene; the American imagery of gentrification is simultaneously cosmopolitan and parochial, general and local. It is general in image if often contrary in detail. For these reasons, the critique of the frontier imagery does not condemn us to repeating Turner's nationalism, and should not be seen as a nationalistic basis for a discussion of gentrification. The Australian experience of frontier, for example, was certainly different from the American, but was also responsible (along with American cultural imports) for spawning a strong frontier ideology. And the American frontier itself was as intensely real for potential immigrants in Scandinavia or Ireland as it was for actual French or British immigrants in Baltimore or Boston.

However, as with every ideology, there is a real, if partial and distorted, basis for the treatment of gentrification as a new urban frontier. In this idea of frontier we see an evocative combination of economic and spatial dimensions of development. The potency of the frontier image depends on the subtlety of exactly this combination of the economic and the spatial. In the 19th century, the expansion of the geographic frontier in the US and elsewhere was simultaneously an economic expansion of capital. Yet the social individualism pinned onto and incorporated into the idea of frontier is in one important respect a myth; Turner's frontier line was extended westward less by individual pioneers and homesteaders, and more by banks, railways, the state and other speculators, and these in turn passed the land on (at profit) to businesses and families (see, for example, Swierenga 1968). In this period, economic expansion was accomplished in part through absolute geographical expansion. That is, expansion of the economy involved the expansion of the geographical arena over which the economy operated.

Today the link between economic and geographical development remains, giving the frontier imagery its present currency, but the form of the link is very different. As far as its spatial basis is concerned, economic expansion takes place today not through absolute geographical expansion but through the internal differentiation of geographical space (N. Smith 1982). Today's production of space or geographical development is therefore a sharply uneven process. Gentrification, urban renewal, and the larger, more complex, processes of urban restructuring are all part of the differentiation of geographical space at the urban scale; although they had their basis in the period of economic expansion prior to the current world economic crisis, the function of these processes today is to lay one small part of the geographical basis for a future period of expansion (Smith 1984). And as with the original frontier, the mythology has it that gentrification is a process led by individual pioneers and homesteaders whose sweat equity, daring and vision are paving the way for those among us who are more timid. But even if we ignore urban renewal and the commercial, administrative and recreational redevelopment that is taking place, and focus purely on residential rehabilitation, it is apparent that where the "urban pioneers" venture, the banks, real-estate companies, the state or other collective economic actors have generally gone before. In this context it may be more appropriate to view the James Rouse Company not as the John Wayne but as the Wells Fargo of gentrification.

In the public media, gentrification has been presented as the pre-eminent symbol of the larger urban redevelopment that is taking place. Its symbolic importance far outweighs its real importance; it is a relatively small if highly visible part of a much larger process. The actual process of gentrification lends itself to such cultural abuse in the same way as the original frontier. Whatever the real economic, social and political forces that pave the way for gentrification, and no matter which banks and realtors, governments and contractors are behind the process, gentrification appears at first sight, and especially in the US, to be a marvelous testament to the values of individualism and the family, economic opportunity and the dignity of work (sweat equity). From appearances at least, gentrification can be played so as to strike some of the most resonant chords on our ideological keyboard.

As early as 1961, Jean Gottmann not only caught the reality of changing urban patterns, but also spoke in a language amenable to the emerging ideology, when he said that the "frontier of the American economy is nowadays urban and suburban rather than peripheral to the civilized areas" (Gottmann 1961:78). With two important provisos, which have become much more obvious in the last two decades, this insight is precise. First, the urban frontier is a frontier in the economic sense, before anything else. The social, political and cultural transformations in the central city are often dramatic and are certainly important as regards our immediate experience of everyday life, but they are associated with the development of an economic frontier. Second, the urban frontier is today only one of several frontiers, given that the internal differentiation of geographical space occurs at different scales. In the context of the present global economic crisis, it is clear that international capital and American capital alike confront a global "frontier" that incorporates the so-called urban frontier. This link between different spatial scales, and the importance of urban development to national and international recovery, was acutely clear in the enthusiastic language used by supporters of the urban Enterprise Zone, an idea pioneered by the Thatcher and Reagan administrations. To quote just one apologist, Stuart Butler (a British economist working for the American right-wing think tank, the Heritage Foundation):[1]

It may be argued that at least part of the problem facing many urban areas today lies in our failure to apply the mechanism explained by Turner (the continual local development and innovation of new ideas)

... to the inner city "frontier." Cities are facing fundamental changes, and yet the measures applied to deal with these changes are enacted in the main by distant governments. We have failed to appreciate that there may be opportunities in the cities themselves, and we have scrupulously avoided giving local forces the chance to seize them. Proponents of the Enterprise Zone aim to provide a climate in which the frontier process can be brought to bear within the city itself. (Butler 1981: 3)

The circumspect observation of Gottmann and others has given way 20 years later to the unabashed adoption of the "urban frontier" as the keystone to a political and economic program of urban restructuring in the interests of capital.

The frontier line today has a quintessentially economic definition – it is the frontier of profitability – but it takes on a very acute geographical expression at different spatial scales. Ultimately, this is what the 20th-century frontier and the so-called urban frontier of today have in common. In reality, both are associated with the accumulation and expansion of capital. But where the 19th-century frontier represented the consummation of *absolute geographical expansion* as the primary spatial expression of capital accumulation, gentrification and urban redevelopment represent the most advanced example of the *redifferentiation* of geographical space toward precisely the same end. It is just possible that, in order to understand the present, what is needed today is the substitution of a true geography in place of a false history.

The restructuring of urban space

It is important to understand the present extent of gentrification in order to comprehend the real character and importance of the restructuring process. If by gentrification we mean, strictly, the residential rehabilitation of working–class neighborhoods, then, in the United States (where the process is probably most dramatic), it shows up clearly in data at the census tract level but not yet at the scale of the Standard Metropolitan Statistical Area (Chall 1984, Schaffer & Smith 1984). For a number of cities, income, rent and other indicators from the 1980 census show clear evidence of gentrification in central tracts. However, the process has not yet become significant enough to reverse or even seriously counter the established trends toward residential suburbanization. Although this is an interesting empirical pattern, alone it hardly amounts to a secular change in patterns of urban development. If, however, we eschew the narrow ideology fostered around gentrification, and see the process in relation to a number of broader if still less "visible"

20

urban developments; if, in other words, we examine the momentum of the process, not a static empirical count, then a coherent pattern emerges of a far more significant restructuring of urban space.

Before examining the precise trends that are leading toward the restructuring process, it is important to note that the question of spatial scale is central to any relevant explanation. We can say that the restructuring of the urban-space economy is a product of the uneven development of capitalism or of the operation of a rent gap, the result of a developing service economy or of changed life-style preferences, the suburbanization of capital or the devalorization of capital invested in the urban built environment. It is, of course, a product of all of these forces, in some way, but to say so tells us very little. These processes occur at several different spatial scales, and although previous attempts at explanation have tended to fasten on one or the other trend, they may not in fact be mutually exclusive. Where authors have attempted to incorporate more than one such trend, they have generally been content to list these as factors. Yet this version of "factor analysis" is quite unambitious. The whole question of explanation hinges not upon identifying factors but upon understanding the relative importance of, and relation between, so-called "factors." In part, this is a question of scale.

But there is a second question of scale concerning levels of generality. We accept here that the restructuring of urban space is general but by no means universal. What does this mean? It means, first, that the restructuring of urban space is not, strictly speaking, a new phenomenon. The entire process of urban growth and development is a constant patterning, structuring and restructuring of urban space. What *is* new today is the degree to which this restructuring of space is an immediate and systematic component of a larger economic and social restructuring of advanced capitalist economies. A given built environment expresses specific patterns of production and reproduction, consumption and circulation, and as these patterns change, so does the geographical patterning of the built environment. The walking city, we have been told, is not the automobile city, but of greater importance, perhaps, the city of small craft manufacturing is not the metropolis of multinational capital.

The geographical restructuring of the space economy is always uneven; thus urban restructuring in one region of a national or international economy may not be matched in either quality or quantity, character or extent, by restructuring in another. This is immediately evident in the comparison of developed and under-developed parts of the world economy. The basic structure of most

Third World cities, and the processes at work, are quite different from those in Europe, Oceania or North America. But equally, within the developed economies, there are strong regional differences. If Baltimore and Los Angeles are both experiencing a rapid transformation of their space economies, there are as many differences between them as similarities. Still other cities, such as Gary, Indiana, may be experiencing a secular decline and little restructuring (as opposed to continued destruction). In short, there is an overlay of regional and international patterns that complicate the extant urban patterns. Although they focus on the general causes and background to the contemporary restructuring of urban space, the explanations offered will be successful only to the extent that they can begin to explain the diversity of urban forms resulting from the process as well as complete exceptions to the apparent rule. This again calls not for a "factor analysis" (a list of factors) but for an integrated explanation; we have to explain not just the location but also the timing of such dramatic urban change. But perhaps the most basic distinction that will emerge is between those trends and tendencies which are predominantly responsible for the *fact* of urban restructuring and those responsible for the *form* the process takes.

The most salient processes responsible for the origins and shaping of urban restructuring can perhaps be summarized under the following headings:

(a) suburbanization and the emergence of the rent gap;
(b) the deindustrialization of advanced capitalist economies and the growth of white-collar employment;
(c) the spatial centralization and simultaneous decentralization of capital;
(d) the falling rate of profit and the cyclical movement of capital;
(e) demographic changes and changes in consumption patterns.

In consort, these developments and processes can provide a first approximation toward an integrated explanation of the different facets of gentrification and urban restructuring.

Suburbanization and the emergence of the rent gap

The explanation of suburban development is more complex than is often thought, and a revisionist alternative to traditional, transport-based explanations is beginning to emerge (Walker 1978, 1981). The point here is not to give a comprehensive account of suburbanization but to summarize some of the most important conclusions.

The suburbanization process represents a simultaneous centralization and decentralization of capital and of human activity in geographical space. On the national scale, suburbanization is the

22

outward expansion of centralized urban places, and this process should be understood in the most general way as a necessary product of the spatial centralization of capital. It is the growth of towns into cities into metropolitan centers.

At the urban scale, however, from the perspective of the urban center, suburbanization is a process of decentralization. It is a product not of a basic impulse toward centralization but of the impulse toward a high rate of profit. Profit rates are location specific, and at the urban scale as such, the economic indicator that differentiates one place from another is ground rent. Many other forces were involved in the suburbanization of capital, but pivotal in the entire process was the availability of cheap land on the periphery (low ground rent). There was no natural necessity for the expansion of economic activity to take the form of suburban development; there was no technical impediment preventing the movement of modern large-scale capital to the rural backwaters, or preventing its fundamental redevelopment of the industrial city it inherited, but instead the expansion of capital led to a process of suburbanization. In part this had to do with the impetus toward centralization (see below), but given the economics of centralization, it is the ground-rent structure that determined the suburban location of economic expansion (Smith 1984).

The outward movement of capital to develop suburban, industrial, residential, commercial, and recreational activity results in a reciprocal change in suburban and inner-city ground-rent levels. Where the price of suburban land rises with the spread of new construction, the relative price of inner-city land falls. Smaller and smaller quantities of capital are funneled into the maintenance and repair of the inner-city building stock. This results in what we have called a *rent gap* in the inner city between the actual ground rent capitalized from the present (depressed) land use and the potential rent that could be capitalized from the "highest and best" use (or at least a "higher and better" use), given the central location. This suburbanization occurs in consort with structural changes in advanced economies. Some of the other processes we shall examine are more limited in their occurrence; what is remarkable about the rent gap is its near universality. Most cities in the advanced capitalist world have experienced this phenomenon, to a greater or lesser extent. Where it is allowed to run its course at the behest of the free market, it leads to the substantial abandonment of inner-city properties. This devalorization of capital invested in the built environment affects property of all sorts, commercial and industrial as well as residential and retail. Different levels and kinds of state involvement give the process a very different form in different economies, and abandonment (the logical end–point of the process) is most marked in the US, where state involvement has been less consistent and more sporadic.

At the most basic level, it is the movement of capital into the construction of new suburban landscapes and the consequent creation of a rent gap that create the economic *opportunity* for restructuring the central and inner cities. The devalorization of capital in the center creates the opportunity for the revalorization of this "underdeveloped" section of urban space. The actual realization of the process, and the determination of its specific form, involve the other trends listed earlier.

Deindustrialization and the growth of a white-collar economy

Associated with the devalorization of inner–city capital is the decline of certain economic sectors and land uses more than others. This is a product primarily of broader changes in the employment structure. In particular, the advanced capitalist economies (with the major exception of Japan) have experienced the onset of deindustrialization, whereas there has been a parallel if partial industrialization of certain Third World economies. Beginning in the 1960s, most industrial economies experienced a reduction in the proportion of workers in the industrial sectors (Blackaby 1978, Harris 1980, 1983, Bluestone & Harrison 1982). But many urban areas began to experience the effects of deindustrialization much earlier than the last two decades. Thus the growth in manufacturing, at the national scale, since World War II was very uneven between regions. Whereas some regions, such as the West Midlands and South-East of England, or many of the southern and western states of the US, experienced a rapid growth of modern manufacturing, other regions experienced a relative disinvestment of capital in manufacturing jobs. At the urban scale the process is even more marked; most of the expanding industrial capacity of the postwar boom was not located in the inner cities, the traditional home of industry in the Chicago model of urban structure, but in suburban and peripheral locations. The result was a period of systematic disinvestment in urban industrial production, dating, in the case of some British cities, as far back as before World War I (Lenman 1977). This was the case despite the overall growth of industrial production in the UK economy, taken as a whole, even following World War II.

The corollary to this deindustrialization is increased employment in other sectors of the economy, especially those described loosely as white-collar or service occupations. Within these broad categories, many very different types of employment are generally included, from clerical, communications and retail operatives to managerial, professional and research careers. Within this larger trend toward a growing white-collar labor force, therefore, there are very different tendencies and these have a specific spatial expression, as we shall see in the next section. By themselves, the processes of deindustrialization and white-collar growth do not at all explain the restructuring of the urban centers. Rather, these processes help to explain, first, the kinds of building stock and land use most involved in the development of the rent gap, and, second, the kinds of new land uses which can be expected where the opportunity for redevelopment is taken. Thus, although the media emphasis is on recent gentrification and the rehabilitation of working-class residences, there has also been a considerable transformation of old industrial areas of the city. This did not simply begin with the conversion of old warehouses into chic loft apartments; much more significant was the early urban renewal activity which, although certainly a process of slum clearance, was also the clearance of "obsolete" (meaning also devalorized) industrial buildings (factories, warehouses, wharves, etc.) where many of the slum dwellers had once worked.

Although the devalorization of capital and the development of the rent gap explain the possibility of reinvestment in the urban core around which gentrifying areas are developing, and the transformation in economic and employment structures suggests the kinds of activity that are likely to predominate in this reinvestment, there remains the question as to why the burgeoning white-collar employment is, at least in part, being centralized in the urban core. The existence of the rent gap is only a partial explanation; there is, after all, cheap land available elsewhere, throughout the rural periphery.

Spatial centralization and decentralization of capital

With the emergence of the capitalist mode of production, that which had hitherto been accidental disappears, is neglected, or is converted into a necessity. The accumulation of wealth had been accidental in the sense that, however much it was the goal of individuals, it was nowhere in precapitalist societies a general social rule upon which the survival of the society depended. With the emergence of capitalism, the accumulation of capital becomes a social necessity in exactly this way. Marx (1967 edn, Vol. I, Ch. 25) demonstrated that both a prerequisite and a product of the accumulation of capital is a certain social concentration and centralization of that capital. In short, this means that larger and larger quantities of capital are centralized under the control of a relatively small number of capitalists.

This social centralization is accomplished only through the production of specific geographical patterns, but the attendant spatial patterns are complex. At its most basic, the centralization of capital leads to a dialectic of spatial centralization and decentralization (N. Smith 1982). If the expansion of 19th-century capital throughout the world is the most visible manifestation of the latter process (decentralization), the development of the urban metropolis is the most palpable product of spatial centralization. Centralization occurs at a number of spatial scales, however, besides the urban. It occurs at the level of plant size and at the level of national capitals in the world economy, and at each scale there are quite specific mechanisms that engender the process. At the urban scale, traditional theories have emphasized "agglomeration economies." The expansion of capital involves a continued division of labor, again at different scales, and thus in order to provide necessary commodities and services, a larger and larger number of separate operations have to be combined. The less the distance between these different activities, the less is the cost and time of production and transportation. Placed in the context of capital accumulation, this explanation is essentially correct concerning the original centralization of capital into urban "agglomerations."

In an interesting insight, Walker (1981: 388) notes that

as capitalism develops, economies of agglomeration have diminished; they are a historically contingent force. But they are in part replaced by economies of (organizational) scale with the concentration of capital, so that gigantic nodes of activity still structure the urban landscape.

The central insight here is that such forces as agglomeration economies are historically contingent. Viewed from the urban centre, the suburbanization of industry represented a clear weakening of agglomeration economies, and was facilitated (not "caused") by developments in the means of transportation. Yet from the perspective of the national economy, the suburbanization of industry represented a clustering of massive and not so massive industrial facilities around established urban cores, and was thus a reaffirmation (at this scale) of the operation of agglomeration economies, however weakened. What Walker senses, though, is real; agglomeration economies operate in a different manner today, leading to clear spatial consequences. The most obvious of these involves the rapidly changing locational patterns associated with the expansion of white-collar employment.

The problem as regards white-collar employment is that a strong tendency toward centralization is matched by an equally strong if not stronger tendency toward decentralization, the movement of offices and other white-collar jobs to the suburbs. How can such apparently opposite tendencies coexist? How can suburbanization and agglomeration be coexistent? The explanation for this seeming paradox lies with a consideration of two interrelated issues. The first is the relationship between space and time *vis-à-vis* different forms of capital, and the second is the division of labor within the so-called white-collar sectors.

It is a cliché today to suggest that the revolution in communications technology will lead to spatial decentralization of office functions. This annihilation of space by time, as Marx had it, has indeed led to a massive suburbanization of white-collar jobs following on the heels of industrial suburbanization. With the computerization of many office functions, this trend continues. But consistent with the ideology of classlessness which first sponsored the notion of white collar, this trend is generally treated as a suburbanization of any and all types of office work from senior executives to word-processor operatives. Yet the further the trend develops, the clearer it becomes that this is not so. Thus the simultaneous centralization and decentralization of office activities represents the spatial expression of a division of labor within the so-called white-collar economy. For the most part, the office functions that are decentralized are the more routine clerical systems and operations associated with the administration, organization and management of governmental as well as corporate activities. These represent the "back offices," the "paper factories," or, more accurately, the "communication factories" for units of the broader system (Wald 1984).

Much less usual is the suburbanization of central decision making in the form of corporate or governmental headquarters. The office boom experienced by many cities in the advanced capitalist world during the past 15 years seems to have been of this sort; it has been a continued centralization of the highest decision-making centers, along with the myriad ancillary services required by such activities: legal services, advertising, hotels and conference centers, publishers, architects, banks, financial services, and many other business services. There are exceptions to the rule, and one of the most obvious is Stamford, Connecticut, which has attracted several new corporate headquarters. Yet Stamford is in no way typical. Rather it is unique, precisely in having attracted the decentralization of ancillary administrative and professional functions central to corporate headquarters, thus resulting less in a decentralization process than in a *re*centralization of executive functions in Stamford. Whether or not this strengthens the tendency to a "multi-modal metropolis" (Muller 1976) remains to be seen.

The question we are left with, then, is why, with the decentralization of industrial and communications factories, there continues to be a centralization of headquarter and executive decision-making centers. Traditional explanations focus on the importance of face-to-face contact. However, although the face-to-face explanation begins to identify the relevant issues, it is too unspecific. It tends to evoke a certain sentimentality for personal contact, but we can be sure that no mere sentimentality is responsible for the overbuilt skyscraper zones of contemporary central business districts. Behind the sentimentality lies a more expedient reason for personal contact, and this involves the very different standards by which time is managed in different sectors of the overall production and circulation of capital. Briefly, in the industrial factory and in the communications factory, the system itself (either the machinery or the administrative schedule) determines the basic daily, weekly and monthly rhythms of the work process. Serious change in this long-term stability comes either from external decisions or from only periodic internal disruptions such as strikes, mechanical faults, or systems failures. The temporal regularity of these production and administration systems, along with their dependence on readily available skills in the labor force and the ease of transportation and communication with ancillary activities, make suburbanization a rational decision. They have little to gain by a centralized location in the urban core, and with high ground rents they have a lot to lose.

But the temporal rhythm of the executive administration of the economy and of its different corporate units is not stable and regular in this fashion, much to the chagrin of managers and executives. At these higher levels of control, long-term strategic planning coexists with short-term response management. Changes in interest rates or stock prices, the packaging of financial deals, labor negotiations and bailouts, international transactions in the foreign exchange market or the gold market, trade agreements, the unpredictable behavior of competitors and of government bodies – all activities of this sort can demand a rapid response by corporate financial managers, and this in turn depends on having close and immediate contact with a battery of professional, administrative and other support systems, as well as with one's competitors. At this level, and in a multitude of ways, the clichéd expression that "time is money" finds its most intense realization. (On time and interest, see Harvey, 1982: 258). Less commonly voiced is the corollary that space too is money; spatial proximity reduces decision times when the decision system is sufficiently irregular that it cannot be reduced to a computer

28

routine. The anarchic time regime of financial decision making in a capitalist society necessitates a certain spatial centralization. It is not just that executives *feel* more secure when packed like sardines into a skyscraper can of friends and foes. In reality they *are* more secure when rapid decisions require direct contact, information flow, and negotiation. The more the economy is prone to crisis, and thus to short-term crisis management, the more one might expect corporate headquarters to seek spatial security. Together with the expansion of this sector *per se* and the cyclical movement of capital into the built environment, this spatial response to temporal and financial irregularity helps to explain the recent office boom in urban centers. "White collar" is clearly a "chaotic concept" (Sayer 1982) with two distinct components, each with a distinct spatial expression.

If, in the precapitalist city, it was the needs of *market exchange* which led to spatial centralization, and in the industrial capitalist city it was the agglomeration of *production* capital, in the advanced capitalist city it is the *financial* and administrative dictates which perpetuate the tendency toward centralization. This helps to explain why certain so-called white-collar activities are centralized and others are suburbanized, and why the restructuring of the urban core takes on the corporate/professional character that it does.

The falling rate of profit and the cyclical movement of capital

Given, then, the spatial character of the process, how are we to explain the timing of this urban restructuring? This question hinges on the historical timing of the rent gap and the spatial switch of capital back to the urban center. Far from accidental occurrences, these events are integral to the broader rhythm of capital accumulation. At the most abstract level, the rent gap results from the dialectic of spatial and temporal patterns of capital investment; more concretely it is the spatial product of the complementary processes of valorization and devalorization.

The accumulation of capital does not take place in a linear fashion but is a cyclical process consisting of boom periods and crises. The rent gap develops over a long period of economic expansion, but expansion that takes place elsewhere. Thus the valorization of capital in the construction of postwar suburbs was matched by its devalorization in the central and inner cities. But the accumulation of capital during such a boom leads to a falling rate of profit, beginning in the industrial sectors, and ultimately toward crisis (Marx 1967 edn, Vol. III). As a means of staving off crisis at least temporarily, capital is transferred out of the industrial sphere, and as Harvey (1978, 1982) has shown, there is a tendency for this capital to be switched into the built environment where profit rates remain higher and where it is possible through speculation to appropriate ground rent even though nothing is produced. Two things come together, then; toward the end of a period of expansion when the rent gap has emerged and has provided the opportunity for reinvestment, there is a simultaneous tendency for capital to seek outlets in the built environment.

The slum clearance and urban renewal schemes in many Western cities following World War II were initiated and managed by the state, and though not unconnected to the emergence of the rent gap, cannot adequately be explained simply in these economic terms. However, the function of this urban renewal was to prepare the way for the future restructuring which would emerge in the 1960s and become very visible in the 1970s. In economic terms the state absorbed the early risks associated with gentrification, as in Philadelphia's Society Hill (see Ch. 6), which was itself an urban renewal project. It also demonstrated to private capital the possibility of large-scale restructuring of the urban core, paving the way for future capital investment.

The timing of this spatial restructuring, then, is closely related to the economic restructuring that takes place during economic crises such as those the world economy has experienced since the early 1970s. A restructured economy involves a restructured built environment. But there is no gradual transition to a restructured economy; the last economic crisis was resolved only after a massive destruction of capital in World War II, representing a cataclysmic devalorization of capital and a destruction prior to a restructuring of urban space. Today, 50 years later, we are again facing the same threat.

Demographic changes and consumption patterns

The maturation of the baby-boom generation, the increased number of women taking on careers, the proliferation of one- and two-person households and the popularity of the "urban singles" life-style are commonly invoked as the real factors behind gentrification. Consistent with the frontier ideology, the process is viewed here as the outcome of individual choices. But in reality too much is claimed. We are seeing a much larger urban restructuring than is encompassed by residential rehabilitation, and it is difficult to see how such explanations could at best be more than partial. Where such explanations might just be conceivable for St. Katherine's Dock in London, they are irrelevant for understanding the London office boom and the redevelopment of the docklands. Yet these are

30

all connected. The changes in demographic patterns and life-style preferences are not completely irrelevant, but it is vital that we understand what these developments can and cannot explain.

The importance of demographic and life-style issues seems to be chiefly in the determination of the surface *form* taken by much of the restructuring rather than explaining the fact of urban transformation. Given the movement of capital into the urban core, and the emphasis on executive, professional, administrative and managerial functions, as well as other support activities, the demographic and life-style changes can help to explain why we have proliferating quiche bars rather than Howard Johnsons, trendy clothes boutiques and gourmet food shops rather than corner stores, American Express signs rather than "cash only, no cheques." As Jager (Ch. 5) suggests, the architecture of gentrified housing is also a product of a specific class culture and set of life-styles. Thus some of the newer, less elite gentrification projects, especially those involving new construction, are beginning to replicate the worst of suburban matchbox housing, leading to a social and esthetic suburbanization of the city.

Sharon Zukin (1982a, 1982b) offers an excellent illustration of this point in her analysis of the development of loft living in SoHo and the entire Lower Manhattan area. Under the Rockefeller-inspired Lower Manhattan Plan, hatched in the 1960s, the old warehouses, wharves and working-class neighborhoods of the area were to be demolished in favor of the usual centralized, high-finance, "high-rise, high-technology modes of construction." The successful struggle against corporate redevelopment was waged in the name of "historic preservation and the arts," and, in 1971, in an extraordinary ruling, SoHo was zoned an "artists' district." However, as Zukin points out, this did not represent a victory of culture (far less "consumer preference") over capital. In fact, it represented an alternative strategy (involving different factions of capital) for the "recapitalization" of Lower Manhattan:

> revalorization by preservation, rather than by new construction, became an "historic compromise" in the urban core ... In Lower Manhattan the struggle to legalize loft living for artists merely anticipated, to some degree, a conjunctural response to crisis in traditional modes of real estate development. In fact, the widening of the loft market after 1973 provided a base for capital accumulation among new, though small-scale, developers. (Zukin 1982a: 262, 265)

Since 1973, of course, larger-scale developers have become involved in the area. Where once loft co-ops were spontaneously put together among groups of prospective residents, today developers will renovate and fit a building, then put it on the market ready-made as a "co-op." And of course fewer and fewer SoHo dwellers today are artists, despite the zoning ordinance which still stands.

The point here is that even SoHo, one of the most vivid symbols of artistic expression in the landscape of gentrification, owes its existence to more basic economic forces (see also Stevens 1982). The concentration of artists in SoHo is today more a cover for, and less a cause of, the area's popularity. This is nowhere clearer than in the exploitation of the area's artistic symbolism in aggressive real-estate advertising.

Direction and limits of urban restructuring

If the restructuring that has now begun continues in its current direction, then we can expect to see significant changes in urban structure. However accurate the Chicago model of urban structure may have been, there is general agreement that it is no longer appropriate. Urban development has overtaken the model. The logical conclusion of the current restructuring, which remains today in its infancy, would be an urban center dominated by high-level executive–professional, financial, and administrative functions, middle- and upper-middle-class residences, and the hotel, restaurant, moving, retail and cultural facilities providing recreational opportunities for this population. In short we should expect the creation of a bourgeois playground, the social Manhattanization of the urban core to match the architectural Manhattanization that heralded the changing employment structure. The corollary of this is likely to be a substantial displacement of the working class to the older suburbs and the urban periphery.

This should not be taken, as it often is, as a suggestion that suburbanization is coming to an end. On the contrary, the flurry of excitement during the 1970s about so-called "non-metropolitan growth" in the US represents less a reversal of established urbanization patterns (Berry 1976, Beale 1977) than a continuation of metropolitan expansion well beyond the established statistical boundaries (Abu-Lughod 1982). There is little reason to assume that suburbanization will not be more extensive than ever, should there be another period of strong economic expansion. Nor should this pattern be seen as excluding absolutely the working class from the inner urban core. Just as substantial enclaves of upper-middle-class residences remained in the largely working-class inner cities of the 1960s and 1970s, enclave working-class neighborhoods will also remain. Indeed, these would be functional in so far as the machinery *transportation !*

and services of the bourgeois playground require a working population. The comparison – and contrast – with South Africa is instructive in this respect (Western 1981).

The opposite alternative (that the central and inner cities would continue their absolute decline toward more widespread abandonment) could appear viable only in the United States. And indeed it *is* a possibility for some cities in the US. In so far as the restructuring of the core depends on a continued concentration and recentralization of economic control functions, it can be expected to happen strongly in national and regional centers. But the situation is less clear with smaller industrial cities, such as Gary, Indiana, where the administrative and financial functions associated with the city's industries are located elsewhere. Detroit provides an even more significant example, because the suburbanization of offices has affected not only the "back offices" but many of the headquarters themselves, and the substantial efforts at recentralization, through the Ford-inspired Renaissance Center, have not yet attracted substantial capital to downtown Detroit.

There is also little reason to doubt that the rapid devalorization of capital invested in the inner-city built environment will continue despite the beginnings of a reinvestment. In the present economic crisis, with interest rates high, it is not just new construction which is adversely affected. The same forces engender a reduction in capital invested in the maintenance and repair of existing buildings, and the consequent devalorization will lead to the outward extension of the "land value valley" of physically decayed buildings; the spatial extent over which the rent gap occurs is thus enlarged. Thus the restructuring of urban space leads to a simultaneous as well as sequent decline and redevelopment, devalorization and revalorization.

In conclusion, we have emphasized that the restructuring of urban space is part of the larger evolution of the contemporary capitalist economy. Thus in the present context of deepening world economic crisis, our conclusions and speculations must be provisional. It is quite possible that the present economic crisis will result in very different political and economic forces, institutions and modes of control, and this could well result in very different patterns of urban growth. In particular, I have focused here on the economic background to restructuring rather than attempting to examine the political "growth coalitions" (Mollenkopf 1978, 1983) which execute specific redevelopment plans. This was in part a choice of scale; no matter how general the process, local experiences differ greatly.

In addition, the emphasis on the logic of accumulation and its role in urban restructuring in no way presupposes a philosophical adherence to a "capital logic" approach rather than one emphasizing class struggle. As a philosophical dichotomy this is a false issue; but as an historical dialectic it is everything. The unfortunate truth is that the comparatively low levels of working-class struggle since the Cold War (with the exception of those during the late 1960s, and in much of Europe during the early 1970s) have meant that capital has had a fairly free hand in the structuring and restructuring of urban space. This does not invalidate the role of class struggle; it means that with few exceptions it was a lopsided struggle during this period, so much so that the capitalist class was generally able to wage the struggle through its economic strategies for capital investment. The investment of capital is the first weapon of struggle in the ruling-class arsenal.

An important exception to the general hegemony of capital concerns the role of European social democratic governments in providing public housing, the struggles over privatization of housing, and the rebellions in several European cities in the early 1980s over housing. These issues are not covered here and that is an important omission. What this experience suggests, however, is a further progression in our understanding of the urban frontier. The urban wilderness produced by the cyclical movement of capital and its devalorization have, from the perspective of capital, become new urban frontiers of profitability. Gentrification is a frontier on which fortunes are made. From the perspective of working-class residents and their neighborhoods, however, the urban frontier is more directly political rather than economic. Threatened with displacement as the frontier of profitability advances, the issue for them is to fight for the establishment of a political frontier behind which working-class residents can take back control of their homes: there are two sides to any frontier. The larger task is organizing to advance the political frontier, and like the frontier itself, Turneresque or urban, there are lulls and spurts in this process.

Acknowledgements

Peter Marcuse, Damaris Rose and Bob Beauregard gave me valuable comments on earlier drafts of this paper. I would also like to thank members of a seminar at Harvard University who offered comments, and members of the geography departments at Rutgers and Ohio State who further helped to refine the arguments.

Note

1   For an assessment of the Enterprise Zone experience, see Anderson (1983).

3

The chaos and complexity of gentrification

ROBERT A. BEAUREGARD

The essence of gentrification is hidden from view. One can walk through Adams-Morgan in Washington, DC, or Queen Village in Philadelphia, through Islington in London, or the Victorian inner suburbs of Melbourne, even Over-the-Rhine in Cincinnati, and visually assess the gentrification process as expressed in rehabilitated buildings, stores and restaurants designed for the new, affluent and well dressed inhabitants. Yet the forces underlying gentrification have yet to be fully uncovered. Different layers of meaning still clothe the historical specificity of gentrification, and mask the particular confluence of societal forces and contradictions which account for its existence. Journalistic immediacy, redevelopment ideology and positivist research have obscured the essential meanings and the underlying causes.

The purpose of this chapter is to present a theoretical analysis of the process of gentrification which penetrates these various meanings, but which avoids a simple explanation of what is essentially a complex phenomenon. In fact, there can be no single theory of an invariant gentrification process. Rather, there are theoretical interpretations of how the "gentry" are created and located in the cities, how "gentrifiable" housing is produced, how those to be displaced originally came to live in inner-city neighborhoods, and finally how the various processes of gentrification unfold given the establishment of these three basic conditions. These different theoretical arguments must be combined in a fashion compatible with the specific instances of gentrification that we wish to explain. The emphasis, therefore, must be placed on contingency and complexity, set within the structural dimensions of advanced capitalism. The substantive focus of the analysis is gentrification as it has taken place in the United States. But before addressing these issues, we should understand how our comprehension of gentrification has been distorted, and then set forth epistemological standards for the subsequent investigation.

Meaning and epistemology

Stratifications of meaning

The thinnest and outermost layer of our comprehension of the gentrification process is that of journalistic and public-relations hyperbole fostered by its "boosters:" redevelopment bodies, local newspapers, "city" magazines, mayors' offices, real-estate organizations, financial institutions, historic preservationists and neighborhood organizations comprised of middle-class homeowners. Each has an interest in increased economic activity within the city and an affinity for the middle class who function as gentrifiers. Their descriptions, analyses and advertising both present and misrepresent the phenomenon as it exists, and convey an ideology meant to foster continued gentrification.[1]

Within this layer we find the theme of the "urban pioneers" who are risking themselves and their savings to turn a deteriorated and undesirable neighborhood into a place for "good living." A new, urban life-style is touted, one which represents the consumerism and affluence of those unburdened by familial responsibilities and economic stringencies (Alpern 1979, Fleetwood 1979). These gentrifiers live in historically preserved or "high tech" domestic environments which reflect their sense of "taste." They shop at specialty stores where unique and higher quality clothing and food convey and reinforce a sense of status. Trendy restaurants provide them with places to be seen and admired. The comforts of "civilized" living are everywhere. Urban culture is now a commodified form, leagues removed from the sense of "community" which it was once meant to convey (Williams 1977: 11–20).

This is one ideology of gentrification, part of its reality, but not representative of its essential form. The image of the city and its neighborhoods is manipulated in order to reduce the perceived risk and to encourage investment. Moreover, to believe that such description objectively captures the process of gentrification is to be deluded.

A portion of the previous chapter was devoted to unmasking this "frontier imagery of gentrification" with its pioneers, invisible natives, urban homesteading, myth of upward (through spatial) mobility and the city as a wilderness to be recaptured and tamed. Elsewhere Holcomb (1982) and Holcomb and Beauregard

(1981:52–64) have discussed the image management generally attendant on urban redevelopment schemes. The resultant hegemonic boosterism makes opposition difficult and attracts investors. More importantly, it erroneously presents gentrification as beneficial for the city as a whole. But rather than becoming implicated in the assumptions and pertinences of this ideology (Ley 1980), the point is to penetrate a way through it.

The next layer is composed of the numerous empirical assessments of gentrification, almost all of which have proceeded from a positivistic methodology which often presents empirical regularities in the guise of causal explanation.[2] These empirical investigations include both survey research (Gale 1979) and case studies (Laska & Spain 1980: 95–235), with fewer attempts to assess gentrification utilizing secondary data (Smith 1979b, Black 1980a, Spain 1980). For the most part, they focus upon changes in the built environment over time but fail to explain the dynamics that bring about these changes. The processes of gentrification are not often emphasized: Richards and Rowe (1977), London (1980), and DeGiovanni (1983), are exceptions. Moreover, the concern is almost wholly with housing redevelopment rather than with the gentrification of neighborhood commercial districts (Aristedes 1975, Chernoff 1980, Van Gelder 1981). Lastly, the intent of most of these works is to create a Weberian "ideal-type" description of a gentrifier, a gentrifying neighborhood or a process of gentrification. Highly salient characteristics are distilled into a simplified form which lacks any sense of historical and spatial contingency.

The ostensibly prototypical gentrifier is a single-person or two-person household comprised of affluent professionals without children (Gale 1979, 1980). These "gentry" are willing to take on the risk of investing in an initially deteriorated neighborhood and the task of infusing a building with their sweat equity. Presumably, they desire to live in the city close to their jobs, where they can establish an urbane life-style and capture a financially secure position in the housing market. Their lack of demand for schools, commitment to preserving their neighborhoods, support of local retail outlets and services, and contribution to the tax base are all viewed as beneficial for the city.

The neighborhoods to be gentrified are deteriorated, and occupied by lower- and moderate-income, often elderly, households. These residential areas are located close to the central business district, and often have peculiar amenities such as views of the skyline, access to parks, or some historical significance. The housing is run-down but still structurally sound, except for the existence of abandoned and gutted buildings more popularly known as "shells." Moderate rehabilitation, for the most part, will make most housing suitable for "gentry," and facade improvements will enhance the architectural qualities and contribute to major increases in its market value.

The gentrification process involves the purchasing of buildings by affluent households or by intermediaries such as speculators or developers, the upgrading of the housing stock, governmental investment in the surrounding environment, the concomitant changeover in local retail facilities, the stabilization of the neighborhood and the enhancement of the tax base. Although residential displacement is recognized and empirically documented by researchers operating at this level, its extent and existence as a problem have been debated (Hartman 1979, Sumka 1979, LeGates & Hartman 1981).

Beneath this, and closer to the essence of gentrification, lies a third level of more theoretical analyses. Notable among these are two papers by Neil Smith. Both begin with a strong theoretical base in marxist historical materialism and attempt to unearth the underlying structural forces that have created and currently drive the process of gentrification. One of Smith's arguments (1979a) focuses upon the uneven development of metropolitan land markets. The basic theme is that disinvestment in certain areas of central cities, a disinvestment paralleling suburban investment and further exacerbated by the financial dynamics of construction and land interests (Smith 1979b), has resulted in residential areas whose capitalized ground rent is significantly below their potential ground rent. The value of the buildings themselves is considered of little moment. In the search for locations of profitable investment in metropolitan areas where suburban land has been almost fully developed, finance and real-estate capital discover these undervalued locations and undertake actions (e.g. rehabilitation, new construction, speculation) to capture the difference between the capitalized and potential ground rents. Thus it can be argued that gentrification results, in essence, from the uneven development of metropolitan land markets.

Neil Smith's second theoretical explanation (1982) is compatible with this argument, but takes place at another layer of meaning. The historically uneven development of national and international capitalism is now the starting point. The cycle of valorization and devalorization in regional land markets is now related to the "... broader rhythm and periodicity of the national and international economy" (Smith, N. 1982: 149). The inevitable falling rate of profit and the overproduction of commodities have led to a crisis of capitalism which can only be attenuated through the discovery of new investment opportunities. Following Harvey (1978), Smith maintains that such crises result in a shift of capital investment from the sphere of production to the built environment. Within that arena, the most profitable opportunities for capital accumulation are those devalorized neighborhoods where capitalized ground rent is significantly below potential ground rent. Thus the two arguments merge. The point, however, is that now gentrification is embedded more deeply in the structural dynamics of advanced capitalism in its organic totality, rather than simply in uneven metropolitan development. Gentrification "operates primarily to counteract the falling rate of profit" (Smith, N. 1982: 151). This is a more incisive statement than that offered previously.

However, although these theoretical explanations are commendable, since they penetrate empirical appearances and unsheath an "essence" of gentrification, they suffer from a number of problems. The "rent gap" argument provides only one of the necessary conditions for gentrification and none of the sufficient ones. Observation shows that many areas of central cities have rent gaps greatly in excess of those areas that gentrify. Thus the theory cannot easily explain why Hoboken (New Jersey) becomes gentrified, but Newark – where capitalized ground rents are extremely low and whose locational advantages relative to Manhattan and transportation facilities are on a par with Hoboken's – does not. Moreover, there is the question of how the potential ground rent is perceived, thus establishing a crucial element in determining the rent gap.

Both the "rent gap" argument and the argument focused upon the falling rate of profit suffer three additional theoretical weaknesses. One is the treatment of uneven development. Uneven development is used to explain gentrification and the rent gap, rather than the latter two phenomena being conceived as attributes of uneven development, all of which have to be explained initially by the structural tendencies of capitalism.[3] Secondly, no attempt is made to address the diverse nature of gentrification. It is collapsed into an "ideal type" concept. Lastly, the arguments are characterized by a lack of attention to the role of reproduction and consumption in gentrification. They begin and end in the economic base, the sphere of production, and do not consider how changes in these other two spheres structure, produce and even represent gentrification. Needless to say, these three weaknesses are interrelated.

Epistemological comments

From the above, albeit brief, overview of the three levels of explanation to be found in the literature, a number of epistemological issues can be identified as a means to guide any theorizing about gentrification. The objective here is to penetrate these successive layers of meaning and peer further into the core of the process. This is the first theoretical requirement: that our theory not be deluded by ideology or misrepresent empirical regularities as causal explanation. Rather, we must look beneath the phenomenal forms of gentrification, as indeed some have attempted, in order to understand both its dynamics and significance.

Secondly, "gentrification" must be recognized as a "chaotic concept" connoting many diverse if interrelated events and processes; these have been aggregated under a single (ideological) label and have been assumed to require a single causal explanation (Sayer 1982, Rose 1984). Encompassed under the rubric of gentrification are the redevelopment of historic rowhouses in Philadelphia's Society Hill initiated by an urban renewal project (Smith 1979b), the transformation of a working-class neighborhood of Victorian houses in San Francisco by gay men (Castells & Murphy 1982), the rampant speculation and displacement occurring on the Lower East Side of New York City involving multifamily structures (Gottlieb 1982), the redevelopment of abandoned housing in the Fells Point area of Baltimore, and the conversion of warehouses along the Boston waterfront to housing for the affluent. Each of these instances not only involved different types of individuals, but also proceeded differently and had varying consequences. The diversity of gentrification must be recognized, rather than conflating diverse aspects into a single phenomenon.

Thirdly, the above observations suggest that a diversity of social forces and contradictions within the social formation cohere in some fashion to bring about various types of gentrification. Moreover, it additionally suggests that gentrification is not inevitable in older, declining cities. In effect, gentrification is a conjuncture of both those structural forces necessary for its general form, and the contingent forces that make it appear at distinct points in time and in diverse ways in certain cities and not others (cf. Althusser 1977: 87–128; Beauregard 1984). Certainly the last 50 years have witnessed numerous instances where people have been displaced from cities; young and affluent households have bought property and even rehabilitated it; neighborhoods have deteriorated; governments have provided assistance to real-estate interests; and financial institutions have manipulated land markets. But only during the 1970s and 1980s did these and other forces coalesce and intensify to produce the diversity of processes referred to as gentrification.

Thus we wish to explain gentrification using both structural tendencies and historical specificities, but without extracting it theoretically from the social formation of which it is a part. More precisely, gentrification must be theorized as part of the organic totality of the social formation. This means, even more precisely, not searching for the causes of gentrification solely in the sphere of production. Rather, it is at the conjuncture of production, reproduction, and consumption, at least initially, that we must theorize (Markusen 1980, McDowell 1983, Rose 1984). Gentrification is not simply a facet of capital accumulation.

Given these various epistemological insights, the following discussion places emphasis upon those individuals commonly labeled the gentrifiers, those who serve as the proximate investors in the gentrified housing. The concern is to explain how they came to be located in central cities with reproduction and consumption needs and desires compatible with a gentrification process. After establishing their potential as gentrifiers, the next step is to explain the creation of "gentrifiable" housing and the prior placement of economically and politically vulnerable (i.e. easily displaced) individuals and families into that housing. With these three pieces of the puzzle in place, we can then explore the various processes by which they are brought together to produce gentrification itself.

The potential gentrifiers

The explanation for gentrification begins with the presence of "gentrifiers," the necessary agents and beneficiaries of the gentrification process, and the directions taken by their reproduction and consumption. First, the demand for inexpensive, inner-city housing is not a new phenomenon, nor is the existence of politically and economically vulnerable social groups. However, the existence of affluent, professional and ostensibly "afamilial" households in central cities has become much more pronounced during these last few decades. Secondly, and more importantly, the gentrifiers are often, though seldom alone, the "agents" of the gentrification process, and thus provide the motivations and aspirations that shape it. In this way, agency is structured into our theorizing (Beauregard 1984). Lastly, without this group the whole process ceases to exist. Different types of housing stock might be rehabilitated, and diverse individuals and families displaced, but the characteristics of the gentrifiers are remarkably similar across specific instances of gentrification.

Changes in the industrial and occupational structure of the United States brought about in part by the international restructuring of capital (Bluestone & Harrison 1982: 140–90), and specifically changes in the types of economic activity which are growing and declining in the cities, have resulted in an increasingly bimodal urban labor market (Black 1980b).[4] Before World War II a strong manufacturing sector dominated central cities and provided semi-skilled, medium-wage jobs with some possibility of advancement. That manufacturing sector has since declined both absolutely and relatively, and has been replaced by personal–service, administrative and professional, retail and governmental activities. In the one mode are the lower-wage service jobs in the retail, office, hospitality and governmental sectors; in the other, the professional–managerial employment in the same sectors but also in corporate headquarters and business and legal services. Many lower-middle-income workers have left the city to locate nearer the manufacturing jobs now in the suburbs, and most of the unemployed poor and working poor remain in the city to engage intermittently in the growing service sector and its low-skill, low-wage employment. The professional–managerial jobs are filled with both city residents and commuters. It is within this urban, professional–managerial fraction of labor that the gentrifiers are situated. rent vs own ?

These changes in the sphere of production are part of a long-term trend embodying the decline of the manufacturing sector and the rise of professional and managerial employment, but it is their spatial manifestation over the past two decades which is pivotal for gentrification. Of greatest importance is the absolute and relative expansion of professional and managerial jobs in the central cities. For example, professional and technical workers, managers, and administrators expanded their share of Philadelphia's labor force from 15.5 percent in 1960 to 22.6 percent in 1977. Craft and kindred workers, operatives and laborers declined from 40.1 percent during that period to 30.9 percent, whereas sales, clerical and service workers increased from 38.4 percent to 46.5 percent (City of Philadelphia 1978). More specific data on these potential gentry exist in a recent analysis of New York City's employment (Stetson 1983). Service industries increased their share of employment from 69.6 percent in 1960 to 83.8 percent in 1982. The fastest growing employment sectors from 1977 to 1982 were social services, security and commodity brokers, legal services, banking, and business services. Similar patterns are discernible in other central cities. The point is that employment opportunities for professionals and managers are becoming dominant within central cities. Admittedly, this could result in no additional professionals and managers living within these cities, since they could commute from the suburbs. It does establish, however, a necessary condition for an urban gentry to arise.

42

In order to explain why these professionals and managers do remain within the city and also engage in gentrification, we must move away from the sphere of production and focus upon their reproduction and consumption activities. Moreover, it is not enough to say that they desire to live in an urban environment. The issue is *why* a fraction of this group elects to remain within the city, rather than to follow the trend of suburban out-migration. What is it about an urban residence, in addition to the proximity to work, which is especially compatible with the reproduction and consumption activities of this fraction of labor?

One part of the answer involves the attitude and behavior of many professional and managerial individuals to biological reproduction. Over the last few decades there has been a trend toward the postponement of marriage and of childrearing, and, in more and more cases, decisions to remain childless, despite a more recent rise in childbearing among women in their early thirties.[5] The implications for gentrification are that these decisions create more single individual households and childless couples whose consumption needs differ from those who have traditionally migrated to the suburbs.

Individual behavior concerning biological reproduction is a complex and diverse phenomenon. One factor is the movement of women into the labor force: from 1960 to 1980 the labor-force participation rate for women increased from 37.7 to 51.5 percent (US Bureau of the Census 1982: 377). Economic necessity, the expansion in service-sector and professional–managerial jobs, feminist pressure and affirmative-action legislation have all contributed to making paid employment an available and acceptable option for many women. Certainly holding a paid job has usually been a necessity for working-class women, but economic decline has required even middle-class women to work. The desire of educated women to establish professional careers, coupled with the continued minimal childrearing participation by men, make it likely that childbearing will be postponed or rejected. This option is facilitated by the widespread availability of birth control and the legalization of abortion in 1973. A career orientation also contributes to the postponement of marriage. A full explanation, however, requires that we consider the sphere of consumption within which both female and male professionals and managers exist.

The consumption style of this urban, professional–managerial group is partly one of conspicuous consumption, the acquisition of commodities for public display (see Ch. 5 of this book). It is facilitated by the postponement of familial responsibilities, and the accumulation of savings. Clothes, jewelry, furniture, stereo equip-

43

ment, vacations, sports equipment, luxury items such as cameras and even automobiles, *inter alia*, are part of the visual and functional identity of the potential gentrifiers. In addition, more and more consumption takes place outside of the household in "public" realms: home cooking replaced by restaurants; home entertainment (with the exception of the video recorder which allows freedom from television schedules) by clubs, movies, plays, and shopping; and quiet respites at home are replaced by travel. Admittedly, these consumption habits are not dissimilar from those of other professional, middle-class individuals not in the city, but what makes them important for gentrification is their intersection with decisions on biological reproduction.

The postponement of marriage facilitates this consumption, but it also makes it necessary if people are to meet others and develop friendships. Persons without partners, outside of the milieu of college, must now join clubs and frequent places (e.g. "singles" bars) where other singles (both the never-married and the divorced) congregate in order to make close friends. Couples (married or not) need friendships beyond the workplace and may wish to congregate at "public" places. Those social opportunities, moreover, though possibly no more numerous in cities than in suburbs, are decidedly more spatially concentrated and, because of suburban zoning, tend to be more spatially integrated with residences. Clustering occurs as these individuals move proximate to "consumption items" and as entrepreneurs identify this fraction of labor as comprising conspicuous and major consumers. Both the need to consume outside of the home and the desire to make friends and meet sexual partners, either during the now-extended period of "search" before marriage or a lifetime of fluid personal relationships, encourage the identification with and migration to certain areas of the city.

At the same time, these tendencies are also and obviously important for the gentrification of commercial districts. The potential gentry represent an "up-scale" class of consumers who frequent restaurants and bars, and generally treat shopping as a social event. The objective for the entrepreneur is to capture the discretionary income of the consumer by offering an experience that is more than a functional exchange. Implicated in the purchase, be it of gourmet ice cream, a nouvelle cuisine meal, or a dance lesson, is the status of being at that shop in that neighborhood and buying that particular brand. Thus the dynamic of capital accumulation, fueled by affluence, is wedded to conspicuous consumption. Moreover, the purchase and rehabilitation of existing commercial establishments as a neighborhood begins to gentrify contribute to further residential gentrification. The two are mutually supportive.

Yet the transformation of urban, middle-class professionals into gentrifiers requires more than conspicuous consumption and post-ponement of marriage and childrearing. It also involves threats to their continued consumption and to their long-term economic security, threats which lead them to purchase housing in the city. This fraction of labor is not immune either to inflation or to reductions in their employment status. Both have differing but serious impacts upon the ability of this class to consume in the ways described here. Moreover, these are "educated" consumers who understand the need to engage in financial planning, whether it be through tax lawyers, voluntary savings, or investments. Even while engaging in conspicuous consumption and, at least initially, post-poning major savings, they are also sensitive to the advisability of planning for the future. The maintenance of their consumption patterns in the long run cannot be left to the workings of the economy. It must be actively pursued. That becomes immediately obvious as this group begins to cluster in certain areas of the city causing a "heating up" of the housing market (and thus rising rents, condominium conversions and the like) and an increase in the price to be paid for consumption items.

As this "potential gentry" establishes an area as desirable, especially for those in similar life situations, the demand increases for housing and for restaurants, bars, movie theaters and other facilities for public but individualized consumption. Prices respond to the amount of money available, and are raised accordingly, reaching what the market will bear. Although this is not a major problem as regards most consumption items, it is as regards housing, par-ticularly rentals. The rental market inflates, and individuals find it more and more difficult to move into these areas. For those who are already there, both "early" gentrifiers and older residents, the costs of staying in place may become onerous, and conspicuous consump-tion for the former is threatened. These factors encourage defensive actions to protect oneself against the vagaries of the housing market and, at the same time, to avoid the ravages of the effects of inflation on one's salary. Yet there is still the desire to live in a location with other, similar individuals and with numerous amenities of a par-ticular quality and style. The combined search for financial security, a desirable location, access to amenities, and involvement with people of similar desires and affluence prepares these individuals to become gentrifiers. That there is a status to be gained from "home" or "apartment" ownership and a potential for high capital gains and tax benefits, not to mention the opportunity to express one's afflu-ence and "taste" in physical surroundings, also contributes to the probability of gentrification as a solution to these problems.

Not all of the "gentry," however, will purchase a rowhouse or a condominium; some will rent luxury apartments in converted single-room–occupancy hotels or formerly working–class apartment buildings. Some of the potential gentry may be unable to amass a down payment, or wish to avoid the responsibility of home-ownership. But they should not be considered as lesser gentrifiers because of this; the conversion of apartment buildings to luxury status is also part of the gentrification process.

Still to be explained is why these potential gentry select an urban location over a suburban one, and how certain barriers to home-ownership direct them to deteriorated or lower-income residential areas. The selection of an urban location is mainly explained by the consumption and reproduction activities described earlier, and also by increasing commuting costs in metropolitan areas as rising energy costs have forced up operating costs for the automobile, and as mass transit systems have become increasingly expensive.[6] Moreover, high commuting costs and long commuting times would interfere financially and temporally with consumption activities. Reinforcing this disincentive toward suburban living is the rising cost of newly constructed housing, both in the suburbs and in urban areas. Throughout most of the postwar period, housing has been a prime investment opportunity, providing long-term financial security, precisely because of its rapid appreciation and thus high resale value, not to mention its use as collateral for other investments.[7] In fact, the average purchase price of both new and existing housing, in the suburbs as well as the cities, has risen faster than wages from 1970 to 1980.[8] Both transportation costs and housing costs, then, serve as barriers to the purchase of a suburban house.

At the same time, these individuals cannot compete in just *any* housing submarket. Both encouraging and discouraging the purchase of housing is the inflation of wages and salaries relative to housing prices. Additionally, since these potential gentrifiers tend to be relatively new to their careers, and young, they are unlikely to have extensive savings. Even though parents may contribute to a down payment, the amassing of the capital needed to purchase a well-maintained house in an already "established" and stable middle-class urban neighborhood is likely to be difficult.[9] There are thus limitations on their demands in the urban housing market.

Given the limited capital of this potential gentry, their desire to be close to their places of employment, their peculiar consumption needs, and the derivative desire to treat "housing" as both an investment item and as a statement of the image of affluence and taste which these individuals are trying to project, it is not surprising that they search for inner-city locations near central business districts, with amenities and with an architecturally interesting housing stock which has the potential to be rehabilitated and redecorated, and where housing costs are, for the moment, relatively inexpensive but prices are likely to rise. That is, the end result of these forces is the demand for a specific type of housing in specific types of residential area. That this is also recognized by developers, real-estate agents, and commercial investors reinforces the housing choices of potential gentrifiers. The point is that this is not the same as the generalized demand for inexpensive, inner-city housing. In most cities, there is a large amount of inexpensive housing, but not very much of it entices the gentrifiers. That which does not is left for lower-income groups, or is simply abandoned.

Creation of gentrifiable housing

The next step in this theoretical penetration of the gentrification process is to explain the existence of inexpensive, inner-city housing capable of being "taken over" by "outsiders." There are two issues here: (a) the creation of gentrifiable housing, and (b) the creation of prior occupants for that housing who can easily be displaced or replaced – that is, who are unable or unwilling to resist. These are theoretically separable but interdependent processes.

The devaluation and deterioration of inner-city housing and land is a much discussed and explored phenomenon (Harvey 1973: 130–47, Smith 1979a: 543–5, 1979b, Solomon & Vandell 1982). Most importantly for the argument here, devaluation may or may not result in gentrification. Rather, the processes of residential change have the potential for numerous outcomes, ranging from gentrification to total abandonment of a neighborhood. Thus neighborhood decline is necessary but is not sufficient for gentrification to occur. Vulnerable neighborhoods may begin as areas of working-class housing, housing for the middle class, or even mixed-use (i.e. industrial, commercial, and residential) structures with a significant amount of housing interspersed.

To take the first case, there are working-class neighborhoods where housing has been well maintained for many decades, with working-class families replacing working-class families of the same or different ethnicity and race. Relative to other parts of the city, the housing may be inexpensive and thus entice the potential gentry. It is worth emphasizing that neighborhoods and housing need not be deteriorated before being gentrified. The price of housing within a given city is spatially relative. Its affordability and "acceptability" are regionally determined by prevailing wage rates, the overall cost of living, and the spatial structure of inflation in housing values. Gentrified neighborhoods of this origin seem characteristic of certain "gay" areas in San Francisco (Castells and Murphy 1982), and of traditional working-class neighborhoods comprised primarily of apartment buildings (Gottlieb 1982).

In the second case, where the residential area began not as a well maintained working-class neighborhood but as a neighborhood of middle-class homeowners, the process leading to the creation of inexpensive housing is different.[10] The devaluation of these areas is often described as one where the original middle-class residents move outward from the central city as they establish families and as their incomes rise. They are replaced by households of lower income. These replacement households may maintain the property for a time, but they soon move on the same trajectory of upward and outward mobility as those they replaced. Reproduction and consumption activities are thus central to the production of deteriorated housing. Eventually, the neighborhood is "invaded" by a group of households with a low and virtually stagnant income stream. The costs of maintenance and reinvestment in the housing exceed their financial wherewithal, and significant deterioration begins.

The result is the further in-migration of households unable to maintain their dwellings, overcrowding, the subdivision of large households into rental units in order to produce a rent roll acceptable to their owners (some of whom may be absentee landlords), and the eventual transition of home-ownership to rental tenure. The landlords may continue to invest in the property, and this process of devaluation might be averted, or at least temporarily halted. If not, disinvestment escalates as the tenants become poorer and poorer, as profits erode in the face of inflation, and as other investment opportunities compete for the landlord's capital. This leads to more rapid deterioration, actual destruction (e.g. "torching" for insurance purposes) and abandonment. The housing stock in this area is now "inexpensive."

Peculiar to even fewer cities than gentrification is "loft conversion," the creation of inexpensive housing from mixed-use districts, particularly industrial or waterfront districts with many small-scale manufacturing plants or warehouses established prior to World War II. This is the third case we shall consider. Often, these mixed-use areas are adjacent to central business districts. Cities such as New York, Philadelphia and Boston have had areas of this type abandoned, but without replacement by other industrial tenants. The buildings have remained empty, or have been rented or purchased by marginal industrial or commercial tenants who have failed to maintain them. The result has been both devaluation and deterioration. Enclosed space in these areas is thus relatively inexpensive, even though it may require significant rehabilitation before being habitable as housing. Nonetheless, the transformation of mixed-use areas and the takeover of inexpensive working-class housing are as much a part of gentrification phenomena as the more prototypical case of the redevelopment of deteriorated but once middle-class neighborhoods.

Locating the gentrified

The people most likely to be gentrified (i.e. displaced) are those living in inexpensive but architecturally desirable housing near central business districts. Many are marginal to the labor market or outside it: unemployed males and working-class white, black and Hispanic youth, the elderly, "welfare" mothers, and many working-class households and underemployed individuals near the poverty line. Some are "redundant" workers, but many are part of the urban labor market.[11] They are living in these locations for a variety of reasons: the rents may be cheap, the location may hold historical and emotional significance, there may be spatial advantages in terms of private and public services needed for reproduction and consumption, or employment opportunities may be nearby. Their location may be a matter of choice; it may have stemmed from a lack of choice. Nonetheless, their existence here is a matter of the creation and location of the inner-city poor.

The explanation for the inner-city poor under capitalism is complex, involving not only the migration of black agricultural workers after World War II but also that of poor whites from rural lands (e.g. Castells 1976b). The lure of low-wage manufacturing jobs in the cities brought them there, and the subsequent diminution of such jobs left them in marginal economic straits. The opportunities for the sons and daughters of these migrants, moreover, are limited. Low-wage, unskilled manufacturing and service jobs compete with unemployment and public assistance. The link between the potential gentrifiers and the potential gentrified begins here in the labor market. The forces that have generated employment opportunities for the professional–managerial class have also diminished low-wage manufacturing jobs with opportunities for advancement, and given rise to service and clerical employment in retail establishments and offices. These latter jobs are often of low pay and with little possibility for career mobility. In the retail and hospitality sectors, for example, turnover is high and employment stability is virtually nonexistent. The restructuring of the urban labor market is thus part of the explanation for the existence of both the potential gentrifiers and the potential gentrified. The former are provided with the reasons and wherewithal to undertake gentrification; the latter are limited to certain neighborhoods within the city and are unable, because of their low economic status, to resist gentrification.

These individuals occupy housing which has the potential to be gentrified and, secondly, are themselves economically and politically powerless relative to the gentrifiers. Because they are in the low-wage sectors of the labor market, or outside it on "fixed" incomes, they have few economic resources and find themselves renting in these neighborhoods, or else barely able to maintain and hold on to houses in which they have lived for years, years that have seen their relative economic influence in the housing market erode. At the same time, their consumption potential is weak relative to other segments of the city's population, particularly the potential gentry, and thus their attractiveness to proponents of redevelopment, usually intent on creating a city of middle-class affluence, is also weak. Many of these households, additionally, are characterized by large numbers of children, or are female-headed and poor, thus requiring a greater share of local governmental services ranging from education to law enforcement. The hypothetical gap between what they demand in governmental services and what they pay in taxes and contribute to the circulation of capital through consumer expenditures combines with their inability to afford decent housing to make them relatively undesirable to local-government officials.

Thus, because these individuals and families lack economic power, and because of related disadvantages in the realms of consumption and reproduction (e.g. low purchasing power and family instability, respectively), they also lack political power. The end result is that these households are easily exploited by landlords if they are renting, unable to resist "buyouts" by the more affluent if they own their housing, and unlikely to mobilize to resist local-government encouragement of gentrification. Of course, it is not uncommon to find in gentrifying neighborhoods older homeowners and small landlords who are anxious to sell and move. However, this has not been shown to be a major proportion of those potentially gentrified, and therefore does not obviate the displacement consequences of gentrification. This group merely points up, once again, the chaotic nature of gentrification. The location of these "powerless" households in gentrifiable residential areas is not a "law" of capitalism, which inevitably produces the conditions for gentrification, nor do those potentially gentrified always succumb without a struggle (Auger 1979). Instead, the location of economically and politically weak households in certain types of neighborhood at a particular historical time combines with the inner-city location of the potential gentry, among other factors, to produce the conjuncture which is labeled gentrification.

Gentrification processes

To this point, a number of components of gentrification have been explained: the production of the potential gentry, the generation of the potentially gentrifiable neighborhoods, and the creation of the potentially gentrified. This analysis has included the possibility that any of these "productions" might not lead to gentrification. It remains to (a) identify the "facilitators" or active agents of gentrification, in addition to the potential gentry themselves, and (b) more specifically to explain why only *certain* inner-city areas with inexpensive housing opportunities occupied by the "powerless' become gentrified. Many parts of any city remain in a deteriorated condition, despite the existence within the city boundaries of potential gentry, and despite the presence of inexpensive housing occupied by the lower class.

Gentrification is partly facilitated by the federal government's inducements to home-ownership, making a housing purchase economically beneficial (Stone 1978). Basic to this policy is the tax deduction for interest payments on mortgages. There are also more recent tax deductions and credits for weatherization and energy-conservation projects (e.g. solar panels), as well as for the rehabilitation of historic structures. The purchase and rehabilitation of a house can benefit the buyer significantly, particularly in the first few years of the purchase when interest rates comprise a large proportion of mortgage payments and when rehabilitation is likely to be done. This applies, of course, to home-ownership regardless of location, though Federal Housing Administration mortgage insurance has historically favored suburban sites.

The local government often plays a more active and direct role in the gentrification process (Smith 1979b). It stands to benefit directly from the dislocation of lower-class groups which burden it through social programs, and from their replacement by middle-class consumers whose income will circulate in the local economy and whose investments will enhance the tax base. Thus one finds local governments advertising the potential for gentrification in certain of their neighborhoods; providing tax abatements for rehabilitation (e.g. the J-51 program in New York City); devoting community development funds to rehabilitation and to improving public services in these neighborhoods; using code enforcement to force landlords and homeowners to rehabilitate or to sell their properties; actively engaging in the designation of historic districts or the labeling of "neighborhoods" (e.g. the "creation" of Tribeca by the New York City Planning Commission); and diminishing public service provision elsewhere in order to encourage decline before then facilitating reinvestment (Hartman *et al.* 1981). Moreover, the local government can rezone a mixed-use district to make it easier to gentrify, or it can fail to enforce zoning statutes in a mixed-use district, thus facilitating an easier transition to residential land use.

The local government and the various tax provisions of the federal government, however, are not determinant, and their actions may not even be necessary. What is necessary, but not sufficient, is for financial and property interests to foresee the opportunities involved in the transformation of a residential area from low to middle income through investment in rehabilitation. Landlords, developers and real-estate agents, both large and small, play an important role in "steering" the potential gentry to a neighborhood, buying property and speculating (i.e. "flipping" a building by purchasing it and then selling it a short time later without adding any value to it), and displacing residents (directly or indirectly) by raising rents in order to empty a building in preparation for sale or for complete rehabilitation. In addition, rental properties are turned into condominiums or cooperatives, and even rehabilitated as rental units (Richards & Rowe 1977, Smith 1979b, Gottlieb 1982). In all these instances, property interests are exploiting those short-term investment opportunities created by other components of the gentrification process. In fact, the ways in which profits may be realized are numerous, as are the combinations of small, medium and large developers, real-estate interests and landlords who might pursue them.

Property interests, nonetheless, cannot operate without the assistance of financial entities able to lend large sums of capital (Smith 1979b). Investments in the built environment are large and usually of long duration. More importantly, the profits to be made from such investments are contingent upon low equity-to-debt ratios, which allow tax advantages, high profits and easy withdrawals (i.e. escape) from both good and bad investments. Savings and loan associations, local banks, and other financial institutions make capital available over long terms for mortgages and over shorter terms for construction and rehabilitation. Insurance companies and pension funds may also buy property and invest in neighborhoods. In the case of large buildings or complexes, new forms of creative financing (such as limited-equity partnerships) allow numerous and various fractions of capital and even labor to provide money for gentrification, and to reap the rewards from the rapid escalation in housing costs.

All of these agents, inclinations and forces must come together in specific spatial locations. These sites are often characterized by architecturally interesting housing or commercial and industrial structures "with potential:" a unique spatial amenity such as access to a waterfront, a hilltop location or a spectacular view; substandard but not structurally unsound buildings clustered relatively close together to allow for a contagion effect to occur and for gentrifiers to "protect" themselves; proximity to the central business district (Lipton 1980) or at least good mass transportation links; and local neighborhood commercial areas with an initial attraction to the early gentrifiers but also with the potential for transformation to the types of shops, restaurants and facilities most compatible with the reproductive decisions and consumption activities of the gentry.

The actual gentrification process, though it may involve all of these actors to varying degrees, has not unfolded similarly in different cities, nor is it likely to unfold in the future. Theory must explain multiple gentrification processes.[12] The most commonly accepted version is that in which a deteriorated neighborhood is initially invaded by "pioneers." Then the process quickens as gentry, along with small real-estate interests, financial institutions and construction firms, participate in the purchase and rehabilitation of single-family dwellings (London 1980). The dynamics are different in those neighborhoods in which large-scale developers and speculators purchase multifamily housing and the area is transformed into luxury condominiums and cooperative apartments (Richards & Rowe 1977, Gottlieb 1982). One can also identify a gentrification process in which the local government takes the initiative through a major urban renewal project (e.g. Society Hill; see Ch. 6) or through homesteading programs (e.g. in Baltimore). Each of these processes (and there may be others) brings together the various actors and conditions in a different manner with varying implications for the distribution of the resultant financial and social benefits and costs.

Recognition of the complexity of processes involved furthers our sensitivity to "gentrification" as a chaotic concept. No one or even two factors are determinant. Conversely, the absence of any one factor does not mean that gentrification will not occur. Just as possible is their fusion into another form of neighborhood transformation unlike what we currently label gentrification. A sensitivity to these various possibilities is what characterizes the present theoretical analysis. It is a sensitivity both to the structural elements of advanced capitalism, which establish some of the necessary conditions for gentrification, and to the specific and contingent factors and historical timing, which must occur for gentrification to materialize. What is essential, nonetheless, is the production of that fraction of labor from which the potential gentry are drawn, the production of areas where gentrification might proceed, and the creation of a "gentrifiable" fraction of labor. That these components may exist without gentrification ensuing attests to the view of gentrification as an historical event created by the fusion of disparate forces and contradictions within a social formation which is itself characterized by both structure and contingency (Beauregard 1984).

Thus, a recognition of gentrification as both chaotic and complex has guided this work. The theoretical goal was to penetrate the layers of ideology and positivist social research which clothe gentrification, yet not to probe so deeply as to pass by its concrete manifestations. The intent was not to rediscover the essence of capitalism, but to use its structure and dynamics to explain a specific social phenomenon. Only by having gentrification clearly in view can it be scrutinized effectively.

Acknowledgements

Damaris Rose, Neil Smith and Briavel Holcomb have been most helpful in shaping my understanding of gentrification phenomena, and how to theorize about them. I would like to acknowledge their contribution.

Notes

1 It is within this layer of meaning that we find the notion that gentrification is a template for the future of urban neighborhoods, despite the obvious fact that, albeit highly visible, it is as yet a small-scale phenomenon.

2 Rose (1984) makes the point that even marxist theorists are prone to a "mix-and-match" methodology in which marxist categories are combined with positivistic empiricism to produce an eclectic and epistemologically inconsistent theoretical argument.

3 Moreover, it is not just capitalist countries that exhibit uneven development of sorts. However, this important theme cannot be discussed here.

4 International restructuring also affects the accumulation potential of different investments and thus influences gentrification. The variation

in profit rates across industrial sectors, however, is always operative at the national level under capitalism and thus is not sufficient for explaining gentrification.

5   From 1970 to 1980 the following changes occurred: the percentage of married individuals fell from 62.4 to 60.8; the percentage of nonfamily, two-person households increased from 8.0 to 11.2 of all nonfamily households, a category which itself increased by 66.4 percent; and the birth rate decreased from 17.8 to 16.2 per 1 000 population (US Bureau of the Census 1981). As for the fertility rate of women in their early thirties, the rate among women 30 to 34 years of age rose 22.5 percent from 60 births per 1 000 women in 1980 to 73.5 births in 1983. In addition, "forty-four percent of the women in this age range who gave birth last year either held jobs or were seeking jobs" (Pear 1983).

6   The consumer price index for public transportation increased by 131.7 percent from 1970 to 1980, and that for private transportation by 148.4 percent. Private non-agricultural gross weekly earnings in current dollars rose by 96.2 percent (US Bureau of the Census 1981: 468).

7   This suggests that sale value, and not ground rent, is a more salient financial issue in gentrification, though primarily for the gentry and not for property or financial interests (cf. Smith 1979a). Of course, the two "values" are difficult to separate in reality.

8   Whereas the consumer price index for housing increased by 122.3 percent from 1970 to 1980, private non-agricultural gross weekly wages rose by 96.2 percent in current dollars (US Bureau of the Census 1981: 468). The median sale price of a new privately owned one-family home increased by 176.1 percent over this decade, and the sale price of an existing, privately owned single-family home by 170.4 percent (US Bureau of the Census 1982: 249).

9   Omitted from this argument, because it seems less important where gentrification has occurred, is the construction of middle-income housing on vacant land in central cities. If such land were to exist, it is difficult to predict whether it would detract from the process of gentrification.

10 This is the case most often discussed in the literature and an example of particular interest to urban sociologists of the human ecology school.

11 To the extent that they are redundant, the displacement of these marginal and working-class households may not interrupt the smooth reproduction of labor for capital. See Smith, N. (1982: 153).

12 DeGiovanni (1983) has demonstrated empirically the discontinuous nature of gentrification and its variability across gentrifying neighborhoods.

4

Class constitution through spatial reconstruction? A re-evaluation of gentrification in Australia, Britain, and the United States

PETER WILLIAMS

The imagery of gentrification, whether in Australia, Britain or the United States, is so powerful today that it is easy to forget how recently this process has become part of the landscape of the city. The terminology of opportunity – "ripe for renovation," "bursting with promise," "original features," and "period charm" – has awakened many to the rich harvest to be gathered in the inner city. Twenty-five years earlier, the language and the locale were entirely different. Talk was of modernity, latest design and simple efficiency, and our attention was on suburbia as the finest expression of urban living, with fresh air and open space, country views and easy access. For many the suburbs remain the dream, and outward spread remains the reality for virtually all metropolitan areas in whatever country. At the same time, gentrification has all the signs of being acclaimed a universal process, albeit varying in scale and importance. Indeed such has been the enthusiasm of scholars to "discover" its occurrence that we now have worldwide reports of "sightings," even though our understanding of this process and its various forms is quite limited. Certainly the same signs of selective social and physical change can be observed in the cities of many advanced capitalist societies, but that can only form the starting point of any evaluation.

This chapter has two interrelated aims. The first is to evaluate critically the nature of gentrification and its image of uniformity in advanced capitalist societies. This question is pursued through an examination of the process in Australia, Britain and the United

States. In making these comparisons it is possible to generate an awareness both of the different contexts in which gentrification arises and of the general (cross-national) and specific (national or local) elements of this process. The second and related aim is to reconceptualize gentrification within the context of the relationships between social structures and human agents, and to break down the narrow structuralist perspective which has been developed in recent years. In particular it is important to consider questions of local politics, the varied responses and capacities of the state, gender, social and economic restructuring, and, most importantly, class relations and class constitution. Let us therefore begin by looking at the gentrification process in three different countries.

Nations and localities: gentrification in Australia, Britain, and the United States

Gentrification as a process of socio-economic change is not restricted to particular cultures or countries. The evidence available suggests it has occurred in towns and cities throughout much of Europe, Canada and New Zealand, as well as the three countries to be discussed here. The reason for selecting Australia, Britain and the United States is largely a function of the availability of material rather than deep-seated arguments regarding their particular importance. The three countries have interesting and important contrasts in terms of economic development, land- and property-ownership, form and structure of cities, social and political relations, and the organization of government, thus offering up the possibility of considerable variations in the operation and impact of the process.

At the level of simple observation, gentrification worldwide seems very much a uniform phenomenon. The experienced "spotter" can detect brass door knockers, pastel colours, paper lanterns, bamboo blinds, and light, open interiors in the inner areas of many cities. Although the extent to which these design features are now supplemented by iron bars, security screens and alarm systems seems to vary considerably, gentrification, like the spread of natural-food shops and exotic restaurants, appears to be common to many advanced capitalist societies. These visual signs coincide with attempts by public and private enterprise to "reclaim" inner areas from decline, perceived racial takeover, and impoverishment. Such campaigns for an urban "renaissance", promoting the historical qualities of the landscape of commercial and early industrial capitalism, its tourist potential and its cultural significance, have become commonplace in Europe and North America. It is interesting to note that these programs are not unlike the urban-clearance campaigns undertaken in the 19th century, which were promoted for reasons of health, security, and the establishment of urban setting commensurate with the importance of the emergent urban bourgeoisie.

Beneath the apparent uniformity of the process lie a number of more important similarities *and* contrasts. We shall now examine these in the context of national housing markets, patterns of state intervention, and economic and social restructuring.

Housing markets

The housing markets in the three countries vary significantly with respect to the relationships between housing supply and demand, institutional structures, the wage–housing cost relationships, market regulation and manipulation and financial organization. Such factors bear directly on the extent and structure of gentrification. In Australia, the housing market is characterized by relatively rapid response to particular demands. Land supply is good and the building industry has been able to provide a steady stream of suburban housing. Home-ownership levels have been high and working-class home-ownership has been much higher than in Britain or the United States, in part as a consequence of high wage levels. There have been acute housing shortages for much of this century (fueled by substantial immigration and a reluctance to build for those on the lowest incomes), with the consequence that many of the inner areas were rapidly colonized by new migrants. The outward spread of the metropolises and the suburban movement of industry have encouraged and enabled inner-city migrants to move out, to be replaced by white-collar professionals. The whole process, though initially the preoccupation of individuals, has become a coordinated speculative activity (Black undated, Roseth 1969, Centre for Urban Research and Action 1977).

The position in Britain is, in many respects, similar to the Australian situation. The much more complex and interlocked urban system in Britain has meant that many of the pressures in the housing and job markets are displaced into the smaller towns and villages surrounding the larger metropolitan centres. Gentrification in Britain is therefore much more pervasive and not confined to the largest inner cities. At the same time it is clearly in these inner areas that the most acute contradictions are posed. The restructuring of these areas has proceeded rapidly in recent years. As available property in the London boroughs of Islington, Camden and Greenwich has been taken over, the process has spread out into other boroughs. The very high proportion of private rental accommodation previously typical of these areas has been an important element in this change. Most inner London boroughs had upwards of 60 or 70 percent of the stock of dwellings in the private rented sector until recently, much of it consolidated into large property holdings (see Ch. 7).

Rent controls that were operative since the early part of the century acted to freeze the stock and its tenants while other aspects of the landscape changed around them. The decline of traditional industries and the rise of white-collar work and service employment shifted the balance of demand. The extensive clearance programs and provision of public housing, the construction of new towns and the promotion of home-ownership as a desirable tenure also influenced market conditions, reducing the stock of purchasable inner-city housing at the same time as making the idea of ownership more desirable (Hamnett & Williams 1980). The more circumscribed nature of the British housing market, reflecting both greater government control and a more hierarchical social and economic structure, has perhaps heightened the tension and conflict around gentrification even though the form of the process is like that in Australia.

Housing in the inner areas of American cities has been dominated by rented property. With racial change and the occupation of this housing by an underclass of black households, there has been substantial abandonment of property and redlining by financial organizations. Abandonment is effectively unknown as a phenomenon in the Australian and British housing markets, though redlining has certainly been widespread. These factors, combined with local fiscal crises, have imbued the gentrification debate in the United States with a significantly different momentum. Although the housing market is generally unregulated and open, in a way not dissimilar to the market in Australia, racial conflict, displacement (Henig 1980) abandonment and fiscal crisis ensure that gentrification is assigned particular importance as a process of change in urban areas.

Local politics and the state

The divergences between the three countries are brought out even more sharply when we consider local politics and the role of the state. It is evident that in Australia, Britain and the United States, gentrification has had considerable impact on local communities and local politics, with local councils at first being "infiltrated" by the gentry and ultimately being taken over. In both Australia and Britain this reconstitution of local politics has pitted working-class politicians against the new middle class, and even against more left-wing councillors within the same local Labour parties (Smith 1976, Bartley 1982, Stephen 1984). The resultant turmoil has been matched by the confusion of local communities concerning whether to welcome or reject the gentry. In both countries the gentry have moved into areas which had substantial immigrant populations. To some long-established residents, gentrification was just another cycle of change, and in some respects it was preferable because it brought people who, at least in appearance, habits and culture, were more like the host communities. There was therefore initial welcome from residents, traders and landlords, even though all might ultimately suffer from the reconstruction of their neighborhood and the reconstitution of local politics.

The situation in the United States is at the same time similar and yet quite different. It is similar because there is abundant evidence of the political struggles fought out in neighborhoods regarding space invasion and displacement (Henig 1982); it is different because these struggles seem to have an intensity which is greater than that in Australia and Britain. The defense of turf (Cox 1984) reflects the absence of government controls and the consequent formation by neighborhoods and their residents of coalitions to protect their interests. One avenue of research on gentrification and displacement has considered the characteristics of neighborhoods which have successfully coped with this process, and so the perception of gentrification in the United States is closely linked to an appreciation of neighborhood politics and the politics of local control. To that extent gentrification is seen as yet another process of change which threatens the balance of power in localities.

The question of local control raises the vital issue of the role of the state. In many respects it is around the question of state control and intervention that the most marked differences arise between the countries concerned. In Britain, the level of intervention is, in relative terms, the highest. The widespread provision of public housing and a traditionally more interventionist style of local government have meant that gentrification has been countered in particular ways. The existence of public housing estates and the maintenance of programs to extend public housing via new building and the municipalization of existing dwellings have meant that there have been strong countertendencies operating in many inner areas which have ensured the retention of existing low-income communities. Equally, because local government is involved in

60

housing provision, it has contributed to (and been a consequence of) the politicization of the housing question at the local level.

The extent to which British local councils have resisted gentrification has varied considerably, however, reflecting different levels of political control and administrative competence. There has been a long-running and substantial aid program to private-sector housing, which is administered by local government, and this has acted as a stimulus to the gentrification process. Aside from the eligibility of particular areas as either historic conservation areas or traffic control zones, or simply as capable of improvement, individuals have been eligible to receive grants for renovating their dwellings (Hamnett 1973). Until checks were imposed on the use of these grants, many instances of abuse occurred, with public funds being used by speculators to renovate dwellings which then passed from working-class rental tenancy to middle-class home-ownership. Alongside these program initiatives has been a sustained promotion of home-ownership by central government, and most recently a central government requirement that local councils offer public housing for sale to tenants. The council-house sales program, along with the rundown of public expenditure on municipalization and new building, is substantially reshaping local housing provision. In the case of inner-city areas it has certainly contributed to an extension of the gentrification process.

In Australia, as in Britain, the abandonment of ambitious government plans for the clearance of areas of older housing and their replacement by new housing, infrastructure and service facilities have meant that a large stock of original dwellings remains available for gentrification. Unlike in Britain, where, until recently, municipalization and public housing construction were used to challenge and reshape the pressures leading toward gentrification, in Australia the process has taken place without any substantial, direct policy response by government (Kendig 1984). There can be little doubt, however, that rent control aided the decline of the dwelling stock and contributed to the proletarianization of Australian inner suburbs. The removal of such controls, the abandonment of large-scale redevelopment plans, and the continued promotion of home-ownership (including strata titling legislation, which contributed to flat breakup) all indicate that government has played a role in creating the conditions which opened up opportunities for gentrification. Equally, by not seeking to control gentrification, government has assisted its continuation, though in doing so it is responding to pressure from a variety of broader social movements.

The strength of central- and local-government intervention in Britain (at least until recently) contrasts sharply with the position in the United States. The dynamics of the housing market, and indeed of American society as a whole, seem to have produced an acceptance of change which, though challenged at the level of the neighborhood, has produced little in the way of strong policy response from government. However, the widespread promotion of gentrification as a solution to the social and financial problems faced by many inner-area municipalities has endowed the American debate with a "national logic" which is absent elsewhere. Indeed what is significant about the United States is the way the twin issues of local fiscal crisis and racial conflict are so central to the gentrification issue. The many small local governments that continue to exist within the framework of large metropolitan areas, and their impoverishment through the loss of the tax base due to the abandonment of property and the outmigration of industry and the "middle classes," has produced a situation in which gentrification is put forward as a means of local salvation. The return of households with considerable incomes, it is claimed, will boost local economies, and through improvements to dwellings it will result in a higher property tax base. Suddenly local municipalities that were facing a slow collapse into bankruptcy have begun to contemplate alternative futures. Although many doubt the ultimate efficacy of gentrification as the solution (e.g. Berry 1980a, President's Commission for a National Agenda 1980), the process has stimulated a great deal of urban boosterism (see Ch. 3).

The debate about the future of the American city has also been intensified by the question of race. The emergence of predominantly black central cities and white suburbs has led to many programs designed to reconstruct the "social ecology" of metropolitan areas. Gentrification, as an apparently spontaneous private process, has been welcomed as one means of reinserting "middle-class" whites into central areas (cf. Schaffer & Smith 1984). It has been argued that the process will have little effect overall in reversing tendencies toward the creation of an urban underclass (Norton 1979, Bradbury et al. 1982), though Downs (1981: 149) has suggested that until alternatives are developed, gentrification should be encouraged:

> Completely opposing gentrification until enough federal subsidies are available to avoid all involuntary displacement amounts to indefinitely postponing most revitalization. In effect, such a policy blocks the single most powerful housing upgrading force now operating within central cities. Consequently prolonged opposition to all gentrification is a short-sight policy in relation to the long-range fiscal, physical and social needs of central cities.

Given that the Reagan government has adopted the policy of "benign neglect" with respect to the cities (Lang 1982), it would seem gentrification is likely to continue its inroads into the stock of dwellings and result in further displacement. Whether Fainstein and Fainstein (1982) are right to argue that older American cities are now converging on the European "model," with the rich at the centre and the poor on the periphery, is another matter.

The absence of any substantial level of public housing provision as in Britain, or the wide opportunities for home-ownership that exist in Australia has meant that, in the United States, the issue of displacement has become a matter of considerable importance. Though it is recognized in all countries that gentrification substantially disadvantages particular groups, the consequences have been most apparent in the United States. As a result, the process of gentrification has been substantially politicized. In formal terms, this contributed to the formation of the 1976 President's Committee and the subsequent 1978 Housing and Community Development Act, although, as already noted, such placatory steps have no place in the aims of the present administration. At street level, gentrification has led to violence, not only between tenants and the landlords keen to get them out, but also between original occupants and newcomers (Cybriwsky 1978, LeGates & Murphy 1981). Ultimately it may be that these events are more powerful than legislation.

Economic and social restructuring

In each of the three countries a fundamental economic restructuring has been underway since the 1960s. Established heavy industry and old industrial heartlands have been in decline, and new industrial and service sectors have emerged, partly based around new technologies, in what can be called the sunbelt areas. These economic changes have been paralleled by equally important shifts in the demographic and social structures of each of the countries. The growth of one- and two-person households, the decline in family size, and the rise in the number of elderly persons have had a considerable impact on the functioning of the housing market, changing patterns of both demand and supply. This is not only a result of the flow of households through the housing stock, but is also a consequence of the important wealth-generating role of domestic property. Part of the impetus behind the gentrification process has been the financial resources passed to individuals and households from the proceeds of parental-property sales.

As already noted, there have been suggestions in both Britain and the United States that gentrification is producing a basic restructuring of the city. Certainly there is evidence to support this argument, but it is essential to think behind the process itself to the changes in these specific societies which are producing an urban restructuring. The reshaping of the economic and demographic structures are of crucial significance, and they are also highly interrelated. Linked to them and in some respects providing the driving mechanism is the matter of changing class structures. A characteristic feature of a number of advanced capitalist societies in the postwar era has been the emergence of new strata of professional and managerial workers, reflecting the contradictions and complexities of maintaining and servicing the production process. This new middle class has many features in common, whether we are discussing Australia, Britain or the United States. What varies significantly is the social structure of which this new middle class is a part.

The strength of government intervention in Britain has already been noted in comparison with that in the other two countries. What is also important to note is the more rigid and hierarchical nature of class relations in that country, and thus the greater importance of all the symbols and processes involved in class structuring. The home is a potent symbol in the process of class constitution, and for the new middle class, who have been active participants in the gentrification process, it seems to have special significance. Despite the obvious connotations of gentrification, class in any active sense has been little used as a concept with which to "unpack" the process in theoretical terms. Consequently there is limited material on which to base a comparison of the three countries examined here.

Reconceptualizing the gentrification process

This brief cross-national discussion reveals a number of important differences and similarities in the way gentrification has taken place and the impacts it has had. How can we make sense of this evidence, and what does it tell us about the nature of gentrification? In seeking to address these questions one is immediately forced to confront the existing inadequacies in the conceptualization of gentrification. In particular it is apparent that the preoccupation with the *description* of gentrification means that we have little sense of the contextual and compositional forces that "produce" this process (Thrift 1983). The purpose of this section of the chapter is to open out and restructure our understanding of gentrification, thus providing a clearer basis upon which to erect a comparative analysis.

Much of the literature on gentrification has directed our attention toward universal processes. Everywhere, we hear, the middle classes are making their return to the city (e.g. Christiano 1982). While research focused upon establishing the empirical evidence of change, it is not surprising that debate should have centred on similarities. Once research shifted toward the reasons behind such changes, the differences began to appear. Indeed, to some extent, they were foreshadowed by the rather intriguing debate over what to call this process. Many American analysts have been uncomfortable with the term "gentrification" (with its obvious class connotations), preferring labels such as the "back-to-the-city movement," "neighborhood revitalization," and "brownstoneing," all of which were indicative of underlying divergences in what was believed to be central to this process.

As other chapters in this volume indicate, gentrification is a complex and varied process which can be conceptualized at a number of different levels. To date, the dominant mode of analysis has been empiricist, with little or no attempt to structure the evidence theoretically. Although such work has captured some aspects of the appearance of gentrification, it has given little sense of the social processes embodied within it. A second approach, and one criticized elsewhere (Hamnett 1984a, Williams 1984a), has been structuralist with an emphasis upon the guiding power of capitalism. Although an essential corrective to the chaotic world of facts provided by the first, it has itself had certain important weaknesses (Duncan & Ley 1982). As Szelenyi (1981:2) has commented,

Structuralists, even the less orthodox ones are likely to identify the "capitalist mode of production" with a set of relatively non-dynamic structural relationships, the essence of capitalism being its logic, how a given set of structural features are related to each other and how, in the last instance, they keep reproducing, in a reasonably pure form, the same system.

Despite the apparent vitality of debate, present attempts to theorize this process have been inadequate in a number of ways (see Holcomb & Beauregard 1981, Hamnett 1984a, Rose 1984, Williams 1984a, for extended reviews). As indicated, much discussion has focused upon the people, property and areas involved, though it is by no means clear what the relative importance of these different components or the processes underlying them may be. Secondly, it is apparent that subsequent attempts to theorize the process have emphasized either production-based formulations stressing the changing requirements of capital (e.g. N. Smith 1982) or the consumption-based questions of urban politics, housing classes and institutional manipulation (e.g. Logan 1982). This separation, essentially between a marxist economic analysis and a weberian sociological analysis, has wrought a considerable cost in terms of our capacity to comprehend the nature of the forces at work. It has separated and counterposed arguments which ultimately require integration (Klausner 1983). These problems are compounded by the considerable silences in the literature, and within urban geography and human geography in general, with respect to questions of class relations, intra-class conflict, politics, culture and history, as well as the more general issues of how to relate and understand social structures and human agency (see Thrift 1983, Gregory 1984, Thrift & Williams in preparation).

It becomes apparent that gentrification as a concept is an underdeveloped and unevenly developed notion (Rose 1984). Rather than conceiving of gentrification as a special and somewhat unusual process, it should be understood as one example of the way social relations are played out in space and how social and economic change is imprinted upon the built environment. As Castells (1983: 302) has recently commented,

> Cities, like all social reality, are historical products, not only in their physical materiality, but in their cultural meaning, in the role they play in the social organization, and in peoples' lives. The basic dimension in urban change is the conflictive debate between social classes and historical actors over the meaning of urban, the significance of spatial forms in the social structure, and the content, hierarchy, and destiny of cities in relationship to the entire social structure.

The reshaped residential environments characteristic of the gentrification process can be related clearly to the changing form and structure of social classes and their articulation with the built environment. Despite the growing literatures on the "new class," the decline of the working class and the growth of professional and managerial strata, few of these ideas have penetrated the gentrification debate. It is as if social relations and spatial form are separate and unconnected (see Saunders 1981 for a useful review, and Castells 1983 for a provocative unifying argument). Yet the importance of gentrification stems partly from the fact that it is a highly visual expression of changing social relations and of the interaction of social classes in space. Debates over segregation, normally carried out by geographers through the sterile medium of data (see Brown 1981 for a useful discussion of this), were thrown into confusion by both the "return" movement of the "middle class" and by the conflicts between them and existing residents. Questions of displacement, constraint and disadvantage could no longer be set aside easily, nor could the apparent politicization of this process with groups vying for the control of or assistance from government at various levels. Thus, not only are issues raised with respect to class structure but also inter- and intra-class relations and capacities, which vary within different national and local contexts.

Questions of changing class structure immediately prompt questions about how the economy is changing and how such changes make themselves apparent. The restructuring of production and distribution has resulted in massive shifts in the types and locations of work. Much of our knowledge of economic restructuring is based upon the experience of the old industrial heartlands such as the North-East of America, the North of Britain and the South-East of Australia (Cameron 1980, Stillwell 1980, Blowers *et al.*, 1981, Fainstein & Fainstein 1982). Much less is known about the new "sunrise" areas and the many smaller cities now undergoing expansion. However, it is plain that many blue-collar jobs have been lost and that a considerable proportion of these have been from enterprises located in inner urban areas. The suburbanization of manufacturing and distribution, alongside continuing tendencies for the centralization and concentration of management and related services, has meant that the geography of the city has undergone considerable change (Hall 1981). Alongside these processes the internationalization of production has resulted in relative and absolute changes in the role of particular economies, and the emergence of what Friedmann and Wolff (1982) refer to as "world cities." The coincidence between such "economic" changes and the emergence of the gentrification issue is too close to be ignored.

Indeed, as Szelenyi (1981), Zukin (1982b) and others make plain, these shifts in production and changes in consumption are both related and quite selective. Alongside decline is widespread renewal: capital outflow is matched by capital inflow (of a different kind) and the generation of new opportunities to accumulate and profit. As Zukin (1982b: 173, 175–6) comments with respect to the loft-conversion process:

> This succession of uses reflects processes of change in the larger society. Not only does it parallel the gentrification of working-class neighborhoods in many cities but it also concretizes – through change in the built environment – the dislocation of industrial production from traditional centres of light manufacturing and its apparent replacement by higher-level, "post industrial" activity.
>
> What is really at stake on this terrain is the heart of the city: the reconquest of the downtown for high class users and high rent uses ... Revitalization really involves putting into place an accumulation and a cultural strategy.

The determination of financiers and other entrepreneurs to exploit the changing function of the built environment, sweeping away the dead labour of the productive era (Harvey 1978) and welcoming in what Zukin terms "the artistic mode of production" is of vital importance. Locked behind the data on social change are such sets of forces, constantly acting to preserve or reshape the landscape; bringing about, as Castells (1983: 302) would term it, "new forms of urban meaning."

The relationship between the built environment and class composition and change has not been the subject of detailed research, not least because of its complexity and the myriad other questions of gender, race and culture which also need to be addressed. Certainly we can offer crude correlations between building types and social groups, but that is hardly adequate, not least because gentrification often involves overturning traditional patterns. However, we can begin to make steps along this path, as Jager (Ch. 5) indicates. The renovation of Victorian or Edwardian houses can be interpreted as being an expression, even a compensatory strategy, by part of the middle class for their contradictory position in the social structure. The search by this particular group for a niche in the physical landscape is not simply related to cheap housing in accessible inner suburbs. It also makes a series of statements regarding their place in the middle class and their relationship to the working classes, and, perhaps more importantly, it is a reflection of the ambiguous nature of white-collar work. As Featherstone (1982: 29) comments,

> There are more and more areas of work in which precise evaluation of an individual's achievement on universalistic criteria becomes impossible. Hence "extra functional elements of professional roles became more and more important for conferring occupational status" [Habermas]. The difficulty of evaluating an individual's competence on strictly rational criteria opens up the space for the performing self . . .

The solidity of a Victorian or Edwardian home, the restoration by which one recaptures the values and imagery of that era, and the very act of living in areas "with history," both reflect and reinforce the processes through which these social groups are seeking a clear identity. Moreover it must be remembered that it is not simply related to where such groups are going (socially) but also where they have come from. For many, gentrification in their adulthood follows a suburban childhood.

The failure to comprehend the importance of culture, both in the specific manifestations given above and in its more general attributes, represents a central weakness in the existing gentrification debate. The changing nature of middle- and working-class life and culture, set within the context of a changing economy and society, provides critical leverage for understanding this process (e.g. Castells & Murphy 1982, Castells 1983). Gentrifying households have typically been two-earner households (both heterosexual and homosexual), with the partners pursuing careers in the professional and white-collar labor markets. The earning capacity of such households is considerable, just as is their rejection of the suburbs as a place in which to earn and spend. The reasons for this are complex and important. The entry of women into certain areas of the paid labor force has been acutely difficult. It has been resisted by many men and inhibited by the family and household circumstances surrounding many women.

The form and location of the home played an important role in that process. The suburban environment is remote from the labor markets of some of these types of employment and is more conducive to a different life path involving childrearing and traditional domestic roles. Many of the female (and male) gentry were beneficiaries of the boom in tertiary education in the 1960s and 1970s. They were also in many cases the children of the "middle-class' suburbanites. Attending universities and colleges not only allowed many women to exercise choice over what roles they took on subsequently (including a working career), but also allowed many of them to experience a very different urban environment. Subsequently, having become familiar with the apparently more solid, intimate and accessible world of the inner city, many were encouraged to reject suburbia physically (just as they were rejecting it mentally) and opt for the world they now understood and preferred. For women, that decision gave them ready access to relatively well paid jobs, a supportive environment and the opportunity to imprint themselves and their newfound status upon the landscape (Holcomb 1984).

The situation for gay households is not entirely dissimilar (see Castells 1983). The defensive and secluded nature of gay gentrification in San Francisco has given way to open confidence as they have consolidated their hold on particular localities and asserted their position within the local labor market, government and political processes. In themselves, sexuality and gender do not explain gentrification even though they are of great importance in some places. The fundamental shifts that have occurred in work, education and life-style provide part of the general context within which these changes have occurred. The growing importance of the service sector in mature economies, the rise in white-collar work and professional servicing, and the growth of self-employment and particular types of small businesses have all contributed to making the space for the developments we observe. Alongside these changes has been the rapid expansion of post-secondary education in the

1960s and 1970s. Little discussed with respect to its impact on the built environment, this has been a significant factor in the production of the new middle class, its values and actions.

We must also recognize that local political, social, economic and cultural conditions will give the process different appearances and consequences in different localities. The political reaction to gentrification is a case in point (Cocke 1983). It is apparent from what little work has been done on this issue that people's reactions to gentrification have varied considerably from place to place (Glassberg 1979, Bartley 1982). Acute political and social conflict has been observed in some areas, but the way it is structured depends crucially on factors such as the form of organization of the state as one of the main mechanisms for expression of such conflicts (McKay & Cox 1979). In part the lack of research in this area reflects our inadequate understanding of local politics and local social relations. Gentrification provides one route for opening out this area of study.

So far we have discussed a number of the silences which surround the gentrification debate, all of which need addressing in order to allow a systematic and penetrating assessment of gentrification on an international scale. Central to that assessment is the question of class and class-and-status relations. It is argued here that it is these relations which stand at the core of the gentrification process and which, if analyzed adequately on an international basis, would provide a key element in understanding this form of change. It is to this question we now turn.

Gentrification as class constitution

Attempts to use alternative concepts of class (relational) have been limited (Mullins 1982; Smith and LeFaivre 1984), in part because of the tension between the conventional marxist two-class model and the apparently more fragmented and complex situation revealed by gentrification. As argued elsewhere (Williams 1984a, Thrift & Williams, in preparation), the production-based class relationship is no longer adequate to the needs of contemporary social analysis, and a more extended concept is required, i.e. one that captures the salience of both production and reproduction-based relationships.

The recognition of the different settings that give rise to varied class capacities and consciousness is an important step in this argument (Baumann 1982), as is the view that "classes do not manifest themselves within the structure" (Urry 1981: 15) but are created in action and reaction. Thus, with respect to the gentry, it has been argued in this chapter and elsewhere in the volume that

70

residential location and the residence itself are not simply expressions of class; they are part of the process of class constitution. LeGates and Murphy (1981: 266) have commented that "gentrification conflicts have a class base, but do not follow classical Marxist categories," revealing the tension between an unreformulated marxist model and the empirical realities they perceive.

It is apparent from all the literature on gentrification that the "middle class" space invaders draw upon a culture, a life path, which in many respects is different from that of working-class residents. In other words the interaction structure (Thrift 1983), within which such individuals gain capacities and develop shared perceptions and actions, draws upon worlds well beyond the locality which they are gentrifying. Typically they and their children are educated outside the area in which they live; they indulge in leisure and recreation pursuits within the metropolis and beyond, rather than in the locality, and they work elsewhere. The suggestion that they have little in common with "the locals" is true in that, aside from having a home in a particular neighborhood, they may have little contact with it. Women, as housewives, might normally function as a link, but with many working, even that chain is weakened. This separation carries with it a considerable irony and an important set of contradictions.

Having, in many cases, been brought up in "classless" suburbs (one class in reality) and gone to higher-education establishments where class was outwardly less relevant (though actually implicated in the very core of those establishments), the move to establish residence in working-class inner areas was an important act. It appeared to mark a break from the class-segregated past and it was presumed to offer the warm supportive communal existence denied in the suburbs, discovered at university or college, and potentially to be lost again. Yet having established such a residence, these groups, by the very sets of structures within which they were already located, have actually found themselves alienated from this comunal classlessness. Far from resulting in a classless society, this alienation, in conjunction with their already established life paths, has resulted in a heightened class consciousness. "Little wonder then that friends and pioneers have moved on to regain their true identities in Chelsea and Hampstead" (Dunn 1982).

When the gentry began to take over parts of inner London they became conscious of the gulf between their own expectations and needs and what the local working-class community provided. It was therefore hardly surprising that, within a short time,

Committees of an improving sort met around stripped-pine kitchen tables. Pressure groups – working-class members welcome – gave local councils expert advice on the improvement of buildings, road safety and derelict sites. Neighbouring was reduced to an earnest, classless essence from which, surely, working-class people would emerge with an enlightened understanding of their environment. (Dunn 1982: 29)

The divergent life paths and capacities of different social classes began to emerge. Improvements did mean different things to different people. The realities of different job markets, education opportunities and communities were increasingly apparent to the different groups involved. As Dunn (1982: 29) continued,

All the meetings, it was soon noted, seemed to be held in middle-class houses. A campaign to do something about a transport cafe whose customers were parking in the fresh trendy streets . . . provoked little enthusiasm from the working class.

No wonder, given that their livelihoods often depended upon such customers. Locality meant more than residence for some. The outward integration of classes (e.g. people from different classes living next door to each other) only obscured deep-seated differences. As one member of the gentry commented, "On the face of it we got on very well, but we really didn't have much in common" (quoted in Dunn 1982: 29). Many of the "middle-class" people who moved into these areas eventually moved on. Taking advantage of substantial capital gains, they moved out to the country or to the established "middle-class" enclaves of inner London. Their replacements, as the prices would dictate, came from more secure and affluent locations in the employment structure. These parts of inner London now appear subdued and eminently respectable. The woman quoted above remarked that

This new lot seem to be more impersonal, not a bit interested in the pigging in or the local life. All their houses are painted the same, which I think is very symbolic. They're much more class-bound than we were. They send their children more to private schools than we did. The new ones are snobs and proud of it. (Quoted in Dunn 1982: 29.)

The process of change never ceases. The displaced moved elsewhere and have made their own impact on localities. Some of the gentry worked out their identity through the gentrification process and, having rediscovered the essential differences between themselves and the working class, they left. Perhaps they maintained that contact through their work as public servants administering programs related to the disadvantaged, but, at home, comfort seems to require familiarity and similarity.

It should be stressed that these class relations are only part of the overall forces at work. Such patterns of outmovement are also influenced by life cycle and housing careers, and it may be that these influences will prove to be very importat in the rise and fall of the gentrification process. This discussion has focused upon class constitution in Britain. This is not to suggest that similar forces are not at work elsewhere; indeed, Michael Jager's analysis of Melbourne (Ch. 5) demonstrates that they are. However, the form, content, and meaning will differ significantly. The point here is to argue the importance of these processes both as a counter to the narrow economism which has been utilized in explaining gentrification, and as one way of opening up the analysis to an understanding of the interrelationships between social structures and human agents. It is conceded that "class" can be used in as blunt a manner as "economy;" however, as will be apparent from the arguments developed earlier, the intention here is quite different. Indeed an understanding of gentrification offers real insights into the nature of class constitution as an active and mediated process.

Conclusion

> The city is the product of history, the reflection of society, the action of man upon space. (Castells 1976b)

The comparison of gentrification in Australia, Britain and the United States has indicated the different causes and consequences that underlie what, at a superficial level, is a very similar process. It demonstrates the importance of reaching behind the appearance of social processes to consider the forces at work and the way these vary across space. At the same time, although it has been possible to expose important distinctions between gentrification in different countries, that comparison has been blunted by the very inadequacies of the research available to be drawn upon. In the second section of the chapter a number of neglected areas were discussed which, it was argued, require development both as counters to crude structuralism and to provide a better grasp of gentrification and the way the process is constituted. A number of conclusions are now appropriate.

Gentrification is an outcome contingent upon an array of social settings and social practices. It cannot be reduced either to the consequence of a set of universal structural forces or to the product of the actions of a multitude of autonomous individuals. Adopting the former position erodes, in large part, any prospect for a comparative study of this process because it renders all variations subordinate to an underlying unified essence. The very high level of abstraction inherent in that approach contrasts markedly with what might be seen as its polar opposite, the social actor. The actions of numerous individuals involved in gentrification have been endlessly studied and compiled into lists indicating the various demands they are seeking to fulfill. This individualized demand-based approach ignores entirely the fact that such actions are carried out in settings which are not of the choosing of the actors concerned. As Gregory (1984) comments, "all social practices depend on conditions and constraints which reach beyond the competence of knowledgeable human subjects."

The solution for some has been to talk in terms of integrated studies, where both demand and supply are considered, or where structure and agents are brought together. The difficulty with these approaches is the way "factors" are brought together into a functional ensemble. The structurationist model as proposed by Giddens (1979, 1981) and others is one attempt to overcome these enforced dualities and this approach deserves further attention. Although it is argued that social life is best viewed as being produced through the recursive interactions of human practices and social structures, it should be acknowledged that this chapter offers only a few tentative gestures in that direction. As will now be clear, much of the essay is concerned with making the necessary "space" for such analysis to proceed.

The form and structure of government, the housing market, race and class relations, and the more general question of restructured economies and the future of particular cities, vary significantly between and within the three countries examined, ensuring that gentrification occurs in quite different ways. In Australia, it has generated a degree of curiosity, but only recently are there signs that its longer-term implications with respect to low-income housing, local politics and service provision are being recognized. In Britain, the interventionist role of government with regard to the housing market ensured early politicization of the process. In attempting to hold a line between preserving low-income housing and revitalizing the housing stock, many local councils have found themselves condemned by all parties and have thus confronted sustained attempts to capture the formal reins of power. In the United States, gentrification has provided one of the main challenges to the prospect of cities sharply divided by race and class (in the short term), and the promise of a partial halt to central-city disinvestment, but at the price of substantial displacement.

Focusing as they do on the policy significance of gentrification, such comparisons should not, however, be allowed to overshadow a whole series of issues and effects which are locked within this process. The debates over capital flight and the recommodification of inner-area property quite rightly focus attention on the implications this process has for accumulation and profit. In the United States, in particular, the abandonment of residential property, the severe decline in profit from central-area enterprises and the subsequent decline in exchanged values have posed a considerable threat to particular interests. Whereas some have cut losses and shifted resources to the suburbs, others have simply been bankrupted. This redistribution of wealth acted against established owners locked into particular investments but opened up opportunities for a number of entrepreneurs. Precise calculation of profits and losses is complex, particularly when applying a marxist value analysis. The constantly changing and uneven nature of the accumulation process ensures the continuous creation and destruction of opportunities to profit.

Gentrification is one such profitable opportunity and the evidence from all three countries reveals the steady expansion of a whole variety of entrepreneurial interests in this process. The image of gentrification as a series of individualized decisions taken by autonomous homeowners belies the reality of a structured process with an array of coordinated interests involved. Moreover, as the debate over capital movements and economic restructuring reveals, these entrepreneurs are responding to circumstances as well as creating their own conditions of existence. Gentrification is not a conspiracy by a set of secretive capitalists. Rather it is a process that emerges from the interaction of a whole set of relations, which include the conscious will of individual capitalists, competition between capitalists, and the capitalist class as a whole.

Just as individual capitalists, and probably particular groups of capitalists, have failed to maintain profits and have lost out in the process of gentrification, so too individuals and groups of residents in areas that have been gentrified have made money gains. Much of the discussion of gentrification has focused on displacement. Certainly the process has imposed enormous costs on particular groups and individuals with regard to housing, everyday life and employment. But so too others have benefited. In Australia and Britain, many low-income migrants have found themselves able to sell their property at prices which allow substantial money gains, sufficient to allow purchase of property elsewhere. This seems to be less common in the United States. *renters* ←

These calculations of the effects of gentrification are important. They point to the ways in which we can objectively assess the recasting of social relations. They can, however, only provide us with one element of the understanding we require. Social relations are much more than a balance sheet of costs and benefits. In these final paragraphs it is therefore appropriate to return to the more general question of gentrification, class relations and the city.

equal dispersion of benefits?

Gentrification has occurred within the context of the postwar baby boom and the rapid and massive expansion of the new middle class. Benefiting from new commitments to health, education and economic prosperity, this generation has firmly imprinted itself on the social, political and physical landscape. As Blum (1983: 7) has commented with respect to New York,

> We have altered the landscape to suit our needs. Our socio-economic status has given us the power to spend, and thus the power to transform neighborhoods once defined by racial and ethnic characteristics. The blacks and the Jews and the Irish have dispersed; we, the baby boom kids, have taken their place.

The political effects of this invasion are now being expressed in the labelling of groups such as the "Yuppies" (the young urban professionals), the emergence in Britain of the Social Democratic Party, and the setting up of community associations and protest groups, all of whom express an earnest rationality regarding contemporary affairs. The economic and social effects are also plainly apparent. Gentrified localities appear increasingly identical, with the result that one can move from Chicago to Boston and find virtually the same neighborhood in which to live (Blum 1983). Moreover this process has spilled outward so that increasingly cities are developing their historic tourist areas with wholesome food, intellectualized environments and "safe" streets. The takeover of neighborhoods is only one step in the whole process of spatial capture and reclamation.

As the "new middle class" has gone from strength to strength, so the working classes, under assault in the sphere of production, now find themselves under attack in the realm of reproduction (Williams 1982). With more locally based and varied cultures formed around the relatively close proximity of work, home and school, the working classes have maintained a degree of localization and thus, in national terms, fragmentation, which has exposed them fully to contemporary trends of restructuring whether of work or of the city. Their capacity to resist gentrification has been varied. Although acutely aware of the conflicts of interest between themselves and newcomers, many working-class residents have been willing to form coalitions with the gentry and even to be led by them. Rarely, however, has the outcome been in their long-term favor. Even where effective local control is possible, e.g. in Britain through powerful local governments, it has been difficult to prevent the remorseless march of the invaders. In the main this is because the working classes have been under siege on many fronts. The loss of residence has been just another facet of the destruction of their class, whereas for the "new middle class" this established base has been essential to its constitution.

Acknowledgements

This chapter has benefited considerably from the advice and comments of Alan Murie, Pat Mullins, Liz Cocke and Hal Kendig. They are not responsible for its failings and I thank them for their efforts. I would also like to express my thanks to the Urban and Regional Studies Seminar group at the University of Sussex who discussed one version of this chapter.

5

Class definition and the esthetics of gentrification: Victoriana in Melbourne

MICHAEL JAGER

As its name suggests, the process of gentrification is intimately concerned with social class, yet in economic, social and political terms, the class dimensions of gentrification are only beginning to be scrutinized. The architectural and internal decorative esthetics of gentrified buildings and neighborhoods have attracted only passing comment and almost no sustained attention. This lack of attention is particularly surprising in that the esthetics of gentrification not only illustrate the class dimension of the process but also express the dynamic constitution of social class of which gentrification is a specific part. Indeed the esthetics of the process are the most immediately visible aspects of its constitution; etched into the landscape in the decorative forms of gentrification is a picture of the dynamics of social class.

It is a tenet of this chapter that social class is not a static object, but a set of social relationships in continual constitution and reconstitution. Commenting on the formation of the original gentry in England, Wallerstein writes

> It is far more than a semantic issue but semantics plays its role . . . It is no accident that the scholars debate furiously here, because the whole point is that this period in English history is not only a moment of economic change and great individual social mobility, but of the change of categories. Not only are we unsure how to designate the meaningful social groupings: the men of the time also were . . . The whole point about "gentry" is not only that it was a class in formation but a concept in formation. It was, however, a case of new wine in old bottles. (Wallerstein 1974: 236–40)

Likewise, gentrification may also involve new class formation as well as a concept in formation.

78

Central to the processes of class constitution and definition is the built environment, as both a container and expression of social relations. The changing social order is both reflected in and reconstructed by the spatial order and the buildings which are part of it. There are numerous dimensions to this. The focus here is upon the interrelationships between class constitution and the conservation of a Victorian built environment; it draws upon a case study of Melbourne, Australia. Inevitably, certain of the features described will be specific to that city and to class relations in Australia, but the general question of class distinction and symbolism through the built environment is of universal importance to an understanding of gentrification and its wider meaning.

Social class and housing form

An active process, urban conservation is the production of social differentiation; it is one mechanism through which social differences are turned into social distinctions. Slums become Victoriana, and housing becomes a cultural investment with facadal display signifying social ascension. Veblen's notion of conspicuous consumption catches the importance of social self-assertion which presides over the urban conservation struggle in Melbourne.

For Veblen's leisure class, servants had a dual function; they had to work and perform, and they also had to signify their masters' standing. Gentrified housing follows a similar social logic. On the one hand, housing has to confer social status, meaning and prestige, but on the other it has to obey the social ethic of production: it has to function economically. This unites the performance ethic and the signifying function; that is, it designates the social position and trajectory of certain class fractions in relation to others. Thus beyond the function as a status symbol (signifying and designating), housing mediates the constitution of class (demarcating and discriminating) (Baudrillard 1981).

For Veblen the leisure class occupied a strategic position, setting a prescriptive example of conspicuous consumption, and thereby providing the norms that organized and gave cohesion to the social hierarchy. Today this task of providing a model of emulation falls to sections of the "new middle classes" (Diggins 1978). "The grande bourgeoisie which shrank a great deal because of the economic process of concentration has had to give over to the petite bourgeoisie its function as the class whose life style was to be emulated" (Pappi 1981: 105). With its inherited if weakened function of vicarious consumption, then, the "new middle class" takes on a societal importance which is not commensurate with its numerical strength. Gentrification promotes neither a new Veblenesque leisure class, nor an equivalent of commensurate social significance, but it does affirm a parallel class tactic and movement. What social tastes are expressed in the gentrification of Victorian terrace housing? From which class are gentrifiers demarcating and separating themselves; which social position is being sanctioned; and toward which class model do they aspire (Baudrillard 1981)?

What permanently characterizes the middle classes, "the class which is neither nor" (Pappi 1981:106), this "class in between" (Walker 1979), is that they must conduct a war on two fronts (Elias 1974:302). On the one hand the middle classes must defend themselves against pressure from the dominant classes, retaining a certain independence and autonomy, and on the other hand they must continue to demarcate themselves from the lower orders. This permanent tension on two fronts is evident in the architecture of gentrification: in the external restorations of Victoriana, the middle classes express their candidature for the dominant classes; in its internal renovation work this class signifies its distance from the lower orders. Architectural form not only fixes a social position but also in part conveys and sanctions a social rise. A change in social position is symbolized through a change in housing.

The ambiguity and compromise of the new middle classes is revealed in their esthetic tastes. It is through facadal restoration work that urban conservation expresses its approximation to a former bourgeois consumption model in which prestige is based upon a "constraint of superfluousness" (Baudrillard 1981:32). But in the case of urban conservation those consumption practices are anxiously doubled up on what may be termed a Victorian work ethic embedded in renovation work. In artistic terms this duality is expressed as that of form and function.

Class demarcation and distinction

"Economic power is firstly the capacity to put economic necessity at a distance" (Bourdieu 1979:58). Leisure is the most direct expression of relief or freedom from economic constraints. This relative freedom or distance from economic necessity is signified through conspicuous waste and superfluity. It is forcefully expressed through the consumption of housing as an esthetic object, through the appropriation of history, and the "stylization of life" as Victorian gentility. Thus for Veblen one of the major signs of prestige for the leisure class is that of waste in either expenditure (conspicuous consumption) or inactivity (conspicuous leisure). Through those wasteful practices (which as Veblen points out are only wasteful from a naively utilitarian perspective), the leisure class for Veblen, and the bourgeoisie more generally, distinguishes and distances itself from the labouring classes.

Societally produced objects may express this same social logic (Baudrillard 1968). They signify prestige through a certain decorative excess, through form rather than function, and it is through that excess that "they no longer 'designate' the world, but rather the being and social rank of their possessor" (Baudrillard 1981:32). Representational excesses and superfluity associated with facadal restorations are not only intended to realize additional economic profits, therefore, but also to affirm social rank.

What is being displayed and proclaimed through such artistic consecration is not simply possession, but successful triumphant possession. Victoriana is victorious possession. Conspicuous display of property is the basis upon which privileges are accorded and won. The distancing from industrial labor through excess and superfluity was achieved in Veblen's time through idleness as opposed to labor, consumption as opposed to production. However, where higher consumption standards and longer leisure time have been generalized, and hence can no longer signify distinction, new distinctive standards are called for.

"This cultivation of the aesthetic faculty" (Veblen 1953:64), therefore, is increasingly associated with an attempt to appropriate history. It is not just conspicuous consumption but consumption and reproduction of past history that comes to signify social distinction. With its architectural renovation and decoration, urban conservation employs this more modern system of social signification. The new middle class does not buy simply a deteriorated house when it takes over a slum, nor does it just buy into future "equity;" it buys into the past.

The predilection of the petty bourgeoisie for antiques is legendary:

> The taste for the bygone is characterized by the desire to transcend the dimension of economic success, to consecrate a social success or a privileged position in a redundant, culturalized, symbolic sign. The bygone is, among other things, social success that seeks a legitimacy, a heredity, a "noble" sanction. (Baudrillard 1981:43)

Both socially and territorially, this may be all the more important for newcomers; history is made the guarantee against modernity, the past becomes a means of acquiring historical legitimation. Thus in a status drive, the function value of certain objects could be overridden or directly contradicted by their symbolic value. Packard (1963: 67) cites certain symbolic goods of "uncertain utilitarian value" whose value as an avenue of social promotion was none the less assured.

The value of cultural commodities may be most fully and prestigiously realized through the consumption of time. The possession of antiques and the consumption of history express a certain power over time. History may be retrieved and reinstated, indeed must be, since legitimate culture is "only acquired with time;" putting time to work (*mise en oeuvre*) "supposes the leisure to take one's time" (Bourdieu 1979: 78). Artistic discernment and appropriation not only demonstrate a certain distance from the world of necessity and rigors of inner urban industrial living, but also testify to the discerning taste of the possessor. They confer the "cultural authority of wealth" (Diggins 1978: 146).

This approximation to a former bourgeois cultural model is most clearly expressed through the emphasis on historical artifacts in housing advertisements: "Historic Carlton home," "retaining many original features," including "superbly ornate cornices and fine surrounds, ceiling roses, register grate fire places and lace iron verandah, original door handles, finger plates, lock covers, and ebony handles." These features combine to produce a "truly magnificent example of Victoriana," "authentic Victoriana," "a Sterling recreation," "opposite a pretty English style park." A note of anxiety – "facsimile of original Victorian wall paper" – is allayed with one of reassurance – "restored under architect supervision" and "retaining all its Olde Worlde splendor." This populist duality of tradition and modernity is more sharply expressed: "Victorian with modern additions," "country life" but "well appointed kitchen." This also introduces the element of kitsch so fundamental to urban conservation in Melbourne. "Secluded by nineteenth century gates," "lush ferneries" and "English styled gardens;" this advertising language from the *Melbourne Times* in 1982 expresses the internalization of nature and domestic decorating which has been historically important for the middle classes.

The lack of an indigenous or established aristocracy in Australia encouraged some early settlers to attain upper-class exclusiveness through the retention of English attitudes (Carroll 1982). This orientation reappears in urban conservation, although the credentials change. The Victorian bourgeoisie and gentry remain the principal referents. Urban conservation in Melbourne retreats into the past as far as possible, feasible, or appropriate. Classes, like historical eras, might disappear, but they leave their residues, remnants, relics and motifs, which may continue to operate. The feudalistic pretensions of "the new landed gentry" are made evident through housing displays, representing an investment in status.

If relatively conspicuous consumption represents one pole of the former upper-class ethos, its other pole was distinction. "What distinguishes the bourgeois is distinction itself" (König 1973: 148). In this manner distinction is to be equated with exclusiveness. However, since this can no longer simply be based on natural criteria, the discriminatory dimension of consumption practices must also be increasingly segregative in order to reproduce class differences. This calls for spatial separation. Residential zoning uses spatial distance to ensure social segregation. Urban conservation zones, historic building registers, and classification by the National Trust are not a functional necessity since the property market had already assured their existence. The necessity of public declaration is that of official recognition and sanctioning from above.

Those displays of artistic consecration and possession which seek to create an esthetic object rather than a simple material-use value indicate the class candidature of the new middle classes and define the limits to their social ascension. Failing to approximate fully to the former cultural model, that is, lacking sufficient economic capital to distance themselves fully from economic imperatives, and yet possessing sufficient cultural capital to ape that bourgeois cultural ethos, the new middle classes are forced back upon the employment of a second cultural model – that of work, investment and saving, the Victorian work ethic. The gentrifier is caught between a former gentry ethic of social representation being an end in itself, and a more traditional petty bourgeois ethic of economic valorization. The restoration of Victorian housing attempts the appropriation of a very recent history and hence the authenticity of its symbols as much as its economic profitability is in the beginning precarious. It succeeds only to the extent that it can distance itself from the immediate past – that of working-class industrial "slums." This is achieved externally by esthetic–cultural conferals, and internally by remodeling.

The effacing of an industrial past and a working-class presence, the whitewashing of a former social stain, was achieved through extensive remodeling. The return to historical purity and authenticity (of the "high" Victorian era) is realized by stripping away external additions, by sandblasting, by internal gutting. The restoration of an *anterior* history was virtually the only manner in which the recent stigma of the inner areas could be removed or redefined. It is in the fundamental drive to dislodge, and symbolically obliterate, the former working-class past that the estheticization of Victoriana took off. Esthetic choices may be constituted through opposition to those groups which are closest in both spatial and social terms.

In Melbourne the new middle class which remained in the inner areas was squeezed by modern urban reconstruction programs and the Victorian Housing Commission (VHC). Metaphorically the urban bulldozers leveling slums for VHC constructions were also the agents of social leveling, which meant social declassment for the new middle classes in the inner areas. The classification of housing as slums created a potential for social de-differentiation, standardization and social descent. Through Victoriana the new middle classes oppose aspects of central urban reconstruction programs. Cultural distinctions, local specificities, historical values, and esthetic standards, are brought to the fore.

The creation of Victoriana possessed the merit of rendering immediately perceptible both those strategies for social differentiation and distinction, and the cultural qualities and claims of the possessor. Housing rehabilitation strategies, together with other key consumption activities in the inner areas, had to be both clearly visible and relatively ostentatious; hence they are conspicuously represented. With a decline in real differences between levels of blue-collar and white-collar wages during the 1970s, together with inflation and higher taxes, status differentials had to be all the more forcefully marked than before. The blurring of social differences in this way elicited a dramatic cultural offensive by the new middle class as a means to reinstate social differentiation.

The crucial architectural notions such as purity and authenticity are there to exonerate the social demarcating drive. This esthetic drive will in several instances (such as a momentary mobilization of urban conservation protagonists to exclude aboriginals from settling in Fitzroy) approximate to what Mary Douglas (1978: 101) has called the purity rule. Increasing social control accompanies a disembodiment of received, antagonistic forms of expression; ritualistic ceremonies cleanse and purify the past while they create and maintain the present social boundaries. Having been isolated and excluded, the lower orders resurface to be patronized as "the local people," the "local community," the "little tenants." Populist nostalgia is the inversion of ethnocentrism and racism, and compensates for social and spatial exclusion.

The stigmatization of slums and their contents accompanies the ennobling of Victoriana and its architects. The social demarcation and distinction of class involve the establishment of social boundaries for determining insiders from outsiders, and the architectural and territorial form of Victoriana is the most visible means of achieving this. Social boundaries are made territorial. Thus Victoriana is a fetish, in Marx's sense, in that the objects of culture are made to bear the burden of a more onerous social significance, and yet retain a distinct material function. This is clearest with internal renovations, where actually the authenticity of the 20th-century working-class home was as undesirable as that of the 19th-century Victorian home was unrealizable. For the economic investment in Victoriana depended upon thoroughly modern renovations, especially in the kitchen, and the provision of modern appliances. The Victorian esthetic had its limits; it legitimates but cannot be allowed to compromise the economic investment. Hence the uneasy recognition in housing advertisements themselves that this esthetic can never be fully realized; the emphasis is upon "combining period charm with modern amenities."

In part the emphasis on and demand for modern amenities reflects the Victorian work ethic, especially when the remodeling is done by the new occupiers themselves. Their work is generally a product of economic necessity, but a necessity which is quickly turned into luxury. The labor expended is the principal safety valve against an initially uncertain property acquisition, and it is the insurance policy for the maximization of investment. Yet it is also the means by which parts of the esthetic are created and by which the esthetic as a whole is domesticated into the 20th century. Inner worldly asceticism becomes public display; bare brick walls and exposed timbers come to signify cultural discernment, not the poverty of slums without plaster. Taking this to an extreme, one study (Hargreaves 1976) defines the quality of housing according to its capacity to sustain maximum remodeling.

In this way "the stigma of labour" (Diggins 1978: 144) is both removed and made other. Remnants of a past English colonial presence survive through the importance attributed to handmade bricks, preferably with convict thumbprints. The latter then become a cultural sign accompanying the presence of the gentry. Modernity for Veblen was always an ambiguous project in which residues of a barbaric past continued to surface. The strategy of the new middle classes is dual: they both appropriate and transform; even stigma can be made into a cultural artifact and sign of historical discernment.

A new consumption circuit

As the industrial middle classes of the first half of the 19th century were influential in the expansion of fashion, as manifested in housing interiors (König 1973), so the new middle classes are influential in the extension of the consumption circuit, in which the historical past, new urban life-style, and culture are increasingly integrated. This is epitomized in Victoriana. Although gentrified housing *per se* is hardly significant enough today to usurp the broad social functions of Veblen's leisure class, it is true that vicarious and conspicuous consumption is increasingly related to property investment and purchase of housing.

The new middle class is assuming the responsibility for introducing new consumption models if not new modes of consumption (Lefebvre 1978: 45); in this they perform as cultural brokers and historical mediators of the National Estate. The emergence of the new middle class occurs at a particular stage of economic development, that of industrial saturation, where the function of this new class is precisely to promote the new consumption ethic. The "trendy" and the "taste-maker" emerge as new social types carrying this new societal function.

What characterizes this new consumption model is an emphasis upon esthetic–cultural themes. Leisure (Mullins 1982) and relative affluence create the opportunity for artistic consumption, and art becomes increasing integrated into the middle-class pattern of consumption as a form of investment, status symbol and means of self-expression. The difference between this consumption model and a more traditional middle-class one is marked. The latter has been described by Gusfield, in the study of a middle-class-status movement, in the following way:

> . . . tied to the values of the sober, industrious and steady middle class citizen . . . they operated with the conviction that such was indeed the case: that abstinence as an ideal was a mark of middle class membership.
>
> As the new middle class has developed cultural patterns distinctive to it and opposed to nineteenth-century values, the place of impulse gratification in work and leisure has been redefined. Self-control, reserve, industriousness, and abstemiousness are replaced as virtues by demands for relaxation, tolerance, and moderate indulgence. Not one's ability to produce but one's ability to function as an appropriate consumer is the mark of prestige. (Gusfield 1963: 85 and 146)

Ostentatious display, exhibitionism, and demonstration are essential for the spread of fashion, but operate only on some given stage. In a previous century the theatre itself was a privileged site of fashion display. "With the advent of the 'bourgeois tragedy',"" according to König (1973: 58), "the middle classes became interested in the theatre and used it to display their wealth and the new fashions." Today the inner urban "scene" has become an important stage for promoting fashion and new urban life-style. The elaboration of consumption techniques is increasingly centred in the private residential and cultural domains, rather than in the public or occupational spheres. Thus the redevelopment necessitated by urban conservation involves the reworking and recycling of consumption objects at an accelerating rate. As the past becomes a commodity for contemporary consumption, the consumption circuit is extended both in time and space. This throws up a new type of cottage industry such as that of Brunswick Street in Melbourne where there is an "increasing concentration of alternative/new wave/avant garde galleries, studios, shops, coffee lounges, theatres, restaurants and the like" (*Melbourne Times*, 1983). This new cottage industry promotes domestic decoration, gastronomy and entertainment as the media for new consumption tastes. In all, the new consumption circuit depends not just on the consumption of objects but on the consumption of history as it is embodied in the objects. Urban conservation not so much conserves or preserves history but reuses and recycles it. This leads to a new and distinctive kitsch.

Kitsch: a new esthetic

In urban conservation, esthetic merit does not inhere so much in a particular object or a particular quality, but rather in the combination of objects and qualities facilitating their designation as "architectural excellence and historical significance." To the extent that certain objects and combinations of qualities become stylized as signs of architectural excellence and historical significance, they become the basis of a new kitsch, as illustrated by the following:

> Individual homes and streetscapes are classified by the National Trust ... and the interior has French doors and the ubiquitous Spanish arch.
> Spacious Victorian residence, renovated to perfection, placing emphasis on elegant living with magnificent French windows. (*Melbourne Times*, 1982)

Counterposed to the kitsch of the European migrants of the 1950s and 1960s with Mediterranean colorings and motifs is the kitsch of the new middle classes. The latter is consecrated as esthetic.

With the consecration of the esthetic as kitsch, the esthetic itself becomes of secondary importance. It is not the esthetic itself but the social distinction it evokes which is achieved in the display of kitsch. In kitsch, imitation takes precedence over authenticity, and this expresses the uncomfortable combination of the economic and social functions of urban conservation – the necessity to produce profit *and* social distinction.

Kitsch may be defined by its simulation of authenticity and art, by its attempted approximation to a former consumption model, and by the need to compensate for market consumption. Victorian rehabilitations are caught between authenticity (high Victorian or authentic Victorian as distinct from modern simulations) and reproductions. The further the authentic dimension is compromised, the greater the facadal salvaging and display. As the cultural intention is compromised, the esthetic realm is reduced to facades, which both proclaim an artistic exhibitionism and an internal cover-up. Products about to disintegrate realize additional values and re-enter the consumption cycle, in a new form, for a second time. This is realized through marketing, which is as essential to cultural commodities as it is to fashion. In this way, Victoriana represents the hallmark of fashion, in which the alternation of obsolescence and innovation constitutes a new dynamic potential. As with Marx's "fetishism of commodities," Veblen's "conspicuous consumption" is seen to serve deeper social ends, and this is epitomized in kitsch.

The combination of modernity and "history" is not conflictual, but rather complementary. For even with renovation, modernization takes the form of a neo-archaism – an attempt to return to a pre-industrial past with handmade bricks, and a refutation of mass products. Victoriana distinguishes itself from an industrial stigma just as contemporary kitsch distinguishes itself from an industrialized low culture. In this way the retrieval of history becomes an instance of modernity. This neoromanticism of urban conservation incorporates the most modern functional elements. History is not restored in urban conservation, but recovered in a distorted and partial form.

Stylization of life

Struggles over art forms are at the same time struggles over the art of living (Bourdieu 1979). This approximate pun catches Weber's notion of status groups which are founded over a common style of life and whose characteristics are themselves significant determinants of life-chances. This struggle we can refer to as the "stylization of life," which we can define as the way in which the new middle class, through its social strength, can impose a manner of living, legitimated as natural, and can also exclude other ways of living (Weber 1978 edn: 387–90). The imposition of conformity in living styles is most evident in the increasing emphasis placed on cultural consumption. This is epitomized in the so-called "new urban life-style." The struggle to achieve this stylization of life is apparent in urban conservation, which represents an extension of initial anti-Victorian Housing Commission conflicts. Efforts to distance ugly and unsightly VHC towers gave way to the imposition of the refined esthetic of Victoriana. "Under modern conditions," wrote Veblen, "the struggle for existence has, in a very appreciable degree, been transformed into a struggle to keep up appearance" (Mills 1972: 255). Although social classes may not be directly defined by distinct styles of life, these may, nonetheless, be an important stake in class struggles.

The cultivation of housing and urban planning through urban conservation represents the imposition of an esthetic way of life which has successfully accorded priority to artistic intentions rather than to social functions, to symbolic forms rather than to economic necessities, and to representational excesses rather than to practical utilities. "As the tendency of distinction of the bourgeois upper class now spread to life as a whole" (König 1973: 149), so the constitution of housing as an esthetic–cultural commodity is extended to the inner urban and natural environments, which become an esthetic arena. This shift in priorities is amply demonstrated through the emphasis placed upon the beautification of the environment and the stylization of local politics, both of which, in budget and ideological allocations, place increasing weight on style and form rather than on content. Architecture and politics follow a similar movement, an estheticization of form, in which style itself is to be consumed. Expressionism in facadal displays, open days, fetes, cultural days and festivals assume increasing importance in daily life and in local politics.

However, the fragility of small domestic capital in relation to other larger economic forces present in the inner areas ensures that the esthetic disposition will be tightly circumscribed. This also explains the continuance of strictly economic imperatives and determinants embedded in the estheticization of Victoriana. The slightly triumphant facades of Melbourne Victoriana are matched by more anxiously modeled interiors.

The consumption of objects becomes generalized in advanced industrial societies. This forces class differentiation to be based upon a refinement of consumption objects, which are not only differentiated but must be consumed in a particular way – demonstratively and distinctively. The style of consumption itself becomes crucial to the maintenance of social differentiation. The reproduction of social differences is no longer simply based on possession, but on being seen to have, perhaps simply in being stylish. "A consumption economy, one might say, finds its reality in appearances" (Bell 1976: 68). Conspicuous consumption is expressed not just through symbolic investment in housing but through more traditional middle-class consumption concerns such as dress, entertainment and restaurants, which are further key components in the new inner urban life-style. It may even extend to the "grammar of forms of life" (Habermas 1981: 33).

In a generalized consumption society, where class distinctions no longer appear so rigid and where consumption habits are not so rigidly dictated by class position, there is a constant jockeying for class position, played out in the sphere of consumption. Ostentatious consumption is no longer imposed directly by such rigorous social constraints, but if anything this enhances the role of consumption in the discrimination of one social class from another. A number of holding and salvaging operations are carried out by this or that class or subclass, and this leads to a displacement of struggles into the cultural, esthetic and consumption spheres.

The importance attached to rehabilitation cannot be explained solely by economic profits. Rehabilitation and urban conservation legislation also served to define and maintain class boundaries in various ways. Rehabilitation symbolized new-middle-class arrival and territorial possession. Urban conservation is a token of social position and an indicator of social aspirations. It marks social relationships and privileges. This explains why heated public disputes could take place over such apparent trivialities as restoration. This is also why Victoriana is so demonstrative. It provides a means of expressing social identity, of representing values, of affirming arrival, of symbolizing possession and of demonstrating presence.

If accumulating social distinctions and privileges was one means of ensuring middle-class identity, the economic valorization of housing was another. The gentry has in the past made fortunes through the acquisition of consecrated property: ecclesiastical property in the 16th and 17th centuries and historical property in the 20th. However, the extraction of value from housing is not simply or solely related to economic profit. Economic gains, working-class "displacement," are not the major dimensions of gentrification in Melbourne. The economic gains are too small, the fractions of capital too local and insignificant, being principally those of small domestic property. They are in themselves insufficient to ground a notion of housing class (Pratt 1982). Where economic capital is insufficient to secure substantial social privileges, then it may, when combined with more substantial cultural capital, perform more admirably. The constitution of historical property, both individual domestic property and a National Estate, has been the basis for the formation of a new local urban elite. Traditional middle-class mechanisms of status defense, such as the procuring of titles,

National Trust classifications and historic zoning, have been accompanied by the securing of local-government posts and offices by the new gentry. The estheticization of the environment, "saving the inner areas," has been their historical mission. Housing representation and local political representation form the two principal activities of the gentry in Melbourne. Where real social advancement is blocked, a concern for display and signs of advancement may substitute for real achievements.

6

The political and social construction of revitalized neighborhoods: Society Hill, Philadelphia, and False Creek, Vancouver

ROMAN A. CYBRIWSKY, DAVID LEY, and JOHN WESTERN

In recent years numerous explanations have been advanced for the emergence of widespread North American inner-city revitalization (Laska & Spain 1980, Holcomb & Beauregard 1981). These have ranged broadly, from factors such as the decision-making behavior of individual households, to the operations of seemingly immutable forces at the national or international levels. These competing theses emphasize on the one hand the autonomy of willed actions (human agency) and on the other the imperatives of demographic and economic structures. However, in this chapter, from a longitudinal perspective on two case studies, we are unwilling to separate the contributions of these two factors in neighborhood change, and instead emphasize their sometimes elusive overlap. The specific lineaments of revitalization in our two case studies arise from an evolving interplay of key individuals and interest groups, shifting finance and property markets, imperfectly orchestrated consumer demands, somewhat unpredictable electoral responses, and changing priorities and intervention strategies by government at different levels. In brief, our emphasis does stress the capacity of human agency to initiate significant urban change, but within a well defined context, alternately constraining and enabling.

One implication of this emphasis might seem to be the partial discounting of "structural" explanations for inner-city revitalization. That is, the shift toward smaller households or the tightening of housing markets, for example (see Berry 1980a), might be portrayed as but a passive backdrop to a stage upon which powerful actors, a civic elite, *will* the new city into being. In like vein, the dominant role marxists claim for "capital" in propelling the restructuring of residential space (Smith 1979a) might be overshadowed or at least redirected by the apparently autonomous actions of civic power-brokers. But we do not wish to overstate the case; rather our interpretation sees any single-variable perspective as insufficient, in as much as it clouds the necessary *interdependence* between the agency of so-called principal actors or interest groups, and various and evolving contextual factors.

Thus, for example, Sanders' clear and even-handed retrospective on urban renewal makes it plain that success depended on the property market, in our view, basically a structural factor: "the burden of new development rested on the private real estate market, with profits as a central motivating force" (1980: 105). Agency, on the other hand, is continuously implicated in the "curious mix" (1980: 104) of private-sector and various levels of public-sector involvement; for the implementation of urban renewal "rested on a trust in local agencies to make wise decisions about such matters as land uses or the form of the city in twenty years, about which they knew . . . very little" (1980: 105). Or again, Mollenkopf (1978) avers that urban renewal has been used as a tool to maintain a city's economic growth even in the face of declining population growth (as in the case of Philadelphia). We do not necessarily perceive in this some superhuman effort on the part of the planners of urban renewal to beat back structural trends, but rather an attempt to manipulate and channel such trends, constrained by them to a degree. So neither agency nor structure is necessarily imperative; each is contingent upon the other.

The two neighborhoods selected for comparative study are Society Hill in Philadelphia and False Creek in Vancouver. This choice is not merely fortuitous. In North America we could hardly have chosen two more seemingly dissimilar cases: in separate countries, divided by the width of a continent, and in cities founded for very different motives two centuries apart. In Society Hill, redevelopment plans date back to the 1940s, and are rooted in the perceived need to rescue Philadelphia from the debilitating effects of decentralization, aging, and disinvestment so typical of older industrial cities in the United States. In False Creek, by contrast, the context is western Canada's rapid urban growth of the late 1960s and 1970s, and confidence in Vancouver's future prosperity; here, therefore, constraints were fewer, so more ambitious objectives could be pursued.

Yet certain important common themes emerge. In both cities a major long-term shift in the urban economy has occurred: the transition from a raw-materials-processing and manufacturing economy to that of the downtown-focused service orientation characteristic of the "post-industrial" city (Bell 1973, Stanback & Noyelle 1982). The reshaping of both the Society Hill and False Creek neighborhoods, each adjoining the downtown area, is part and parcel of this change. Another similarity between the two neighborhoods is that planning and design innovations were developed here so successfully that they have received considerable professional praise and endorsement as prototypes of urban redevelopment. Society Hill has come to be considered a textbook example of good city design, and early reviews of the still-evolving False Creek project point to similar renown, as in an evaluation in the *Architectural Review* which claimed that it "encapsulates, probably better than anywhere else in the world, the housing dream of the 1970s" (Wright & Collymore 1980: 323). Both projects are consequently providing models for the revitalization of other districts and cities. Moreover, both of these projects were, despite such latter-day imitation, initiated in an atmosphere of considerable skepticism, and involved at least in part the problem-solving creativity of a body of articulate and politically mobilized visionaries.

Philadelphia's Society Hill: the political context

The present elite character of Philadelphia's Society Hill district belies the neighborhood's status only 40 years ago (Fig. 6.1). It was part of a city which Lowe (1967) characterized as then being "a donut: a vast metropolis built up around a hollow center." This, she contended, was as true of the commercial core, the downtown, as of nearly all inner-city neighborhoods. "These were being submerged in slums . . . [having] streets which were the dirtiest in the country." Moreover, physical dilapidation seemed to be matched by an inept municipal leadership, "the most quiet and crudely wasteful city government in the U.S." (Lowe 1967: 319). Nearly all the rich and powerful had fled the city limits for elite suburbs, leaving in their wake a concentration of the metropolitan area's poor, aged, and minority groups. Yet it is these same center-city "donut" precincts that stand today as illustrious models of successful urban revitalization.

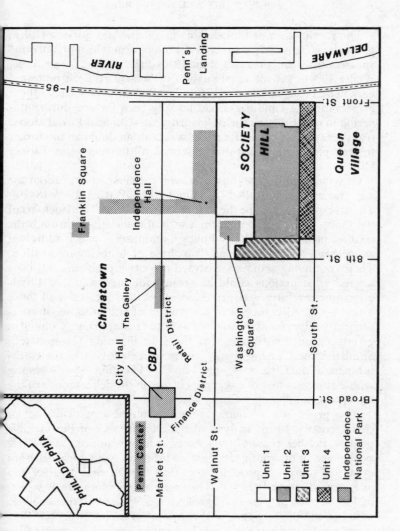

Figure 6.1

The reanimation of Philadelphia in general and Society Hill in particular is frequently portrayed as a movement which first became apparent from the latter part of the 1940s onwards (see, for example, Weiler 1974). Yet the rehabilitation of Society Hill can be traced back in part to as early as the 1930s. The Philadelphia Society for the Preservation of Landmarks had initially been formed during this period in order to save the noteworthy late-Colonial Powel House from decay. This particular effort was without doubt an important first chapter in the "historic preservation" movement in Society Hill.

Of wider significance, however, was the emergence at about the same time of the so-called "Young Turks" (Petshek 1973: 18–20). These persons were to be the advocates of the "new" Philadelphia of the 1950s. They began to form a web of associations through the establishment of their "City Policy Committee," which addressed altogether broader questions than those of historic preservation. Their continuing seminars analyzed the city's problems and considered what options could be created for their solution. Local-government reform was perceived as essential (Scattergood 1956: 5–8, 12–13). Also they were convinced of the promise of comprehensive city planning, and by 1942 had pressured City Council to greatly enhance the powers of the City Planning Commission. Similarly, the "Young Turks" were prime movers in the establishment of the Citizens' Council on City Planning, a body among whose aims was that of engaging citizens in the deliberations of the now powerful Planning Commission.

As a group, the "Young Turks" possessed a particular set of characteristics. In his analysis of the reform years of Philadelphia politics, Petshek tells us "they were . . . full of enthusiasm." There was an accent on youth, designed to bring in "young leaders from untapped sources," provided they had "intellectual capacity and integrity" (Petshek 1973: 19). They were also predominantly white, male, and from patrician backgrounds. As Walter Phillips, a charter member and major figure of the group, wrote in retrospect, they were "persons who for their age had gained unusual recognition . . . in their respective vocational activities." Because, he claimed, "most of the civic leadership in Philadelphia . . . had in the past [been furnished by] a small, downtown, unrepresentative circle of people," the City Policy Committee consciously included "not only lawyers and businessmen but also labor leaders, social workers, doctors, architects, teachers, and government employees" (Phillips undated: 4). One early recruit to the City Policy Committee was Edmund Bacon, recently graduated from the Cranbrook Academy of Art under Eliel Saarinen, and previously at Cornell University;

96

another was future Philadelphia mayor and US Senator Joseph Clark.[1] The City Policy Committee soon made its influence felt in successful lobbying for the hiring (in 1943) of Robert Mitchell as the first executive director of the new City Planning Commission.

The City Policy Committee again played a major role in the organization of the landmark Better Philadelphia Exhibition. Held in 1947 in the downtown Gimbels department store, it was the brainchild of Bacon and Phillips, and was supported also by the City Planning Commission. The exhibition displayed how Philadelphia *could* look in the not-too-distant future, and proved to be a veritable public relations coup. Over 400000 people – representing the remarkably high proportion of perhaps one in every ten persons in the metropolitan area – visited the appealingly produced exhibit, whose sights and sounds caught the imagination of the public, especially a 14 ft by 30 ft scale model of center-city Philadelphia, parts of which moved in order to demonstrate "before-and-after redevelopment." Widespread enthusiasm was engendered: as Mitchell, the City's Planning Director, said, "it made people see the city as solvable" (quoted in Lowe 1967: 323). Indeed, the degree of public response had not been anticipated. It seemed to indicate the possibility of broad citizen support for interventionist city planning in general, and created particular expectations of a better downtown Philadelphia to come.

At the same time as the citizenry was gaining an appreciation of the potentials of comprehensive city planning, so, too, many of the leading business people of the metropolis were, from their own specific standpoints, becoming equally convinced of the need for an ambitious reshaping of the city. The business establishment's agenda for change had been particularly conditioned by the evident need to turn the city's reputation around. To illustrate, a highly symbolic vignette from Philadelphia commercial folklore which came to be reported across the nation concerns the 1948 visit to California of Harry Batten, director of Philadelphia's N. W. Ayers Advertising Agency. In endeavoring to convince certain West Coast business interests to establish their eastern offices in his city, Batten was sobered by the damning response: "We've surveyed 20 of the biggest American cities ... and Philadelphia would be our *last* choice" (Havemann 1962: 244). This spurred Batten on his return to mobilize other business leaders toward the goal of thoroughgoing physical and political improvements in the city. Encountering in their view only limited positive response from the more conservative, laissez-faire Philadelphia Chamber of Commerce, they founded the Greater Philadelphia Movement on December 16 of that year.

Self-limited to 35 board members, the Greater Philadelphia Movement represented a significant segment of Philadelphia's commercial elite. In addition to Batten, the group composed the top executives of several of Philadelphia's leading banks in particular, and also of law firms, investment companies, railroads, and other commercial concerns. This is entirely consistent with a 1965 analysis by the *Philadelphia Bulletin*, which describes the organization as the "Cream of the Civic Group Giants":

> Sixteen of GPM's present 33 members are in the Philadelphia *Social Register*. All but a few are in *Who's Who in America*. Six are on the University of Pennsylvania trustee boards. Three are on the boards of the Philadelphia Orchestra and the Academy of Music.
>
> There are 24 GPM members who have "Ivy" undergraduate or graduate school backgrounds. Eleven belong to the 131-year-old Philadelphia Club, a sure mark of the patrician. Eight more are members of either the Racquet Club or the Rittenhouse Club.
>
> There are some whose ancestors were signers of the Declaration of Independence or delegates to the First Continental Congress. Many have followed the path of the Proper Philadelphian through the New England boarding schools of St. Paul's or St. Mark's, then on to Princeton or Harvard or Yale. (McCullough 1965: 4)

The Greater Philadelphia Movement and the City Policy Committee found themselves, from their differing perspectives, espousing a common cause. "Confidence in the City's government," asserted a position paper of the Greater Philadelphia Movement,

> is essential to the development of this area. Therefore, the movement is deeply interested in helping to create an improved municipal government under a modern and efficient charter – a government characterized by honesty, competence and high type performance.

Or as William F. Kelly, a major Movement figure and former president of the First Pennsylvania Bank, put it yet more unambiguously, "the future of our companies, all of them, is tied to the growth of our city. When I spend time on civic affairs I'm in effect working on the bank's business too" (McCullough 1965: 3).

In brief, the combination of business power, political influence, and civic vigor which the two interest groups of the City Policy Committee and the Greater Philadelphia Movement commanded was sufficient to overcome the entrenched Republican city machine, torpid and corrupt from decades of uninterrupted sway. By the mid-1950s, the City Charter had been reformed (1951), among other things to confer greater executive powers upon the mayor; Joseph Clark, Democratic candidate and member of the City Policy Committee, was elected mayor on a reform platform and took office in 1952. Richardson Dilworth, another central member of the City Policy Committee, was elected District Attorney in that year, and was to succeed Clark in the mayor's office in 1956, when the latter was elected to the US Senate. These electoral successes permitted the implementation of a planning agenda, thus transforming what had previously been merely intriguing possibilities (as with the Better Philadelphia Exhibit) into concrete proposals for remaking the city. The successes revealed also that elite initiatives found substantial popular support.

Among the salient provisions of the city's new charter was its insistence upon the preparation of an explicit and comprehensive physical plan for the city by the Planning Commission. The consequence of this insistence is that planning, especially as applied to the downtown area, has become a major force in the reshaping of the city over the past 30 years. Such well known projects as downtown Philadelphia's Penn Center office complex, the creation of Independence National Historic Park, the distinctive enclosed retail mall named The Gallery,[2] and numerous other center-city physical improvements are all constituent outgrowths of an overall planning scheme for a new Philadelphia (Halpern 1978). These major improvements were largely conducted and overseen by Edmund Bacon, appointee of the reform City Policy Committee, who by 1949 had become Executive Director of the Philadelphia City Planning Commission.

Society Hill: strategies and implementation

It is in this context of confidence in the practicability of planning that we place Society Hill's redevelopment. The neighborhood was consciously selected for transformation into a district of prestigious homes in order that it be occupied by Philadelphia's elite classes. Dilworth himself, while mayor, said straightforwardly, "We've got to get the white leadership back..." Society Hill, then, represents a symbolic and key *residential* component of the strategy to revitalize center city. In this it was intended to complement parallel efforts geared to office uses, retailing, tourism, and recreation (Cybriwsky & Western 1982).

The selection of Society Hill was calculated, and revolved around its perceived potential for successful revitalization. It is almost as if revitalization had to be seen to work here first, if it was to gain any credibility as a possible strategy for other portions of central Philadelphia. Here in Society Hill was a neighborhood with immanent advantages: Philadelphia's oldest district, a repository of

American history, easily accessible by foot to downtown, within view of the Delaware River, and containing much significant period architecture. Immediately adjacent to Society Hill stood several of America's historic shrines: Independence Hall and the Liberty Bell, Carpenter's Hall, and the First and Second Banks of the United States. Yet in the 1940s these noteworthy structures were in a setting of decline, surrounded by incompatible land uses associated with the older, discarded edge of a westward-shifting downtown: warehouses and wharves, light manufacturing, overcrowded rental properties, multitudinous small retailing establishments, and other aging elements of the so-called "Zone of Transition" around the downtown core (Pace 1976).

The redevelopment of this square mile called for massive surgery, which had been made possible by the previous passage of federal and state urban renewal legislation. In 1956 the Washington Square East renewal program, overseen by Edmund Bacon, was officially launched. It envisaged a metamorphosis of the built environment, especially in what was designated as Unit One of the renewal scheme, the first phase of the project. Unit One was the largest segment of the total Redevelopment Area (Fig. 6.1), and, to reiterate a point made earlier, represented a site where upper-income renewal *had* to succeed in order that further renewal might be seen to be practicable. Thus, as opposed to the somewhat "looser" more pluralistic strategies employed for Units Two and Three, no chances were taken.

The Unit One district was totally condemned by the Redevelopment Authority in 1959, giving that body absolute control over its reshaping. Those land uses now considered by the planners to be incompatible, such as industry and warehousing, had to be removed altogether. The single largest such facility, occupying several entire blocks, was the long-established Food Distribution Center. It had been described as rat-infested, lacking in sanitary facilities, overcrowded, and altogether grossly unhygienic, and therefore commended itself for resiting.[3] Other uses, such as retailing, were reshuffled into carefully delineated, compact districts.

Much more land was to be devoted to higher-quality residential uses, interspersed with a generous provision of green spaces, pedestrian paths, and small sequestered parks. Wherever possible, painstaking care was taken over historical preservation, not just of recognized landmarks, but also of the rank-and-file residential blocks and storefronts which, once their facades had been refurbished, were to provide so-called authentic neighborhood ambience. Where demolition was followed by new construction, efforts

100

were made to harmonize scale and texture with that of the pre-existing Colonial fabric. The striking exception (see below) was the trio of luxury high-rise apartment buildings, Society Hill Towers, on the site of the Food Distribution Center.[4]

This redevelopment was a remarkably bold initiative. It presupposed investment on a grand scale, of both public and private monies, in the very face of the powerful countervailing forces of decentralization. The inner city, after all, seemed no place to sink large sums. Indeed, an elaborate marketing survey of center-city real estate conducted in the late 1950s concluded that there was only limited demand for high-rent residential provision there (Rapkin & Grigsby 1960). Yet, upon a base of federal and state grants, the planners sought to underwrite their proposals by inducing significant investment from precisely those interests which were presently financing the suburbanization of Philadelphia: the elite classes and the major banks, corporations, and real-estate brokers. The plan, then, took as a premise that a major investment, if well formulated and executed, could bring back enough elite households to Society Hill to serve as a catalyst for further return, in a reversal of centrifugal trends. The opening passage of Bacon's *Plan for Center City* (Philadelphia City Planning Commission 1963) reads "that center city [was to] serve as a springboard from which waves of revitalization [would] spread outward as suburban families [were] attracted to urban living."

Thus, the transformation of Society Hill may be viewed as in significant measure an act of will on the part of a small and creative group of civic strategists, in the face of apparently daunting constraints: "Everyone thought the idea was screwy," recalled Bacon. And in an article entitled "Renaissancemanship," David A. Wallace, Professor of City Planning at the University of Pennsylvania, wrote that "it will be a long time before the project is surrounded by anything but junk, and only a planner will ever walk from Society Hill to Wanamakers [a major downtown department store] or Penn Center" (Wallace 1960). In such a climate, Mayor Dilworth's moving house in 1956 to Washington Square East (the square was described by Jane Jacobs (1961: 98) as "completely taken over by perverts") takes on a particular symbolism; to the elite, this was a pioneering gesture. As Bacon noted in 1974, "Dilworth's decision to build ... was a very important act in opening up the whole possibility of making Society Hill work" (Bacon, November 7, 1974, in Phillips interviews). Likewise, former board chairman of the New York Stock Exchange, Henry Miller Watts Jr., was another early arrival.

There were other leading citizens who participated in such

demonstrations of long-term confidence. They moved in self-consciously as "pioneers," rehabilitating a "slum" dwelling, and thus lent publicity and cachet to the Society Hill project. Next door to Watts, for instance, C. Jared Ingersoll, multimillionaire lawyer and railroad financier with numerous civic credentials (e.g. Greater Philadelphia Movement member, sometime president of the Philadelphia Museum of Art), came into Society Hill from an elite "Main Line" suburb to rehabilitate a historic Society Hill townhouse:

> My wife and I . . . bought from the Redevelopment Authority a lovely old house built in the early eighteenth century which had gone completely to rack and ruin. The filth was beyond belief, the fleas were such and the stench was such that you couldn't stay in the house about ten or fifteen minutes because the fleas would eat you alive. There were two dead cats found in the bathtub. (Ingersoll, June 28, 1977, in Phillips interviews)

Such doings were detailed in the local press, which often reported on the progress of rehabilitation, sometimes with before-and-after photographs. Before long, some owners were giving tours of their refurbished period houses. Thus the *Sunday Bulletin* (May 10, 1959), in an article entitled "Come and See the Flowering of Society Hill," invited its readers to see what "the new pioneers" had accomplished: "Many of them have worked on their own houses, scraped floors, painted walls, or haunted antique shops to find an old door knob or a special hinge . . ."

Such publicity was sought, and orchestrated, in order to overcome Society Hill's negative image. As another figure in the neighborhood's redevelopment, James Martin, said, "we sort of had to salt the mine . . . It was a bombed-out area . . . [with] more houses than there were buyers" (Martin, March 16, 1977, in Phillips interviews). Bacon himself has spoken of "twisting people's arms" that they might move into Society Hill, and upon finding "wealthy potential old-house buyers" he would personally conduct them through the neighborhood, lauding its history and selling its future.

By this time, too, Albert M. Greenfield, whom E. Digby Baltzell subsequently described in *Philadelphia Gentlemen* (1958: 379) as "the most powerful single individual in the city," had become convinced of the potential of center-city renewal, and was in 1956 appointed chairman of the City Planning Commission.

> [He] had owned or brokered, at one time or another, half of Philadelphia, and had vast holdings in department stores, office buildings and hotels in downtown Philadelphia as well as other cities . . . He talked at length to every top industrialist, banker, merchant and businessman to

win personal and financial commitment . . . [Greenfield stressed to them that] retail sales on Market Street, the main shopping area, had fallen 15 percent in the past eight years, even while the region had grown. The Society Hill project would be only the first step in a comprehensive plan. He told the banks and insurance companies that carried the mortgages on the stores and buildings in the area that they would be the long-run losers if downtown withered. (Lowe 1976: 341, 344–45)

In order to assume the public office of City Planning Commission Chairman, Greenfield, who had until then been Chairman of the Board of the Philadelphia Chamber of Commerce and in fact had been opposed to public-sector involvement in any renewal programs, needed formally to distance himself somewhat from his Philadelphia property investments. Then, as publicist and overseer, with his unparalleled acumen in real-estate matters in Philadelphia, he made a substantial commitment in time and energy to the Society Hill redevelopment. (He could even wax "lyrical about the project's significance to 'this beloved city – this lot of one thousand acres that combines all that civilization has to offer'" (Lowe 1967: 345).) One especially significant action was, at his urging, the founding in 1956 of the Old Philadelphia Development Corporation, a body of business and banking leaders. Its aim would be to contract with the Redevelopment Authority (the city agency which, through eminent domain, was to gain title to the Society Hill properties) to redevelop the historic buildings and certain of the vacant lots.

Further impetus was given to the Society Hill project through the idea of introducing luxury high-rises into the redevelopment, in striking counterpoint to the area's restored (or simulated) Colonial- and Federal-era two-story townhouses. Not only did the final choice fall on I. M. Pei's "brilliant design" (Bacon's expressed opinion (1976: 265), but the very nature of the nationwide architectural competition with its contending proposals attracted much attention, as was intended. Even so, necessary funds for development were initially hard to come by, as was the required approval of the Federal Housing Administration (FHA) for the scheme. Because of the increasing costs of building to such rigorous design specifications as Pei's proposal demanded, the resultant increasing rents to be charged for the eye-catching tower apartments seemed unrealistic to the FHA's cautious Philadelphia evaluators. The towers were too far from any other high-rent residential district, and were surrounded by a still largely deteriorated neighborhood. It took a year to achieve an agreement for FHA mortgage guarantees, and this only after the chief executive of the FHA in Washington had intervened.

In the meantime, however, the trend toward private rehabilitation in Society Hill started to catch hold; this caused developers of townhouses to begin to see gainful opportunities. In part they advertised their wares selectively. It is in a programme from Philharmonia Hall at New York's Lincoln Center, for example, that we read

> This is Society Hill . . . the new fashionable Philadelphia community . . . famous for its prominent citizenry since before the Revolution . . . [We have] carefully preserved this tradition. The houses are 20th century in design and materials, but retain all the charm and flavor of Colonial America.

Or, in a less targeted manner, we read in the *Philadelphia Inquirer* of May 18, 1958, a property advertisement which hymns the

> new parks, a marina, green pathways, expressways and nice people, all coming to enhance gracious living in Society Hill.

Or again, in the April 4, 1965, *Philadelphia Inquirer*, "Delancey Mews" are marketed by the Albert M. Greenfield Corporation: "AMERICA'S MOST HISTORIC AREA, revitalizing quietly with dignity".[5]

In the end, the combination of advertising hype, face-to-face cajolery by major civic figures such as Bacon or Greenfield, and the "demonstration effect" of such incontestably elite personages as Dilworth, Ingersoll, and Watts residing there apparently unscathed gained a favorable image for the Society Hill redevelopment project. This aided the appreciation of real estate in the area, and soon both developers and private individuals clamored to participate. In this regard Smith (1979b) has shown how, with increasing surety of return, the sources of capital invested in Society Hill properties shifted from state grants to high-risk ventures, and then to savings-and-loan bodies who were now prepared to finance mortgages in a district they perceived as established.

Social planning and social costs

The physical appearance itself of the redeveloped Society Hill manifests the special difficulty of marketing this inner-city neighborhood in the midst of the suburban age. Previously cited advertisements highlighted stereotypically nonurban attributes of the neighborhood, such as marinas and green pathways. The conscious re-sorting of heterogeneous into homogeneous land-use patterns, unlike any of the other older neighborhoods of the city, is, we claim, drawn from a prominent motif in suburban design. The anthropologist Constance Perin, in *Everything in its place* (1977), an exploration of cultural and social symbolism in metropolitan land-use patterns, argues that one of the keys to the successful marketing of American suburbia has been the appeal of clearly ordered and discrete land-use units. Prospective homebuyers, who were not only purchasing shelter, but also deeply committing themselves financially, were reassured by the evident presence of neighbors "just like themselves." Thus in the design of Society Hill, residential tracts were separated from most other uses, and also were internally sorted by cost and tenure type. In addition, building design was such as to maximize both privacy and physical security. The inward-facing plans of several new housing clusters, for example, with parking and entrance on the interior of blocks, exemplify one of the earliest applications of "defended space" principles.

Having ensured that "everything was in its place," so too the Society Hill concept carefully saw to it that everybody was in their place; social homogeneity, equally a stereotypically suburban attribute, was relentlessly pursued. Part of the appeal of homogeneity was to snobbery: the advertisements previously cited invited one to come live with Philadelphia's top people: a 1957 advertisement (early in Society Hill's redevelopment) insinuates "The mayor is, why can't you?" (*Philadelphia Inquirer*, May 19, 1957). Just as important was the need to assuage fears about stereotypical in-city subcultures. ("See, you have to understand [that] the fundamental feeling in suburbia is fear [of the impingement of the city], let's face it," a realtor had informed Perin (1977: 87).) So, in a suburban age, the advertisements felt they had to stress "nice people . . . coming to live in Society Hill." Some years later, a leading center-city realtor felt it possible to sell the neighborhood in terms of who had already arrived there, and implied that the new inhabitants were creating supportive solidarity among themselves. "It has become a neighborhood in the fullest sense of the word, and a classy one at that" (*Philadelphia Inquirer*, April 26, 1965). More baldly, security was also being offered to buyers by assuring them that undesirable pre-existing locals had been removed. With remarkable command of euphemism, the ad's previous sentence read "Society Hill is no longer a haven for ferocious misanthropes."

It is a commonplace that the Society Hill renewal, so evidently "top-down" in conception and execution, imposed social costs upon pre-existing residents of lower socioeconomic status. The prior residents of Unit One could remain only if the Redevelopment Authority was disposed to resell their property back to them with inevitably expensive contractual stipulations: a timetable for any of a number of specific repairs, mandatory upkeep requirements, plus remodeling to exacting and detailed "historically authentic" standards for facades. Unbending application of these criteria expelled all but a few of the original lower-income residents. Thus, at the public meeting held in conjunction with the unveiling of the Unit One plan (April 28, 1958), the complaint was heard from one resident that it was "a plan for an area of wealthy poodled people," and it was reported that "many [residents] . . . didn't like what they saw, or thought they saw, looming in the future.' John P. Robin, president of the Old Philadelphia Development Corporation (the body which had contracted to implement the renewal) responded that "residents would have to compromise their desires with those of others and the city" (*Evening Bulletin*, April 29, 1958). This captures the general tone; in many cases the record documents a degree of insensitivity to or lack of concern with the special needs and claims of pre-existing Society Hill residents.

It was high-income people that were required in Unit One; any possibility of income mix was intendedly minimized. The later developments of Units Two and Three did give a nod in the direction of socioeconomic heterogeneity. Blanket condemnation of property was no longer invoked. Selective renewal left a much larger proportion of original residents in situ. Moreover, there was even a minor provision made for the rehousing of some displacees from the condemned portion of Society Hill. However, even such a token increment of subsidized housing has proved to be the subject of much controversy in the neighborhood, and after nearly 20 years only some of the 19 units projected had actually been built (Pace 1976).

Vancouver: False Creek

Vancouver is a younger and smaller city than Philadelphia. In origin it is a railway town incorporated in 1886 with the completion of the transcontinental Canadian Pacific Railway, and it rapidly evolved into a port city whose characteristic industries were lumber mills, fish canneries, and metalworking. These activities created a distinctive industrial landscape along the waterfront and in the zone of transition encircling the central business district on the downtown peninsula.

However, from the 1930s onwards, Vancouver's economy gradually changed from purely industrial toward increasing tertiary and quaternary occupations in the downtown core. Unlike Philadelphia, Vancouver had maintained an overall level of economic and population growth through the 1970s; the metropolitan area's population

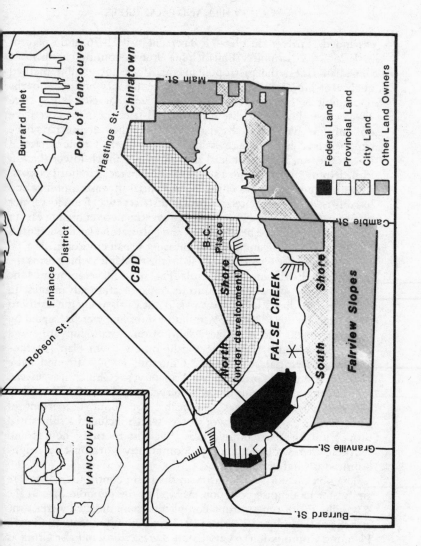

Figure 6.2

expanded 21 percent in 1966–71, 8 percent in 1971–76, and 9 percent in 1976–81. Also unlike Philadelphia, but in common with most Canadian cities, the metropolitan area does not exhibit marked quality-of-life disparities between the center city and its suburbs (Goldberg & Mercer 1980). Demand levels for city living have always been high, and elite residential districts near the core have not only survived but have expanded; other inner-city districts have experienced considerable revitalization (Ley 1981). Crime levels and most other measures of social pathology are much lower than in Philadelphia, and although a substantial Asian racial minority exists, it has in the postwar era enjoyed substantial upward mobility and has diffused into integrated residential districts away from its former ghetto in Chinatown. Careful public investment over many years in parks, waterfront and beach access, and cultural and leisure activities has helped to create an unusually pleasing urban environment.

The name False Creek is taken from the tidal inlet which turns the downtown district into a peninsula (Fig. 6.2). Development of the Creek's banks was closely tied to its transportation advantages. In 1892 the Canadian Pacific Railway laid out yards along the northern shore, and by the 1920s all 5½ miles of shoreline were occupied by industry: metal and machinery fabrication, small shipyards, and especially sawmills. Both the Bartholomew town plan (Bartholomew & Associates 1929) and Churchill (1954) affirmed False Creek's industrial primacy in Vancouver. Churchill's survey revealed that the 81 firms on the waterway employed 5 400 workers and the whole basin was responsible for about 12 percent of Vancouver's payroll. The workforce, which included a substantial proportion of Asian millworkers, lived in rooming houses and working-men's cottages in the predominantly working-class neighbourhoods ringing False Creek.

The noxious form of industry in the basin contributed to severe air, water, and noise pollution, as well as the periodic fires in the sawmills. From time to time complaints were directed against the esthetic of the industrial basin; a 1937 memorandum from the Town Planning Commission to City Council was critical of False Creek as "unsightly, offensive, and a menace to the community's health" (Churchill 1954). Despite this, postwar policy continued to advocate industrial land use, albeit more space-intensive forms of industry, and in 1967, under pressure from industrial leaseholders whose leases would shortly expire, City Council passed a motion that "the land abutting False Creek be retained as an industrial area" (Elligott 1977). The physical landscape had changed very little over 80 years, as was apparent from an 1968 description of False Creek as "a garbage dump, a sewer outlet for the city of Vancouver . . . It is, first and foremost, the industrial heart of the city" (Fukui 1968). It seemed as if this pattern was to be sustained into future decades.

TEAM: an urban social movement

In effect the overt commitment by Vancouver City Council to an industrial future for False Creek ensured the very opposite. For it unwittingly provided the stimulus around which emerged an articulate opposition which advocated a totally different use for the tract, that of a landscaped, model, in-city residential neighborhood. Although there was no single visionary comparable to Society Hill's Edmund Bacon, a leading proponent of the transformation of the Vancouver site was Walter Hardwick, an urban geographer, whom Kemble (1980) credited with being "the pivotal person in the development of False Creek as it stands today." The constituency for which Hardwick was a major spokesman might be described as "the new middle class," including such professionals as teachers, professors, architects, lawyers, and social workers. Their opposition to industry in False Creek was fueled by their vision of "a livable city" at odds with the Creek's existing landscape. The ideological conflict was sharpened by concerns over the very real issue of severe industrial pollution at the core of a city with so striking a natural site, on a maritime inlet surrounded dramatically by mountains.

Critics such as Hardwick worked to bring these concerns before the Vancouver citizenry through public education and media debates. By 1967–68 a groundswell of popular opposition to Council's pro-business, status quo policies for the Creek was emerging. This was consolidated in 1968 by the formation of The Electors Action Movement (TEAM), a liberal reform party concerned to a significant degree with such planning and development issues in Vancouver as the False Creek question (Ley 1980). In the city elections of 1968, TEAM placed two aldermen on City Council; one was Hardwick.

A specific call in TEAM's 1968 electoral platform included an innovative proposal to transform False Creek "from purely industrial use to a combination of residential, recreational and 'clean' industrial uses" (TEAM 1968). Over the next 12 months leaders of TEAM continued to chastise the majority council for its inactivity over False Creek, noting for example that no financial provision for any False Creek redevelopment was included in the City's proposed borrowing plan for 1971–75 (*Vancouver Province*, September 25, 1969; *Vancouver Sun*, October 2, 1969). As public awareness continued to grow, Council felt the need to authorize the City Planning Department to set out a brochure which pointed alternative future scenarios for False Creek, and to seek citizen reaction, a public relations gesture reminiscent of, if less dramatic than, the Better Philadelphia Exhibit of 1947. Reporting on the responses, including 36 written submissions, the city's Planning Director remarked that "the numerous public meetings, calls on the Planning Department, and in particular the high quality of the replies have indicated widespread awareness and interest by the citizens in the future of Vancouver" (Vancouver Planning Department 1970).

The character of the 36 submissions is instructive. They comprised 9 briefs by citizens' groups, 11 from business groups, 2 from labor organizations, 2 from municipal boards, and 12 by private individuals. The public was presented with 5 different redevelopment packages, comprising varying mixes of industrial, commercial, residential, and recreational land uses. The two proposals which particularly emphasized industrial land use received no support from any of the 36 submissions. This unambiguous statement of popular intent across a wide spectrum of interest groups seems to have been a decisive event in propelling a reluctant Council toward a nonindustrial redevelopment strategy. The most popular proposal had the largest acreage of parks and community facilities, the smallest acreage of industrial land, substantial residential development, and moderate commercial space.

Although this apparent consensus was sufficient to advance the redevelopment process substantially, a more careful examination of the submissions reveals some important differences of emphasis within the broad-brush design categories set up by the planners. The proposals of citizen groups, including labor unions, contrasted with those espoused by the business sector. Predictably, the latter advocated a more commercial function for the Creek, a major theme of their submissions being the promotion of Vancouver as an executive city, as a center of office-based quaternary functions and of tourism. Thus the Greater Vancouver Real Estate Board called, as did the Downtown Business Association, for a development "consistent with the City's role as the principal executive city in western Canada." The Vancouver Board of Trade commented that "Vancouver has paid insufficient attention . . . to providing the type of downtown environment that will attract the Continent's decision-makers and it is in this context that we consider the future of False Creek so vital to the long-term wellbeing of our community." Moreover, the Building Owners and Managers Association favored in addition greater provision for tourism: False Creek should have "hotels, [a] swimming pool, [a] gymnasium, indoor track, covered tennis courts, theatres, restaurants, etc. interspresed with parkland." On the issue of housing, the business briefs were largely silent, implicitly accepting the high densities included in the planners' concept, and, with an executive city in mind, presumably endorsing market housing on the highly valued land.

In contrast the citizens' groups were most concerned with the housing component of redevelopment. There was a consensus that the densities proposed in the planning concept were too high, "a typical businessman's view of development" according to the Vancouver and District Labour Council. A preoccupation with economic issues, notably tax returns to the city, was challenged by several briefs. The Neighbourhood Services Association of Greater Vancouver urged that social and environmental as well as economic criteria be incorporated into a False Creek plan, and the Citizens Council on Civic Development advocated "a truly living community where people's wellbeing is considered more important than the raising of land values." The citizens' briefs, echoing the by-then influential planning philosophy of Jane Jacobs, also valued social diversity in housing, urging the inclusion of units suitable for families as well as for small households. They also favored the provision of subsidized dwellings, but not in "ghetto concentrations" as had so often accompanied urban renewal in the past. To maintain control of the style of development and its property asset, a number of submissions recommended that the City lease rather than sell its own land holdings in False Creek.

The submissions by business interests still seemed in 1970 to be the most acceptable to the City Planning Department. "Highest and best use" would after all render the greatest estimated tax revenues to the city. The City's concept plans paid particular attention to estimated tax revenues, and its design sketches included a wall of high-rise apartments with densities leading to an eventual population of 50000–60000 in the False Creek basin. Indeed in its brief, one large private landholder, Marathon, noted "fair consistency" between the City's plans and its own high-density development proposals for its property in False Creek.

But events were to change. Within two years the projected maximum population following redevelopment had been reduced to 30000. Marathon submitted three consecutive development plans for its own substantial False Creek property and, encountering negative political response, had each rejected: in consecutive submissions the housing capacity for its project was reduced from 20000 to 14000 to 9000. Finally, in 1977, rebuffed once more by Council (this time over its failure to provide low-income housing), Marathon withdrew as an active participant, and in 1980 sold its holdings to the provincial government. We see, then, that the City's reform politicians were casting a new mold for the planning and design process, and were responding to citizen submissions which had "[become], in effect, bottom line principles . . . both explicit and implicit bases for the planning studies" (Rodger 1976).

Constructing a reform landscape

At the beginning of 1970, before the industrial option for False Creek had been discarded, one of the TEAM aldermen on Council introduced a motion that, should a residential future for the Creek be determined, subsidized housing should form an essential ingredient. This initiative was symptomatic of reform-group leadership over redevelopment, though until the end of 1972 it controlled only three votes on the 11-person council. In January 1972, another TEAM alderman, Walter Hardwick, had been appointed chairman of a Special Council Committee on False Creek (for which he had actively lobbied) in order to develop momentum and focus for the redevelopment.

Then TEAM swept to power on City Council in 1972, winning 9 of the 11 seats. Their campaign material had promoted "inner city living at its best" for False Creek, while promising that "the waterfront [there] should be a continuous system of parks and marinas for all the people to enjoy" (*Vancouver Province*, October 5, 1972). During the critical phase of redetermining planning and design criteria for redevelopment, subsequent to this victory, "the politician became the dominant force in the process . . . Members of Council, through the Special Council Committee on False Creek, in effect became the planners, legislators and administrators for False Creek" (Elligott 1977).

The new city councillors found capable allies in the consultants who were contracted to develop design and planning policies. The chief urban designer, Richard Mann, saw his challenge as the creation of a landscape in harmony with the physical environment and sensitive to social needs. There was a quite deliberate and unusually direct transfer of prevalent social science theses concerning the built environment, a process encouraged by the four academics on the TEAM Council. In this exercise, the design team's working model was Christopher Alexander's pattern language, even if the underlying philosophy was compatible with that of Ian McHarg (*British Columbia Business Journal*, 1972). So, too, other designers and social scientists advocating humane planning sensitive to user needs were cited and drawn upon: Jane Jacobs on social diversity, Herbert Gans on neighboring, Terence Lee on spatial aspects of community. False Creek would indeed provide a landscape where the new class ideology would be writ large.

Like Society Hill, the False Creek redevelopment was devised to erase the stigma of a low-status tract. In both cases, therefore, plans had to address every aspect and all parts of the neighborhood comprehensively. However, in False Creek, redevelopment began on a clean slate: all previous structures were demolished, and even the contours of the land were modified. The plans called for a quality human-scale environment, but as was partly the case in Philadelphia, many developers and financial institutions evidenced skepticism, wary of the innovative character of the project (Rodger 1976). Just as in Philadelphia the taken-for-granted model saw a poor urban core opposed to an affluent suburban ring, the conventional wisdom in Vancouver conceived of a high-rent, high-density centre as a natural counterpart to lower-density suburban single-family units. Thus one of the business submissions to the 1970 concept plans by Eaton's, a major downtown department store, emphasized a proposal giving the highest return to city taxes and favoring tourism. Implicit here was a model including private-sector high-density housing; the Eaton submission noted that there would be a decrease in family units over other proposals, but rationalized this in terms of the land being "too expensive" for family housing. By contrast, the creation in False Creek – that is, in the inner city – of a "middle landscape" of medium density and social mixing stood in direct contradiction to this conventional wisdom on city form.

There was much else in the False Creek design which flouted the traditional development patterns of the early 1970s. The motor car was relegated to peripheral and underground locations; a fundamental premise was that False Creek would be a non-automobile-oriented environment. The project would face toward the water, and a continuous seawall for walking, jogging and cycling would provide public waterfront access and an integrating edge to the long linear site. Jane Jacobs' views on diversity and mixing were applied to land-use types, house forms, and architectural design and materials. The dominant post-modern style and preference for authentic building materials (exposed cedar, quartzite rather than asphalt walkways) implied a statement hostile to the stern modernist architecture which through the 1950s and 1960s had become synonymous with city texture. Moreover, meticulous attention, almost to the extent of romanticism, was paid to the ecologically sensitive re-creation of a "natural" environment reflective of the British Columbian coast: in a 16-acre park are a garden of *native* plants, a

113

waterfall, a stream and a lake. A 60-foot-wide pedestrian overpass to the adjoining neighborhood is so guilefully landscaped that one is quite unaware of crossing above rail tracks and a busy street.

So too the redevelopment by the federal government of erstwhile industrial Granville Island on a site adjacent to the False Creek lands (Fig. 6.2) has broken with precedent. The island's uncompromisingly industrial heritage has been almost patronizingly retained within a new, trendy matrix of retail functions to serve both the False Creek residents and visitors. Here is found the improbable juxtaposition of relict industrial premises (a chain company, a nail factory, and a cement plant) with an art college constructed around them, built in a self-conscious industrial and high-tech vernacular style. Other new arrivals are theaters, restaurants, a community center, and a farmers' market (Kemble 1980). Next to new tennis courts, a children's adventure playground is enclosed within a deliberately preserved industrial structure; the play equipment incorporates salvaged factory-era detritus.

Clearly, False Creek was designed to be "a beautiful addition to Canada's most beautiful city" (False Creek Development Group 1977). The sensuous character of the project offers a striking impression: views of water, of the downtown skyline, and of enveloping mountains have been maximized. There are extensive design features to control noise pollution, and the inlet's water pollution has been cleared up. A range of colors, textures, and materials adds visual diversity to the built form. According to architectural peers the impact is "too good to be true and in this has some of the character of a film set" (Wright & Collymore 1980).

Equally, False Creek was designed to be innovative in social goals. The reform landscape explicitly embraced the mixing of life-styles, income groups, and tenure types. The mandate that False Creek be a residential development for "all the people" rather than a gilded ghetto had been presented in a TEAM Council motion as far back as January 1970. Moreover, such a concern was prominent in citizens' submissions in 1970, again in the TEAM-dominated Council's 1977 rejection of the Marathon proposal for its site on the northern shore of False Creek, and it continues to be a live issue now in continuing disputes concerning the social mix in the planned redevelopment of provincial government property on the site it purchased from Marathon (Fig. 6.2) (Ley 1982b). The 865 units of False Creek's first phase were to include housing for families, couples, the elderly and singles; the income mix was to reflect that of the metropolitan area, with approximately one-third low income, one-third middle income, and one-third high income; tenure types included subsidized rentals, market condominiums, and cooper-

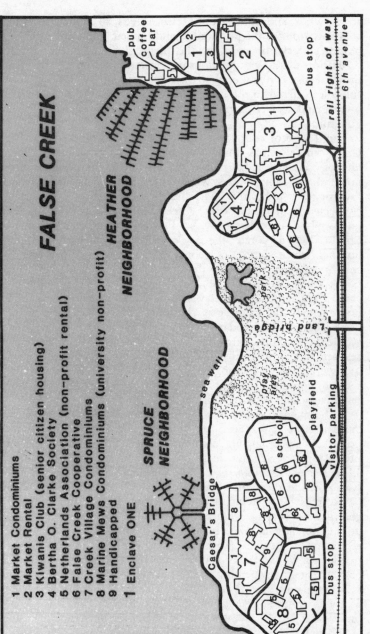

1 Market Condominiums
2 Market Rental
3 Kiwanis Club (senior citizen housing)
4 Bertha O. Clarke Society
5 Netherlands Association (non-profit rental)
6 False Creek Cooperative
7 Creek Village Condominiums
8 Marine Mews Condominiums (university non-profit)
9 Handicapped
1 Enclave ONE

FALSE CREEK

HEATHER NEIGHBORHOOD

SPRUCE NEIGHBORHOOD

pub
coffee
bar

bus stop

rail right of way

6th avenue

Land bridge

Park

sea wall

play area

playfield

school

Caesar's Bridge

Visitor parking

bus stop

Figure 6.3

atives, whose sponsors included service clubs, an ethnic association, an association for the physically handicapped, and even a floating-homes society. In addition, the financial arrangements for the realization of the various housing clusters differed greatly, from more-or-less conventional market investment by developers, to subsidies offered to the nonprofit sector via markdowns on city-owned land, as well as grants from the housing programs of senior governments.

The degree of conscious social mixing is so marked that False Creek can be seen as almost a celebration of diversity. Here liberal ideology could not have been more explicit; the design concept noted that "communities which offer little social and physical diversity are unhealthy ... [;] health in any form is invariably connected to diversity" (False Creek Study Group 1971: 72). This philosophy was consistent with TEAM's housing policy, which as early as 1968 deplored "the low cost housing ghetto ... [;] public housing which segregates people does not work." In order "to support rather than destroy the vast mosaic of subcultures" (False Creek Study Group 1971: 58), the designers found their solution in small circular housing enclaves, each constructed both to shelter homogeneity *and* to serve as "building blocks" toward a broader pattern of neighborhood heterogeneity.[6] Within each enclave, space would be carefully partitioned into a gradation from private to semi-private, semi-public, and public. Together these spatial strategies were to aid in creating neighborhood character, and provide a sense of communal identity and territory, regarded by the design team as socially desirable (Fig. 6.3).

With a major part of the project now completed, some measure of evaluation of False Creek can be attempted, from various standpoints. As a planning and architectural achievement it has received professional recognition in North America and Europe (Kemple 1980, *Progressive Architecture* 1980, Wright & Collymore 1980). As was noted earlier, one evaluation even claims that the visual landscape is "too good to be true." As a living environment, a consultant's survey reported a generally well-satisfied resident population, now in excess of 3000. Residential turnover is very low, around 5 percent a year (Visher, Skaburskis, Planners 1980). For the public as a whole, the project is perceived as a success, with up to 35 000 visitors frequenting the commercial development on Granville Island on a Saturday or Sunday. Moreover, a report on citizens' attitudes to development goals and priorities in Vancouver, based on 7500 responses, revealed a set of objectives fully consistent with the False Creek design criteria (Vancouver Planning Commission 1980).

Conclusion

The revitalization of older neighborhoods in the "grey areas" of North American cities has today become commonplace, so much so that some commentators observe a radical restructuring of the city's social geography in the making (Allman 1978, Rouse 1978). The copious literature to this effect most frequently attributes such transformations to major shifts in the urban economy or demography, or again to changing tastes in life-style. Our analysis of Philadelphia and Vancouver meshes with such arguments, but in addition highlights the often overlooked ability of organized interest groups to define the character of urban revitalization. As Bacon himself has written, under the heading "The City as an Act of Will,"

> Recent events in Philadelphia have proved incontrovertibly that ... the multiplicity of wills that constitutes our contemporary democratic process can coalesce into positive, unified action on a scale large enough to change substantially the character of a city. (Bacon 1976: 13)

The Society Hill case is particularly significant because such a total neighborhood transformation was without precedent. No inner-city area had, especially in a climate of such uncertainty about the very viability of the city itself, ever been identified for so massive a turnabout. Its transformation was predicated upon the faith of a few civic leaders, but there was no guarantee that their hopes for revitalization would be realized unless the state, the private sector, and popular demand responded to their initiative. Much of the private sector in particular, however, was not prepared to take the initiative itself in revitalization schemes that seemed too audacious, too lacking in guarantees of profitability. Thus the Philadelphia Chamber of Commerce, with over 1000 members and a Board of Directors of 65, kept its distance. The more activist Greater Philadelphia Movement, however, was an early supporter of center-city renewal. Not only was it a much smaller and less ponderous body, but it also over-represented city banking interests and to a lesser degree major city law firms. Kleniewski (1982) has shown how such finance capital interests in particular, as opposed to the general interests of capital inhering in the broad spread of the Chamber of Commerce, stood to gain most directly from projects like the Society Hill renewal (see also Smith 1979b). Then, as we have shown, after much persuasion from civic leaders and the demonstration of early successes, property interests and the business community in general *were* drawn in, to their eventual benefit. That is, the success of this "designer neighborhood" has been permitted within the constraints of the property market; at the same time that self-same market has been significantly reshaped, and its constraints realigned, by the neighborhood's very success.

The False Creek case is even more explicitly a "designer neighborhood." Here, in a context of urban growth and underpinned by confidence in its continuance, revitalization has been taken a stage further. Not only has a very large tract of derelict and polluted land, long the site of noxious industry, been reclaimed, but also the tract's transformation is a notable and venturesome experiment in both physical and social planning: a pioneering medium-density residential environment with a mixture of tenure groups, social classes, and life-styles. Again, large developers and financiers were at first reluctant partners who kept their distance until a liberal elite had demonstrated the success of an improbable vision. Improbable or not, that vision evidently struck a responsive chord among much of the citizenry. This indicates that although reform politicians may indeed have been animators and leaders, they were also both constrained and produced by the lineaments of broader, perhaps latent, public preferences. In both Society Hill and False Creek the role of senior governments was critical in financing the project, and the urban electorate made the necessary endorsement of the vision for change at the ballot box.

Whereas capital was inevitably implicated from the beginning, the involvement of capitalists was far more equivocal. In Philadelphia there was clearly a split among them: certain members of the business elite seeing the possibilities early on, most (as with the Chamber of Commerce) only after market trends had become established. In Vancouver's case it is an important debating point as to whether private-sector corporatism could have accomplished as varied a set of social, economic, and environmental objectives as was accomplished in False Creek by public-sector corporatism. If not, then a further argument is raised concerning the place of public land ownership in the mixed economy. There are, of course, examples enough of public mismanagement in urban redevelopment; that False Creek has not added to this dismal record suggests that it may provide a model which rewards more careful consideration.

The elites active in Society Hill and False Creek were not identical. Although generally they were reform Democrats, Philadelphia's civic elite remained closely connected with the city's upper class, and whereas their civic and business lives were often somewhat separate, there remained some individuals, like Albert M. Greenfield, who understood that the saving of Philadelphia was also good for business. Thus in Philadelphia's "top-down" model, political and economic power generally acted in concert, although a patrician sense of civic responsibility dulled the edge of economic self-interest. The reform movement in Vancouver, however, was more clearly separate from the city's business leaders, and in civic politics displaced the pre-existing pro-business party; this might be termed a "middle-up" model. Its professional, new-middle-class orientation identified a broader agenda where tax returns to the city would be moderated in the pursuit of an esthetic environment and social mix through housing subsidies. Thus, the redevelopment of False Creek was but one facet of TEAM's redistributive agenda for Vancouver, whereas the strategy of which the new Society Hill was part had no such immediate aim for Philadelphia. All in all, however, one can observe in the contrasting studies presented here a single pervasive theme: the undeniable impact that a small number of individuals can have in guiding – or even partly reversing – established urban trends.

Acknowledgements

The authors would like to thank the following for their comments on earlier drafts of this paper: Carolyn Adams, Bob Beauregard, Douglas McManis, John Mercer, and Bob Warren.

Notes

1 Interview with Roger Scattergood, one of the four charter members and first Secretary of the City Policy Committee, by John Western, November 8, 1983.
2 To the existing 125 shops, a planned extension, which opened in October 1983, added an additional 105, thereby making this the largest such retail mall in the USA.
3 As the chairman of the city's Redevelopment Authority, Gustave Amsterdam, later described it, "[it was here that] all the food of Philadelphia . . . was dragged through the dirtiest part of town. Anyone who watched the food being processed down there would never eat in Philadelphia, I can tell you that" (Amsterdam, December 20, 1975, in Phillips interviews). Further discussion of the resiting of the Food Distribution Center, and indeed of the entire topic of center-city Philadelphia's renewal, was pursued in interviews with Edmund Bacon by John Western, January 21 and March 29, 1983.
4 The other exception, across a street bounding Unit One, was the establishment during redevelopment of an entire block given over to a dairy and ice cream plant. The buildings, however, were hidden from view by intentionally high brick walls, mandated in the zoning agreement whereby the Abbott's Company was permitted entry. Today,

some 20 years subsequently, the block in question has been redeveloped again. Given the achievement of secure and high market values in Society Hill, the block is now under development as "Abbott's Square," "a landmark in city living, for a very fortunate few."

5 Clearly, questions arise over possible conflicts of interest in Greenfield's public versus business roles. Petshek (1973: 222) went so far as to suggest that Greenfield's enthusiasm for the Society Hill project (to which he had previously been strongly and vocally opposed) stemmed from the fact that his firm's real-estate holdings were concentrated in the southeast quadrant of the central city, where Society Hill was to be located and where property values were thereby expected to rise. Fuller discussion of Greenfield's personal role can be found in Kleniewski (1982: 103–4, 110, 113, 119–21).

6 The echo of Alexander's *A Pattern Language* is pronounced. For Alexander has written that, to enrich city life, it should be disaggregated into "a vast mosaic of small and different subcultures, each with its own spatial territory, and each with the power to create its own distinct life style . . . so that each person has access to the full variety of life styles in the subcultures near his own" (Alexander *et al.* 1977: 50).

7

Tenurial transformation and the flat break-up market in London: the British condo experience

CHRIS HAMNETT and BILL RANDOLPH

That gentrification is a "chaotic concept" (Sayer 1982) was discussed in Chapter 2 of this volume. Although the process is commonly seen to involve the physical renovation of dilapidated housing in inner-city locations along with an upwards socioeconomic transition, a tenure transformation from renting to owning, and a demographic and possibly a racial transition, it is quite clear that not only are all these analytically distinct processes, but that also they can be identified as operating in isolation from one another in different areas of different cities at different times. To this extent, therefore, gentrification, as it is currently understood and defined, must be seen as constituting no more than an historically and spatially specific manifestation of a set of more general transformation processes which are not always found to be acting in conjunction and which can and do take other forms.

The focus of this chapter is on one spatially and temporally specific form of the tenurial transformation process known in London as the flat break-up market. Like the allied processes of condominium conversion in North America (US Department of Housing and Urban Development 1980, Van Weesep, 1981a, b), flat break-up involves the sale for individual owner-occupation of what were previously purpose-built blocks of privately rented flats or apartments. Although the economics are essentially similar on both sides of the Atlantic, the form of the process differs considerably.[1] In both places, however, tenurial change commonly results in a degree of both demographic and upward socioeconomic transition, as younger, more affluent owners replace older, poorer renters. To this extent, the process possesses a number of similarities to gentrification as commonly defined. It differs, however, in two key

121

respects. First, although it frequently involves an element of physical renovation, this is by no means a necessary element of tenurial transformation and, where it does occur, it can often be of a fairly superficial and cosmetic nature, involving no more than external repainting and the installation of an entry-phone system with a view to improving saleability. Secondly, although flat break-ups are concentrated in central and inner London by virtue of the prior concentration of the appropriate property type, the great majority of which was built in two periods from 1880 to 1905 and from 1933 to 1939, it occurs throughout London wherever blocks of privately rented flats are to be found.

Background

The tenurial transformation process in Britain

It is no exaggeration to say that the transition from private rental to owner-occupation and (particularly in Britain) to public housing represents, along with suburbanization, one of the most important transformations of the housing market and residential space in Western capitalist cities since World War II. The importance of the tenure transformation in most Western capitalist countries has been identified by a variety of authors (e.g. Harloe 1980, Kemeny 1981).

Nowhere have the scale and the rapidity of this tenure transformation been greater than in Britain. In the United States, for example, the home-ownership rate was already 47 percent by 1900 and did not increase significantly until the 1950s, reaching 65 percent in 1976; the privately rented sector declined from 53 percent in 1900 to 35 percent in 1976 (Bourne 1981: 43). In Britain, by contrast, the privately rented sector accounted for almost 90 percent of households by 1914, owner-occupation taking only 10 percent. By 1945, the share of private renting had fallen to 62 percent, and owner-occupation had risen to 25 percent; the newly emergent publicly rented tenure took the remaining 13 per cent. By 1981, owner-occupation had risen to 56 percent and the local authority or state sector to 31 percent, private renting accounting for only 13 percent. The decline of private renting has been of massive proportions and it has two contributory aspects. First, virtually all of the new housing in Britain built subsequent to World War II has been for owner-occupation or for local-authority renting. Secondly, the growth of owner-occupation has involved an equally massive tenurial transformation of the existing stock from renting to owning.

The privately rented sector in Britain declined from 7.1 million units in 1914 to 2.9 million units in 1975 (a loss of 4.2 million dwellings), and no less than 3.7 million or 88 percent of these were sold for owner-occupation. Conversely, these 3.7 million units from the privately rented sector accounted for 41 percent of the total growth of owner-occupation between 1914 (0.8 million units) and 1975 (9.9 million units) (Department of the Environment 1977: Vol. I, Table I.24). This process is by no means unique to Britain. Such shifts have manifested themselves wherever there is a buoyant owner–occupier sector and where subsidies have favoured home-ownership at the expense of private renting (see Grebler & Mittelbach 1979, US Department of Housing and Urban Development 1980).

The role of investment and disinvestment in the production and transformation of urban residential space

The scale, extent, timing, and purpose of capital investment play a key role in the production and evolution of the residential environment. Although the role of capital investment has long been recognized by urban and economic historians (Dyos 1961, 1968, Lewis 1965, Reeder 1965, Chalklin 1968, Thompson 1974, Cannadine 1977, 1980), it has not generally been appreciated by most contemporary urban analysts. So great and all-pervasive has been the intellectual hegemony of ecological and neoclassical approaches to the study of urban areas that, despite the pioneering early work of Form (1954), the built environment has been regarded as having sprung out of nowhere. Like Topsy, it has been treated as though it "just growed." The social relations of ownership and production have been almost entirely ignored. So vast has been the intellectual gulf separating the contemporary focus on abstract general models of urban land use from the historical analysis of specific development processes that it would be easy to conclude that history stopped just prior to World War I. Only relatively recently has the advent of urban political economy brought the realities of these processes back into the forefront of concern from the historical backwater in which they have languished (Lamarche 1976, Harvey 1978, Walker 1978, 1981, Boddy 1981). Not until 1974, when Harvey and Chatterjee's seminal study of the structuring of space by governmental and financial institutions in Baltimore was first published, was the role of differential patterns of investment and disinvestment pushed toward the centre of the urban residential stage.

The broad thrust of their work is by now too well known to warrant repetition here. Much subsequent work has focused on the role and effort of institutional lending policies (or "redlining" see Williams 1976, 1978, Boddy 1976a, b, Dingemans 1979, Wolfe *et al.* 1980), but what concerns us here is the attempt by Harvey and Chatterjee to locate the changing operating structure of commercial private landlordism within the wider context of housing-market transformation. Referring specifically to the large commercial landlord who is "very sensitive to profits, losses and the rate of return on capital," they concluded that

> it is evident that landlords "structure" their behaviour according to their decision-environment. There is a "rational" (profit-maximizing) adjustment of landlords' behaviour to sub-market characteristics. This behaviour, in turn, structures outcomes with respect to the renter, the maintenance of the housing sector, reinvestment and disinvestment, neighbourhood decay and the like. (Harvey & Chatterjee 1974: 32)

As we shall attempt to show, landlords do indeed adjust their behavior according to their decision environment in a "rational" profit-maximizing manner, but not necessarily in the rather passive way outlined by Harvey and Chatterjee, where landlords are largely responding to externally determined circumstances outside their own control. Where the demand for owner-occupation is strong and where owner-occupied house prices are rising relative to rents, the incentives for landlords to disinvest and sell for owner-occupation are positive rather than negative. The decline of private renting must therefore be viewed within the context of the structure and operation of the wider housing market. In these circumstances certain types of landlord can play a much more active role in fostering and encouraging conditions favorable to the maintenance or enhancement of profit levels. They can, in other words, actively mediate, if not necessarily initiate, the processes of transformation (Williams 1976). This should not surprise us, for, contrary to neoclassical economic theory, 'markets' are not autonomous objects. They are created and shaped. Equally, tenure transformations do not simply happen; they are produced.

The flat break-up market in central London: its nature and scale

The central-London housing market is unique in a number of respects. First, it has long been dominated by the privately rented sector. In 1961, 80 percent of all households rented privately and as late as 1971 the figure was still 70 percent compared with only 21 percent in England and Wales as a whole. Secondly, the nature of the

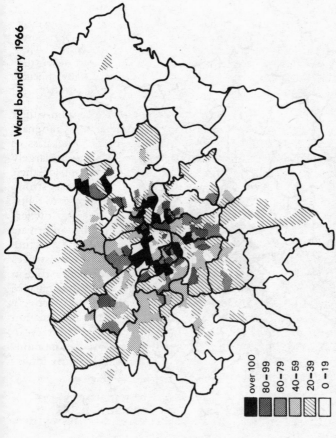

— Ward boundary 1966

over 100
80—99
60—79
40—59
20—39
0—19

Figure 7.1 The distribution of purpose-built privately rented flats in London, by ward, 1966.

Source: 1966 10% sample census.

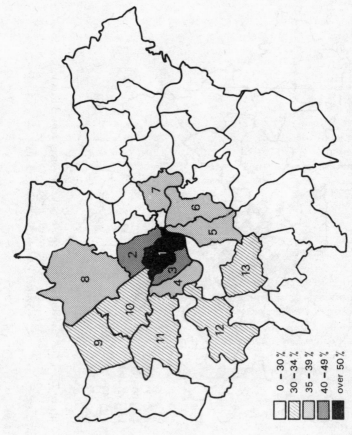

Figure 7.2 Purpose-built privately rented flats as a proportion of all privately rented unfurnished dwellings, by London borough, 1966.
Source: 1966 10% sample census.

0 – 30 %
30 – 34 %
35 – 39 %
40 – 49 %
over 50 %

housing stock in central London is atypical. Whereas nationally, the privately rented sector consisted largely of either single family or multi-unit houses, London, and central London in particular, has long possessed a large number of purpose-built privately rented flats. It was estimated in 1962 (Department of the Environment 1977: vol. III, 83, para. 8) that there were only 350 000 flats in England and Wales as a whole that were built for private owners, including owner–occupiers. Yet, in 1966, prior to the onset of break-up, there were 222 000 such flats in Greater London, of which 174 000 were privately rented. Of these, some 48 000 or 28 percent were concentrated in the three central London boroughs of Camden, Kensington and Westminster, where they accounted for no less than 55 percent of all privately rented dwellings (see Figs 7.1 & 2).

The third distinctive characteristic of central London's housing market is its high proportion of the higher socioeconomic groups. This is even more marked in the purpose-built flat sector, which was built primarily for the growing number of professional, managerial and other nonmanual workers. In 1971, 25 percent of households in the three central boroughs were classified as professional and managerial. In the blocks of flats the figure was 40 percent. Taking the nonmanual groups as a whole, 71 percent of households in the blocks were so classified in 1971, compared with 43 percent in Greater London as a whole. On the face of it these figures present a problem. If the blocks were built for the higher socioeconomic groups in the first place, how can their subsequent history be understood in terms of gentrification? The answer is that the sale of flats for owner-occupation has resulted in an intensification of these characteristics as older, relatively low-income, intermediate non-manual tenants have been replaced or displaced by younger, high-income, professional and managerial households.

The fourth and final distinguishing characteristic of central London's purpose-built privately rented blocks of flats is their ownership structure. Whereas most of the privately rented sector in Britain is characterized by a plethora of small landlords, the pur-pose-built flat sector in London is dominated by larger commercial and institutional landlords (Greve 1965, Milner-Holland report 1965, Paley 1978). All these surveys confirm Kemeny's description of the privately rented sector as "a predominantly small-scale tenure run by late middle aged or elderly individuals who own one or, at most, a handful of tenancies" (Kemeny 1981). The small number of large landlords, who collectively own a considerable number of properties, are strongly represented in the purpose-built flat sector.

From registers kept by the Rent Officer service for each borough, it appears that two-thirds of the 500 landlords identified (who owned an average of 70 flats apiece) were property companies who between them owned 77 percent of the total number of flats. A further 10 percent of all landlords comprised insurance companies, pension funds and other institutional owners, who collectively owned 14 percent of all flats. Between them, therefore, corporate and institutional landlords owned 91 percent of all the flats identified, and the 20 largest owners (3.9 percent) accounted for 54 percent of all flats. Individual landlords and private trusts and executors accounted for only 7 percent of all flats.

Their findings are of considerable importance for our analysis for two reasons. First, as Allen (1983) has pointed out, it is possible to identify categories of landlord on the basis of their particular property relations. The large "economically rational" profit-maximizing commercial investor landlords studied here constitute but one type of landlord. They are, however, extremely important, and our focus on the purpose-built privately rented flat sector in central London therefore offers a unique opportunity to examine both the various responses of such landlords to changing economic and financial conditions, and their role in actively initiating and mediating the transformation of a large part of the central-London private-housing market from private rental to owner-occupation in the space of little over 15 years.

The scale of the transformation has been quite remarkable, and is, in part, a product of the prior spatial concentration of these blocks in central London in the first place. In 1966 the sector was still largely intact, for reasons we shall discuss later. By 1981, however, a major tenurial restructuring had taken place in both central and inner London which had transformed a functioning rental sector into a buoyant owner-occupation market with a large "frozen" rump of flats which, though still rented to sitting tenants protected under the Rent Acts, will not be relet on vacancy. The 1981 Census shows that, in the 15 years since 1966, the number of households in unfurnished, privately rented, purpose-built flats in central London decreased by 50 percent from 43 000 to some 22 000. Meanwhile owner-occupation increased from just 3300 households in 1966 (6.5 percent of the total) to 15 000 or 36 percent in 1981 (see Table 7.1). Even these figures do not tell the whole story, however, for only half the decline in the privately rented unfurnished sector in central London is accounted for by the growth of owner-occupation. The other half is largely accounted for by the number of dwellings held vacant pending sale.

Although the 1981 Census provided no data on vacancies by building type, it proved possible, by comparing those blocks in

128

Table 7.1 The changing tenure structure of central London's private purpose-built flat sector. (*Source:* 1966 and 1981 Censuses.)

	Owner-occupied	Privately rented	Total
1966	3 290 (6.4%)	47 800 (93.6%)	51 090
1981	14947 (36.1%)	26463 (63.9%)	41410
change	+11 657 (+354%)	−21 337 (−44.6%)	−9 680 (−18.9%)

central London large enough to constitute a census enumeration district in their own right, to calculate the increase in vacancy levels (see Hamnett & Randolph 1984 for further details). Altogether 101 such blocks were identified, and collectively they accounted for almost 13 000 flats or 30 per cent of the central-London total. As Table 7.2 shows, the decrease in the number of privately rented household spaces (47 percent) is very similar to the rate of decline across all the blocks in central London from 1966 to 1981. It is significant, however, that the number of vacant units in these blocks increased almost fourfold from 1971 to 1981, from 1137 household spaces or 8.8 percent of the total to 4300 or 33 percent. Although these blocks are unrepresentative by virtue of their very size, the fact that they account for 30 percent of the central-London total cannot be ignored, and if the vacancy level of one-third were to prevail across the board, then vacancies would more than account for the difference between the decline in the number of privately rented households and the increase in owner-occupied households. It cannot be stressed too strongly that these vacancies are not a result of any normal process of household mobility. They are not temporary vacancies which have arisen subsequent to the departure of one tenant and the arrival of the next. Nor are they the product of a shortfall in demand. As the next section makes clear, the vacancies arise from a combination of two forces: first, the capital gains to be derived from sales for owner-occupation; and secondly, the unwillingness of landlords to relet upon vacancy, given both the financial rewards from sales and the existence of security-of-tenure legislation. One effect of the latter is to "lock up" a landlord's potential capital gains for an indeterminate period if the property were to be relet.

Although these figures indicate the magnitude of the tenurial restructuring that has already occurred, they reflect no more than the current stage of what is a continuing process. Just as the majority of vacant units will eventually be sold, so will the overwhelming majority of the remaining tenanted flats as and when they become

Table 7.2 Changes in tenure of 101 blocks in central London, 1971–81. (*Source:* 1971 and 1981 Censuses.)

	Owner-occupied	Privately rented	Local authority	Vacant	Total household spaces
1971	814 (6.3%)	10 666 (82.4%)	320 (2.5%)	1 137 (8.8%)	12 937 (100%)
1981	2969 (23.0%)	5214 (40.3%)	436 (3.4%)	4302 (33.3%)	12921 (100%)
change	+2155 (+265.0%)	−5 854 (−47.0%)	+116 (+36.3%)	+3 165 (+278.0%)	

vacant. Security-of-tenure legislation has helped produce the high level of vacancies, and it has also kept the residual privately rented sector in being.

What has caused this remarkable, and seemingly irreversible, shift in the structure of the purpose-built flat market? The explanation lies both at the general level, in relation to the decline in the private rental sector as a whole since World War I, and, at the more specific level, to the conditions emerging during the 1960s that stimulated the sale of previously rented purpose-built flats to individual owner-occupiers.

The decline of private landlordism

Turning first to the declining importance of the private rental sector as a whole, it is important to note that housing in capitalist economies is a commodity produced for profit. It is, however, a rather unusual commodity in many respects, not the least of which is its high cost relative to income. For the great majority of households, housing cannot be purchased outright. It has instead to be paid for out of income over a period of years. If builders themselves had to rent out or sell their houses on some form of hire purchase, their capital could only be realized extremely slowly, which would, among other things, result in a considerable slowing of the rate of new housing construction. Some mechanism is therefore clearly necessary for the producers of housing to recoup their capital outlay and profits reasonably quickly. As Boddy (1976a: 15) and others have pointed out, the differentiation between various tenure categories functions to speed up the realization of capital involved in housing production. Historically, this function was performed almost exclusively in Britain by the development of a rentier class who purchased property on a mortgage and rented it out (see Greve 1965, Dyos 1968, Kemp 1982). Only after World War I was this function increasingly taken over by individual purchasers using building-society finance and by local-authority housing provision. A discussion of the origins of these developments lies outside the ambit of this chapter, and full treatments can be found in Pawley (1978), Merrett (1979), Boddy (1980), Merrett and Gray (1982) and Ball (1983). Suffice it to note here that prior to the development of the building-society movement from the early 1920s onwards, there was no readily available source of mortgage finance for widespread individual house purchase. Only after the development of a mortgage market could the market itself accelerate the realization of capital invested in housing.

To understand the economics of private rental and the relative financial advantages of rental versus sale, it is necessary to understand the basis on which the exchange value of housing, and hence the returns or levels of profitability, is calculated. In Britain prior to 1914, the ownership market was only little developed and was relatively insignificant, and the great majority of new housing was produced for sale to landlords (Dyos 1968). Equally, the great majority of sales of existing property were transacted between landlords.

Traditionally, private rental property functioned as a source of long-term investment income. As such, it should be viewed in the same light as other income-yielding investments (shares, bonds, treasury bills, and so on (Harvey 1981)). As with those other types of investment, rental property was capitalized on the basis of its current and potential yield, i.e. its periodic rent. Thus the value of a rental property was related to the yield the landlord/investor expected to derive from the property. The yield was equivalent to an "interest rate," and varied depending on competing interest rates elsewhere in the financial system, as well as the rate of inflation, the risk involved in the investment, the potential for rent reversions, the costs of finance, and so on. The important point here is that investment property values were determined by levels, or expected levels, of income.

We can define the *tenanted investment* (TI) value of a property as its value when held as a tenanted property producing rental income. As a simple example, a property on which a 10 percent yield is to be expected would be valued at ten times its annual rental, or ten years' purchase (YP) of the rent. So, for a property producing say £1000 a year in net rent, its value at ten YP would be £10 000, which is the amount of capital a landlord would be prepared to lay out in order to derive the required income. This is the basis on which rented residential property was traditionally valued and traded between landlords for purposes of long-term capital investment.

In the infant owner-occupied sector, the basis of valuation was quite different and related to the *vacant possession* (VP) value to the owner-occupier. This value can be viewed as a combination of both use value and investment value for the occupier (Saunders 1982), and is a function of the level of effective household income and purchasing power as mediated by the cost and availability of mortgage finance (Department of the Environment 1977, Boddy 1980). This opened up the possibility of two divergent methods of valuation for residential property, one based on a multiple of annual rental income for tenanted property, and the other based on the vacant-possession sale value for owner-occupation. So long as the two sets of capital values remained closely linked, and so long as the owner-occupied sector remained insignificant in size, the two systems of valuation did not impinge greatly on one another, and the two sectors were able to coexist. Indeed, it is likely that the price an owner–occupier would be willing to pay for a property would be closely related to its value as a tenanted investment, given the dominance of this sector.

Where the two sets of values diverged, however, a *value gap*[2] could open up, thereby creating the possibility of a profitable transfer of residential property from one tenure to another. Pawley (1978: 62) perceptively noted the existence of such a possibility in Britain immediately after 1919:

> Delayed and expensive repairs coupled with controlled rents presented post-war landlords with a poor return on their investments; there was thus a strong incentive for them to sell as soon as their property became vacant, or alternatively to try to sell to the tenants they could not remove ... Furthermore, with the appearance of two sets of values for houses – those with and those without vacant possession, there were clearly opportunities for speculation. Rent controlled houses could be bought cheaply and sold expensively, provided the tenants could be induced to depart.[3]

The rapid development of the building societies and the owner-occupied market in the 1920s and 1930s was to transform the situation dramatically by establishing the existence of a value gap on an almost permanent footing. The reason is simple. Although it can be argued that, in the final analysis, property values depend on the ability of the housing consumer, whether tenant or owner–occupier, to pay a rent or meet mortgage repayments, the considerable subsidies given to owner–occupiers, through the tax relief on mortgage interest payments and the low composite tax rate levied on the interest paid to building-society depositors (passed on to the owner–occupier via lower interest rates), have served to give the owner–occupier a considerable cost advantage over both the landlord and the private tenant. Not only does the landlord have to borrow at higher commercial rates of interest and meet maintenance and management costs out of rents, but also, until recently, the absence of rent rebates for tenants has meant that the rents paid by the tenant have inevitably been higher than the mortgage repayments made by the owner–occupier on the identical or equivalent property. The result has been, as Nevitt noted, that "Under our existing tax arrangements, an owner–occupier can always afford to pay a higher capital sum for his house than can a landlord who intends to let to a tenant with the same income as the potential owner" (Nevitt 1966: 20).

From the 1920s onwards, it thus became increasingly possible in some areas and on certain types of property (almost exclusively house property) to sell rented property for owner-occupation, either directly to the sitting tenant or, where vacant, on the open market. These differences in property value between the two sectors hold the key to understanding the rationale for the virtual cessation of building for private rental since the 1920s and the transfer of rental property to owner-occupation whenever conditions have proved suitable and mortgage finance has been available.

The development of this dual-value system in the private residential sector as a whole, since the inter-war period when owner-occupation became firmly established in Britain, had a fundamentally debilitating effect on the viability of the private rental sector. Over this period the value gap was compounded by (but *not* created by) the effects of house-price inflation (which has pushed up VP values) and rent control (which has limited rent increases below their "market" rates and hence depressed TI values). At the same time the historic rise of general interest rates and inflation have also had a significant impact on the ability of rental property to produce acceptable yields in comparison with other investment opportunities, and have also in effect helped to depress TI values. Nevertheless, the resulting *value gap* between the VP value of a property (i.e. its value in the owner-occupied market) and its TI value (i.e. its value as an income-yielding investment) is arguably the principal underlying mechanism that has provoked the inexorable transfer of much rented property into owner-occupation. The pressure on landlords to capitalize their properties on the basis of VP values in the owner-occupied market rather than on their existing TI values is now overwhelming in the majority of cases. As Kemeny has pointed out, "In a home-owning society the market for dwellings is dominated by the home-ownership sector, and so the sale price of rental property is determined by the state of the home-ownership market" (Kemeny 1981:28). In the process, the basis of valuation of rental property has been inverted. Instead of capital values being determined as a multiple of rented income, rental incomes are now calculated as returns on the current vacant-possession sales values (not, it should be noted, on historical values). The unavoidable result of this conflict has been the sale of rental property to individual owner–occupiers. In effect, the growth of owner-occupation has recapitalized the existing rental sector, allowing the landlord who can effect the transfer of his property into owner-occupation the possibility of an alternative and much more immediately profitable short-term capital gain. This can in turn be reinvested in other perhaps less troublesome property sectors, or elsewhere in the financial market, or it can merely be distributed as profit.

Although this brief discussion has oversimplified what is in reality a much more complex chain of events and influences, the overall undermining of the position of residential investment landlordism and the opportunities for profitable capital gains through sales into owner-occupation should be clear. It is this process which has turned the tenure structure of the private purpose-built flat market on its head in the past 15 to 20 years. By way of illustration, rent and vacant-possession value data were collected for the purpose-built flat sector in central London in mid-1980. At this time the average registered rent for an unfurnished flat was £1375 per annum and the generally accepted investment yield on this type of property was about 8 per cent. This suggests the tenanted investment value of an average flat to be £1375 × (100/8) = £17 188. At the same time the average vacant-possession sale value of a flat in central London was £63 000. Thus the notional 'value gap' between the tenanted investment and vacant-possession values of this average flat is in the region of £45 000. Quite clearly this represents a substantial capital gain for any landlord able to effect the sale of a previously rented flat into owner-occupation. Furthermore, the effective return on a vacant-possession value of £63 000 was little over 2 percent, hardly a viable yield at a time when money on deposit was earning 15 percent.

However, the actual situation is not so straightforward as this, for many landlords have held their property for a considerable period and the historical costs will be far below even the current TI value. The value gap between this historical cost and current vacant-possession values will therefore be even wider. On the other hand, more recent purchasers of rental property will have paid more than the basic TI value for their flats, for blocks are now traded between landlords at a value which discounts a proportion of the future capital gains to be derived from the eventual break-up of the property through sales at vacant-possession values. In practice this has varied depending on the demand for blocks by break-up speculators, but averages no more than 40–50 percent of the full vacant-possession value of the property. This value, which may be termed the *speculative investment* (SI) value, is based not on rental income but on the expected capital gains to be derived in the future. In our example, the average SI value for a three-room flat in central London in mid-1980 would therefore be about £28 500, leaving an effective value gap of £35 000 gross to be obtained by sale in the owner-occupied market. No landlord buying on this basis is buying to rent, however. Indeed, the term "landlord" is a misnomer, for such property-trading activity is carried out purely for speculative capital gains, renting being a rather unfortunate, albeit necessary, by-product of the search for such gains. In fact, for many break-up operators, flat sales are a vital necessity, as rental incomes will be unlikely to provide enough cash flow to meet the interest repayments on the finance obtained for the initial purchase. Nevertheless, providing the pitfalls of such deficit financing can be avoided, flat break-up can provide the possibility of a substantial profit.

In this respect, it is often presumed that disinvestment from the private rental sector has been carried out on a loss-cutting basis. As we have seen, nothing could be further from the truth. Flat break-up should not be viewed as the final despairing gesture of a landlord class faced by a hostile and unrewarding future, the picture so often painted by the landlords' lobby (see British Property Federation 1975). Rather, the rationale for the process has been the substantial profit to be made from this form of residential–property trading. In fact residential "disinvestment" has been immensely profitable for the many landlords who have capitalized on the opportunities generated by the evolution of the value gap. Moreover, if the capital gains realized by sale are added to rental income, then the "total returns" to be derived from residential property can be considerable. When these "total returns" are discounted back on a yearly basis over the entire period of ownership, then yields compare favorably with those available in alternative investment sectors (Prior 1980). Indeed this process of overall disinvestment has been accompanied by a considerable quantity of *investment* as property speculators have bought into the sector in order to exploit the emerging value gap. Unfortunately, the unavoidable consequence of this activity has been the wholesale loss of rented accommodation through its transfer to owner-occupation.

The switch to break-up in central London

We need, however, to explain why the break-up of this particular sector started when it did, and the factors which have continued to force the transfer of rented flats into long-leasehold owner-occupation ever since. Significantly, many of the earliest flat sales in central London took place at the top end of the market where rent controls had been minimal or non-existent, as rateable values were above the limit under which controls applied. The point is of course that in these cases there was no obvious incentive for landlords to disinvest, given that rents were at their "open market" levels. On the other hand, there is no reason to believe that the high-income tenants in these blocks would have had any great difficulty in obtaining finance to purchase their flats had they been free to do so. Why then did sales only begin in the early to mid-1960s? The answer lies in the changing conditions within the housing and investment markets during this period, changes that affected the behavior of both landlords and tenants and fundamentally restructured the relative profitability of flat blocks as corporate investments.

From the supply side, relatively few blocks of flats for private renting were built in the postwar period. Building controls and rent restriction generally deterred any large-scale development outside the high-rent luxury market in central London. Even here, postwar blocks are few. Although the lifting of restriction on building controls in 1954 and the impact of the 1957 Rent Act may have reinvigorated the sector to some extent, by the early 1960s, returns on developing new blocks for rental had become too small, except in the luxury market or on cheap land in the suburbs. This was partly due to the fact that finance for residential development for investment was both difficult to obtain and expensive, as the institutions largely eschewed lending for such activity, preferring instead to fund the more rewarding commercial development market that reached its peak by 1960.

However, perhaps the single most influential factor which militated against new investment for rent, and which led toward the eventual development of the break-up market in existing rented property, was inflation. From 1950 onwards the investment climate became increasingly distorted by accelerating inflation within the economy as a whole. This had a critical impact on the perception of corporate residential landlords for it shifted attention away from their traditional concern with the long-term prospects for investment income growth to one in which the maintenance of current capital values over the short term became increasingly important. Flats were let on fixed-term leases of five, seven or nine years, or even longer, over which time the rent levels were fixed (or only increased in line with costs of services). The capitalization of the property therefore remained static over the period of the lease. Coupled with rent control in the lower end of the market, this became an increasing constraint. Quite simply, as inflation increased, rents did not keep pace, and in consequence capital appreciation was undermined.

There resulted a growing pressure to switch investment away from the more limited growth potential of flat blocks into alternative sectors offering greater and more immediate returns on capital. This was achieved either by the expansion of the non-residential side of property investment portfolios or, as the inflationary spiral built up, by active disinvestment in residential holdings toward the same end. The commercial property boom of the 1957–62 period certainly helped to persuade most corporate landlords that the assets tied up in residential property could be more profitably reinvested in higher-yielding office and commercial property. At the same time, landlords attempted to maximize the yields they were obtaining from their remaining residential investments by measures such as the exclusion of rates and service charges from rents, the reduction of new leases to three years in order to increase their reversionary potential, or conversion to high-rent furnished lettings. Despite these moves, inflation made it much more difficult to sustain a long-term perspective on residential property investment. At the same time inflation resulted in higher interest rates, which also deterred borrowing for long-term investment purposes.

An important consequence of these tendencies was that by the late 1950s a market had begun to develop involving the building of blocks of flats for sale to long leaseholders in the more select areas of central London, as well as in the suburbs. From the point of view of the corporate investor this sort of "development-for-sale" scheme provided the opportunity of an immediate capital gain and therefore a much quicker return on capital than did building for rent. The profits realized could then be reinvested in further development, or directed into any other investment that offered the maximum short-term potential. Although limited in extent, the development of this market in new flats for sale was to have a significant impact on the established flat rental market, for it suggested to the more astute landlords and property speculators that if a flat could be built for sale, then existing flats could also be sold.

Political factors also played a part in the processes that led towards break-up. The predictable abuses by a minority of landlords following the rent decontrol measures of the 1957 Rent Act resulted in equally predictable responses from others in the rental market. Uncertainty as to the political future of the rental market following the Rachman scandal helped to dampen the remaining enthusiasm for residential investment, especially in terms of obtaining credit.[4] Funding, which had been scarce beforehand, became even scarcer. More directly, the return of a Labour government in 1965 saw the introduction of a system of rent regulation to cover much of the property decontrolled in 1957. The effective impact of this 1965 Rent Act on the profitability of residential investment is difficult to assess accurately given the rapidly changing conditions in the rest of the economy. At least one major landlord openly welcomed the measures, claiming that the three-year periods for which the "fair rents" operated were little different from the three-year lease arrangements which had become accepted procedure. Others noted that the levels at which rents were fixed differed little from expected levels. Perhaps the greatest impact of the Act was psychological, finally convincing the remaining corporate investors that residential property would never be free from some form of government control which might hinder its future growth potential.

In fact, the incoming Labour administration delivered a much more direct and far-reaching blow to the residential investment sector than that of rent regulations. The new fiscal provisions of the 1965 Finance Act, in particular the introduction of the Corporation Tax, had an immediate impact on the property market. Property companies, which traditionally distributed the majority of their earnings, were particularly heavily penalized by this new tax, which was actually aimed at stimulating the reinvestment of profits by manufacturing companies into new production. Faced with increased taxation and the consequent need to increase earnings to maintain dividends, most quoted property companies attempted to rationalize their investment strategies by concentrating on the highest-yielding investments. The pressure to disinvest from the lower-yielding residential market therefore intensified. At the same time the new tax system tipped the balance in favor of property trading as opposed to property investment. Whereas investment income was subject to corporation tax, trading income only attracted capital gains tax, the lower of the two. The door was now open for flat break-up to begin in earnest.

On the demand side several changes in the taxation situation of owner-occupation had a particularly marked effect on higher-income taxpayers during the early 1960s. First, the exclusion of domestic owner-occupied property from capital gains tax greatly benefited higher-income taxpayers who viewed the purchase of residential property as much in investment terms as for its use value.

It made more sense to invest a proportion of personal capital in tax-free domestic property rather than elsewhere. Secondly, the abolition of "Schedule A" taxation on imputed rental values of owner-occupied property was also most keenly felt at the higher end of the market. The net result was that by the mid-1960s the relative merit of buying compared with rental in this sector of the market was becoming readily apparent. For example, at this time a person earning over £10 000 a year, obtaining full surtax relief on an endowment mortgage from a private trust or life-insurance company, no longer subject to "Schedule A" tax and exempt from capital gains tax on any increase in property values, would pay less to buy a flat worth, say £20 000 on the open market than he or she would pay to rent it.

More general economic processes were also having an impact during this period. The central-London housing market was coming under increasing pressure from growing numbers of higher-income white-collar households. As a result, the flat-breakers were operating in a seller's market in which buoyant high-income demand for accommodation of any form underpinned the success of the process. The growth of this professionalized labor force is of course related to wider changes in the economic structure of the metropolis. Although this shift in the structure of demand has not been considered here (see Hamnett & Randolph 1982), it must be stressed that it has played a fundamentally important role in determining the conditions in which flat break-up has developed. At the same time, rapidly rising rents, the declining real cost of mortgages over time in a period of rising incomes, and the capital gains to be made by ownership in a period of escalating domestic property prices, all served to induce those able to buy their own property to do so.

However, we would argue that this "preference" for ownership is to a large extent a constrained preference, for the potential central-London resident will have to buy his or her accommodation in the absence of a functioning private rental sector, outside of the limited high-rent, short-stay luxury end of the market. As Kemeny (1981:63) has rightly observed, "To a great extent ... current tenure preferences are the product and not the cause of tenure systems." Quite clearly, if landlords prefer to sell in order to extract capital gains rather than let out properties, then prospective occupants have little alternative but to buy. That the impetus for break-ups came from the landlord's side is plainly evident in the manner by which they overcame the major barrier to transfer, namely the absence of a functioning domestic mortgage market for leasehold flat property.

Priming the pump: the role of mortgage finance

A critical factor in the rate of transfer has been the availability of mortgage finance for purchase, in which the building societies have played a major role (Nevitt 1966, Boddy 1980). For house property, this process has been in progress since at least the 1920s when the mass owner-occupied market funded by the building-societies movement began to grow rapidly (Pawley 1978). In the case of flats, however, the transfer to owner-occupation had to wait until such time as mortgages for the purchase of flats in multiple-unit properties by individual householders became an accepted risk by the financial institutions. It could be argued from this that the sale of flat properties was therefore a product of consumer demand made effective by changes (under consumer pressure) in mortgage lending practice. However, such an explanation ignores both the complexity of conditions that were necessary for flat break-up to take place, and the ability of landlords themselves not only to perceive and react to changing market conditions, but also to actively mediate changes in those conditions.

As we have seen, by the mid-1960s, conditions were becoming favorable for the development of a demand for leasehold owner-occupation in the central-London flat market, and the incentives to sell on the part of landlords were intensifying. However, in the absence of a widespread mortgage market to allow individual flat ownership on a large scale beyond the high-income submarket, possibilities for the transfer of rented flats into owner-occupation and for the consequent capital gains remained essentially limited. The reluctance of building societies to lend on such property necessitated those property companies who initially entered the break-up market to prime their sales drives by providing would-be purchasers with internal financing, often in close relationship with the secondary banking system. The merits of buying the flat they rented were extolled to sitting tenants, and the pressure exerted was usually aided by substantial discounts on estimated VP values and more active attempts to increase rents. The point here is that flat break-up was not a "spontaneous" reaction to changes in the decision environment of the central-London flat market, but an actively mediated response to changing circumstances by a group of profit-maximizing intermediaries who saw the possibilities for substantial capital gains (Williams 1976). It was only when a market had been actively created and VP values established, principally as a result of the sales to sitting tenants, that an open market in flats became possible, thus allowing households to buy into the sector on a large scale.

Once such a market had been established, flats rapidly became a more acceptable risk for the traditional mortgage lenders, and the market was able to take off on its own. Again, wider societal processes had a substantial influence on the subsequent development of the phenomenon, for although the rate and extent of flat break-up began to build up in the late 1960s, the whole sector was one of the major beneficiaries from the relaxation of credit controls in 1971 and the subsequent flood of money into the property sector. The funneling of finance into speculative break-up operations, principally from the secondary banking system, as well as the rapid expansion of mortgage lending to would-be owner–occupiers, fueled what has become recognized as one of the more notorious examples of speculative activity during the property boom of the early 1970s as flat values escalated.

Though partial, this overview of the development of the flat break-up market in London should indicate the crucial role of finance in the process of creating the conditions in which sales could be effected and capital gains thus appropriated. In this respect, it proves an intriguing comparison with Harvey and Chatterjee's (1974) study of the Baltimore housing market where landlord disinvestment was related to the difficulties of obtaining mortgage finance in the inner city, the net result apparently being housing dilapidation and abandonment. In direct contrast, whereas residential disinvestment and flat break-up in central London have also been dependent on the availability of mortgage finance, in many respects (as the events of the early 1970s show), it has been stimulated by too much rather than too little finance, both for the "disinvesting" landlord and the potential owner–occupier. This is not to imply criticism of Harvey and Chatterjee's analysis, but rather to emphasize that apparently comparable phenomena, in this case landlord disinvestment, in reality may reflect and result from widely differing processes in differing locations, and elicit widely differing responses from apparently similar "actors." Indeed, even within the central-London purpose-built flat rental market itself, there has been a considerable variety in the responses of individual landlords to the changing conditions of profitability which have developed over the past 20 years or so. This variety of responses can be seen in the major changes that have taken place in the structure of landlordism in the sector since the 1950s.

Changes in ownership structure: investment and trading landlordism

As the preceding analysis has indicated, the existence of a "value gap" between the tenanted investment value and the vacant-possession sale value of privately rented residential property has resulted in the transfer of the majority of the conventionally privately rented sector into owner-occupation since the early 1920s. It is significant, however, that the purpose-built flat sector remained almost untouched by the process until the mid-1960s. The point is that the changing general conditions of profitability in the private rental sector did not manifest themselves either equally or evenly in all sectors of the market. On the contrary, they were essentially uneven in their impact between type of property and type of owner. Thus, merely because, for half a century, the economics of continued renting *vis-à-vis* sale for owner-occupation had generally favored sale, this did not necessarily ensure that sales would take place. The conditions of profitability are not a steamroller, uniformly forcing all before them into a certain pattern of response.

Market responses cannot simply be "read off" automatically from the changes in the general underlying conditions of profitability, not least because these conditions are general. Though changes in the general conditions of profitability will be apparent in a market, they do not necessarily manifest themselves as such to individual companies. As Harvey and Chatterjee observed (1974: 30), "Professional landlords make their decisions in terms of a structured decision environment and closely gear their operations to the characteristics of sub-markets *as they perceive and experience them*" (emphasis added). At one extreme it can be argued that landlords who fail to perceive changing market conditions may, like other entrepreneurs, eventually lose their market share, experience declining profitability, or even go out of business, but there is a certain amount of leeway in the accuracy and speed with which individual companies perceive and respond to such changes.

Equally important, the form of the process by which rented flats have been transferred to owner-occupation has also varied considerably. The term "disinvestment" used here to describe the net effect of the process is in fact somewhat misleading, because whereas some landlords were quite obviously disinvesting from a long-term commitment to residential property, others, for very different reasons, were actively investing in the self same properties. The point here is that, within an overall process, which on the face of it appears to reflect declining commercial profitability, we can discover examples of the reverse process. But the rationale on which this apparent newfound profitability is based is quite different from that which prevailed before. The conditions that created a situation of declining profitability for one form of residential property-ownership actually created the opportunity for increased profitability for another. As one commentator remarked at the time, "While the last generation of property developers are licking their wounds a new generation may be buying into cheap situations and laying down the basis of new fortunes" (Chown 1967). Thus not only will the rationale and motivations of existing landlords change as conditions of profitability change, but the rationale and motivations of new landlords entering the market will mirror these changes, and the nature of their operations will differ radically from those of their predecessors.

This shifting pattern of responses is reflected very clearly in the changes in the attitude and behavior of existing landlords toward their residential investment portfolios during the past 20 to 30 years, as well as the behavior of landlords who have entered the market during this period. Although there were arguably as many responses to these changing conditions of profitability as there were landlords, it is possible to identify the major trends in corporate policy as landlords reacted to the developing market. These trends reflect various combinations of the two main bases on which residential property has been held over this period, namely its traditional role as a source of medium- to long-term investment income, and its more recent role as a source of short-term capital gains.

Overall there has been a long-term withdrawal from investment landlordism and a concomitant rise of residential–property trading (trading landlordism). However, the two should not be seen as hard-and-fast categories, and the status of any individual company within this broad schema may change over time as conditions of individual profitability change. In reality, of course, both rental income and capital gains will play a part in the calculations made by any landlord, but the important point is that the role of rental income and capital gains in the purpose-built flat market has shifted fundamentally since the 1960s in favor of the latter. The net effect of the changing conditions of profitability has been a shift from investment to trading. This is sufficiently marked that landlords, whose principal objective is investment for long-term rental income, have been reduced to a residual presence in this sector of the residential market and are mainly confined to the few private trusts and estates which have owned their property for some considerable time and for whom a steady rental income remains important. Even with these landlords it is highly likely that capital appreciation plays an important part in their attitude toward residential property investment, representing as it does a source of future income. Here, however, we have concentrated on changes in the pattern of corporate and institutional ownership since the 1960s. The dominant position of commercial landlordism in the purpose-built flat market means that changes in ownership policies in this subsector will in all likelihood also dominate the trends in the sector as a whole.

The shifting structure of ownership can be illustrated by a typology based on the dual extremes of investment versus trading landlordism. First, those landlords whose principal objective was long-term investment yield represented the established residential property landlords who had held their properties for some time, often since well before World War II. These were pure 'investor' landlords who calculated the rental yields on their residential portfolios in relation to competing yields in the property sector, and tended to disinvest en bloc, literally, by selling off their flat blocks to whomever would purchase. As such, these companies were not interested in generating dealing profits by breaking up their own blocks, and indeed many of them were actively disinvesting well before break-up got underway in the post-1965 period. Residential blocks were simply not providing an acceptable yield in relation to the possible alternative uses that would be made on the capital they represented.

This more or less pure disinvestment strategy was characteristic of the very earliest reaction to increasingly problematic relative investment yields in the flat-block market, and was the general attitude taken in the early 1960s by numerous major established residential landlords. This is an important point because it represented a strategy adopted by such companies before trading profits became both possible and acceptable. Beaumont Properties, British Land, Berkeley Properties, Alliance Property Holdings, Central and District, Bernard Sunley, and Artagen are all examples of such companies. Invariably the capital raised from the sales of residential property was reinvested in commercial property sectors, particularly for office and industrial development. Sales of residential holdings not only freed such companies from an increasingly troublesome and low-yielding investment, but also provided a source of capital in a market where interest rates and therefore finance costs were increasing steadily.

To this group we can also add the major insurance companies such as the Norwich Union, the Pearl, the Prudential, the Co-operative Insurance Society and Legal & General, who have also disinvested in a similar manner. Again their principal concern has been over relative investment yields, although here disinvestment has continued over a longer period of time and in a more sporadic manner, reflecting the differing investment rationale of this group of traditional landlords. In the late 1970s there were still several major institutional landlords in the rental market, but with the recent resurgence of the flat break-up market they too have been selling off their remaining flat blocks.

Most important, the decision by this group of investment land-lords to disinvest released onto the market the blocks that were to fuel the flat break-up phenomenon. Thus, through their decision to sell off their residential investments, these companies provided the opportunities for others to enter the market and exploit their trading potential as the flat sales market developed.

The second major group consists of established landlords who, rather than selling off their residential holdings en bloc, held on to them, or at least the most profitable parts of their portfolios, and then proceeded to break up the blocks themselves. The major policy orientation with those companies has therefore been a switch from investment into trading. Again, not all companies in this group responded at the same time or for the same reason to the opportuni-ties for sales. Some began to break up blocks at the very beginning of the trend, whereas others did not become active until well into the 1970–72 boom period, or after. Others may have been disinvesting en bloc before they themselves recognizing the profitability of breaking up, and then switched to a trading strategy. Moreover, whereas some of this group were active in stimulating the break-up market as part of a deliberate sales strategy, others were more or less forced into break-up in order to generate income during periods of crisis within the company itself – in many ways a defensive disinvestment strategy.

This point also reflects the use to which profits generated through flat sales were put. For the more active breakers, profits were reinvested in alternative property or investment sectors, but those on whom break-up was forced used the income either to meet debts or to generate income for fending off takeovers (not always success-fully). In many respects, this group was probably the most diverse in terms of their response to changes in market conditions. A large number of established companies eventually adopted a self-breaking strategy, including New London Properties, Grovewood Secur-ities, Property Holding and Investment Trust, Peachey Property Corporation, London County Freehold, London City and West-cliffe, and Trafalgar House.

The third major group of landlords which characterized the sector during the period are the companies that have come into the market to exploit the value gap, and whose principal business was the purchase of blocks of flats solely to break up the individual units for sale. Thus their strategy was based on property trading rather than investment, and these specialist traders were active in mediating the break-up market from the beginning. Some of the earlier break-up specialists were relatively autonomous companies, who relied on close links with sources of finance to fund acquisition and sales. However, flat traders, who began to appear as the market picked up, were often little more than the property-trading subsidiaries of secondary and merchant banks. These links, whether indirect or direct, were crucial in the build-up of the market, for they not only provided the finance for purchasers from those established landlords who were disinvesting en bloc, but also allowed the breakers to prime their sales with internal financing.

Few of these companies had any specific interest in property *per se*. Rather, their involvement in the residential sector was purely for trading profits, which were often just distributed as income for the major shareholders and directors, or in the form of interest to the funding banks. The close coincidence with asset stripping is not accidental, for many of the names associated with that form of enterprise have been involved in flat break-up at one time or another. This group adopted a strategy towards flat blocks opposite to that of the first group of companies we described. Here, active investment rather than disinvestment was pursued. However, the rationale on which this investment was based was quite different from that of the disinvestment strategies of the established residential landlords. The latter's main criterion was the relative yield to be derived from the continued ownership of a rent-producing asset, while the former's concern was solely about the capital gain to be derived from transferring rental property into owner-occupation through the exploitation of the value gap. For this group of residential-property owners, rental income plays at most only the marginal role of contributing to overhead and interest payments while trading profits are awaited.

Generally speaking, the specialist breakers based their business on higher gearing and deficit financing, a practice shunned by most established property companies. This was quite acceptable so long as finance was cheap and plentiful, and flat sales could be expected to be completed at an adequate rate. The potential profit in a well-managed break-up operation was immense, especially when property inflation was continually increasing the underlying value of unsold flats. However, when these favorable conditions were reversed, as they were in 1973–75 and in the post-1980 period, many specialist breakers found themselves in serious difficulties.

Nevertheless, a plethora of trading companies has emerged over the past 15 years or so, some more cautiously run than others, but their principal business has been the derivation of trading profits. Early trading companies include Dorrington Investments and the various subsidiaries of First National Finance Corporation. As the break-up market developed, companies were formed solely as vehicles for flat trading activity, several in spectacular stock-market flotations within the shells of defunct companies (favorites being bankrupt Malaysian rubber plantation businesses), which were reconstituted with large injections of residential properties bought from disinvesting landlords with funds supplied by secondary banks. Regalion Securities, backed by First National; Peureula Investments, backed by Keyser Ullman and Dalton Barton; Consolidated Securities, backed by London and County Securities; and Buckingham Properties, a Slater–Walker subsidiary, were notable examples. Many of the earlier publicly quoted breakers became victims of the property crash of 1974, and the tendency in more recent times has been for flat traders to take the form of private companies, often registered in tax havens such as the Channel Islands or the Dutch Antilles. However, the people behind these anonymous breakers are very often the same entrepreneurs whose earlier activities greatly contributed to the property debacle of the mid-1970s.

The fourth and final group comprises the two major property empires of the Freshwater and Berger families. Although their involvement in residential blocks of flats dates back to the immediate postwar period, and they have both been selling flats since at least the early 1960s, their involvement in the central-London market does not fit in particularly well with any of the three groups outlined above. During the 1950s and 1960s, Freshwater and Berger were purchasing blocks of flats at a time when many landlords were adopting a disinvestment strategy and withdrawing from the sector. As a consequence, they bought much of their property at relatively favorable prices. By the late 1950s they both seem to have adopted essentially similar strategies of rapid asset expansion founded on high gearing in a period of steadily rising inflation. Flat blocks played a central role in this process, forming a strong asset base which, through continued rent increases and consequent capital revaluations, could be remortgaged to finance further property acquisitions.

The major consequence of this strategy was that interest charges accounted for much, if not all, of the rental income derived from the properties purchased. The solution to this problem was to generate additional income through an active but closely controlled property trading policy. This was accomplished by the purchase and sale of more readily marketable house properties or lower-value flats in suburban locations. For Freshwater in particular, central-London flat blocks were purchased and retained to form the core of the investment portfolio where rents and therefore capital values could be expected to increase by the greatest amount. Both companies only really entered the central-London break-up market in earnest in the post-1974 period when financial difficulties resulting from the property crash necessitated a rapid increase in trading income. Thus, although both Freshwater and Berger switched from a predominantly investment-oriented strategy with regard to their central-London flat blocks, toward one in which trading predominated, the rationale for the investment was originally that the blocks were utilized as an asset base to boost borrowing potential rather than as rental income, and both companies had been actively trading flats and houses for a considerable period in other sectors of the residential market.

As this rather crude classification indicates, the net effect of policy decisions taken by these various companies and institutions has been the sale of rented flats to individual long-leasehold owner-occupiers, but the actual causal mechanisms by which this process has been effected varied widely. They ranged from active block disinvestment by companies concerned to improve investment yields, to active investment in the same properties by companies seeking to exploit capital-gain potential. Between these extremes, other landlords have varied their attitudes and policies, depending on the external state of the market and their internal conditions of profitability. Some have implemented sales due to favorable market conditions, and others have been forced into a sales policy as a defensive reaction to adverse conditions.

Thus what appears to be a simple and uniform pattern of disinvestment in reality turns out to have resulted from a wide range of specific reactions to a variety of causal structures reflecting both internal and external conditions of profitability. As Massey and Meegan (1982) have stated regarding industrial disinvestment,

> It would be wrong to try to establish empirical "rules" of behavior, of ways of responding to different comparative rates of profit, for different kinds of company. What is clear however, is that behavior may vary substantially; it is not a question of some immediate and automatic response as might be predicted by theorists of perfect market situations. (Massey & Meegan 1982: 97)

This is exactly the point we wish to make here. As the recent Review of the Private Rental Housing Sector concluded, the motivations of landlords are extremely diverse. "Landlords provide accommodation for many different reasons, receive very different rates of return on their property . . . have different incentives to remain in the sector and have very different choices available to them" (House of Commons 1982: xxi).

Even within as apparently homogeneous a subsector as the central-London purpose-built flat market, we thus find a diversity of behavior and attitudes. Underpinning all these decisions, however, was the eventual necessity for the companies concerned to evaluate the potential of residential property in light of competing returns on the capital investment they represented and the search for greater profitability. Those that were reluctant or hesitant to adopt profit-maximizing strategies toward their residential holdings often found themselves the object of acquisition by others who were not so hesitant. Companies whose experience and tradition prompted them to view residential properties as a troublesome and low-yielding investment found ready buyers for these properties among those whose perception of their potential was based on entirely different criteria.

As we have seen, the major underlying factor that generated these changes was the possibility of creating and exploiting the potential value gap resulting from the dual-value system in the residential property market. This in turn has restructured the pattern of ownership within the sector as a whole. Without the possibility of sales to owner–occupiers, existing block owners would either have remained in the market deriving a steady income from rents, or disinvested to other companies who were willing to continue letting. The specialist speculator–breaker would not have had the opportunity of capital gains and would not, therefore, have entered the market. This is not to say that the sector would have remained as it was. In all likelihood there would have been a rundown of the sector – the very opposite of the gentrification trend seen today. In turn this would have resulted in a completely different structure of ownership change than that actually experienced. The point is that it is not possible to conclude that the trend toward flat break-up was inevitable. Rather it was only one of a range of possibilities. The actual form that these changes have taken can only be explained in relation to the historically contingent social, economic and political processes operative over the period in question.

Consequences

Flat break-up has had a profound impact on the functioning of the central-London housing market and has resulted in a number of important consequences for those accommodated in the sector.

First, a functioning conventional private rental market in this sector has to all intents and purposes virtually ceased to exist. Its place has been taken by long-leasehold owner-occupation. A small proportion of the remainder has been converted into high-rent short-stay luxury furnished lettings catering mainly to tourists or visiting businessmen. Here rents are sufficiently high (£5000+ per annum) to provide a viable return. The remaining unfurnished tenancies constitute a relic tenure, which is in effect merely awaiting a profitable transition into owner-occupation; but it is currently protected from a more immediate fate by security-of-tenure legislation. The consequence of this is that affordable private renting in central London today is no longer a possible option for many. Those who cannot rent here have in effect been displaced to alternative locations beyond the central area, or to alternative housing tenures (for example, local-authority housing or lower-income owner-occupation). In the process, a significant proportion of flats are held vacant pending their sale, again adding to the pressure on the remaining (and inadequate) rental-housing supply elsewhere.

Secondly, the resident population of the central-London flat sector has become increasingly differentiated as tenure-specific polarization has restructured the existing social characteristics of residents. Although the residential structure of this sector has always been predominantly white-collar, the owner–occupiers who are moving into the sector are drawn overwhelmingly from the managerial and professional occupational groups. The market has therefore become closed to all but those in the higher-status non-manual occupations. A substantial proportion of flats have also been sold to foreign buyers, especially from the Middle East, for use as *pieds-à-terres*, a reflection of London's renewed role as a key city in the international economy.

However, it is the age-and-income polarization which is most pronounced. The newly arrived owner–occupiers are typified by high incomes and more youthful age ranges, but an increasing proportion of the remaining conventionally renting tenants are both elderly and on fixed or limited incomes. These tenants face a future of steadily escalating rent charges as landlords press for substantial rent increases, to cover their interest charges and maintenance costs as well as to encourage tenants to buy or move. To the extent that tenants are constrained to buy or move, rent increases serve to aid the realization of capital gains by the resulting sales of the flat.

Third, these changes have also resulted in a growing conflict between tenants, whose primary interest is to keep rent increases to a minimum, and owners, who see themselves as "subsidizing" the tenants by paying an apparently disproportionate amount toward the upkeep of their properties through escalating service and maintenance charges. In fact the question of service charges and inadequate maintenance in many blocks is becoming a growing problem.

The cost of long-delayed repairs to these aging properties is now falling increasingly severely on the backs of the new owner–occupiers, rather than on the speculators who have made their profits from the process. The cost of maintaining some of the more neglected blocks will form an increasing financial burden for many residents. Alternatively, problems also arise where landlords are reluctant to engage in any maintenance at all, especially where a sizable proportion of the flats in a block are still rented. In this situation there is little a tenant or owner–occupier can do without recourse to expensive high-court action. There are already signs that building societies are becoming increasingly wary of lending on flats where maintenance could prove expensive or problematic. This could have potentially serious implications for those owners who wish to move, both in terms of the value of their properties and their ability to sell them. Thus, even for the "gentrifying" owner, leasehold flats can be far from an ideal housing alternative in some cases.

Notes

1   English property law allows of no absolute right of property-ownership, independent of the ground on which property stands. Instead it distinguishes between freehold (absolute title to land and buildings) and leasehold (right of use for a specified period). What this means in practice is that in England and Wales there is no legal necessity to convert whole buildings into strata-titled condominiums as there is in North America, where the buyer has absolute and permanent title to the individual unit and owns the common parts and structure of the building collectively (hence the origins of the term condominium), and where titles to all the individual units in a building have to be registered prior to sale. In England and Wales it is possible for long leases of individual flats within a building to be sold while others remain rented. In Scotland, where the property law is quite different, the position is more akin to that in North America, and so called "flying freeholds" can be sold. Taken in conjunction with the British security-of-tenure legislation, which guarantees a tenant a permanent right to occupancy provided the rent is paid and other conditions of the tenancy are complied with, the ability to sell individual flats has had profound consequences for the nature of tenant protest. Such protest has, in general, been far more muted than in North America where tenants are faced with the prospect of mass eviction when a building is converted to a condominium. It is singularly ironic that legislative attempts to regulate and control condo conversions have in consequence been far more marked in free-enterprise California than they have been in England, where the process has proceeded largely unchecked and uncontrolled. In Britain the real losers have not been the existing protected tenants, though they have

suffered from sharp rent increases, inadequate maintenance, etc., but the potential tenant who finds there is nowhere to let. In the nature of things potential consumers are atomistic and unorganized. The rights to a leasehold can be sold or passed on by the leasehold owner in much the same way as freehold ownership rights. The crucial difference is that when the property has less than 40 or 50 years to run, the property becomes unmortgageable. Toward the end of the leasehold term, the sale value falls rapidly to zero, since what is being sold is not ownership in perpetuity but the right to occupy a property for a limited number of years. The full effects of this have not yet been felt in the long-leasehold apartment market in England and Wales, although as time goes on and leases expire, this will become an increasingly severe problem. The Leasehold Reform Act of 1967, which gives the long leaseholders of house property a statutory right to purchase the freehold at an agreed sum, was specifically introduced to deal with the consequences of the termination of 99-year leases granted in the building boom of the late 19th century. Unfortunately, it does not apply to flats since flat break-ups were scarcely underway in 1967.

2 Cf. the parallel between this "value gap" and the "rent gap" proposed by Smith (1979a) in a broader explanation of gentrification.

3 For those familiar with condominium and cooperative conversion in the United States, the contemporary parallel is unmistakable.

4 Peter Rachman was a notorious slum landlord whose activities in London received considerable publicity in the early 1960s. The exposure of Rachman and other such landlords led to new legislation in the private rented sector.

Acknowledgement
The authors would like to acknowledge the financial support of the Economic and Social Research Council.

8

Abandonment, gentrification, and displacement: the linkages in New York City

PETER MARCUSE

Abandonment and gentrification seem polar opposites. Abandonment seems to result from drastically insufficient demand, gentrification from high and increasing demand; abandonment from a precipitous decline in property values, gentrification from a rapid increase. Yet in New York City (and not only there) the two processes seem to be going on simultaneously. How can gentrification and abandonment take place at the same time, often practically side by side? This chapter will try to answer this question, and in doing so will focus on the relationship of each to the problem of displacement.

The policy relevance of the issue should be clear. Existing policy in the United States is premised on three assumptions (see, for example, US House of Representatives 1977):

(a) Abandonment is painful but inevitable. Public policy cannot reverse it; at best it can confine it to certain neighborhoods. Therefore a policy of planned shrinkage, of triage, is necessary, abandoning certain neighborhoods completely in order to try to save others.

(b) Gentrification improves the quality of housing, contributes to the tax base, and revitalizes important sections of the city. The displacement it causes (if any) is trivial. Therefore a policy of encouraging gentrification, through tax benefits, zone changes, or whatever other means are available, should be pursued.

(c) Gentrification is in fact the only realistic cure for abandonment. Especially in a time of fiscal stress, the public sector cannot hope to counter abandonment (see (a) above). Only full use of private-sector resources can do so. Thus the gentrification of abandoned neighborhoods is particularly desirable.

This chapter takes strong issue with each of these assumptions, and consequently with the policy prescriptions based on them. In

153

summary, the argument runs as follows. Abandonment drives some (higher-income) households out of the city, others to gentrifying areas close to downtown, still others (lower-income) to adjacent areas, where pressures on housing and rents are increased. Gentrification attracts higher-income households from other areas in the city, reducing demand elsewhere and increasing tendencies to abandonment, and displaces lower-income people, likewise increasing pressures on housing and rents. Both abandonment and gentrification are directly linked to changes in the economy of the city, which have dramatically increased the economic polarization of the population. A vicious circle is created in which the poor are continuously under pressure of displacement and the well-to-do continuously seek to wall themselves in within gentrified neighborhoods. Far from being a cure for abandonment, gentrification worsens it. Both gentrification and abandonment have caused a high level of displacement in New York City. Public policies have contributed to this result, but are also capable of countering it. Whether they will or not hinges significantly on political developments.

The meaning and definition of gentrification have been established earlier in this volume. However, less attention has been paid to abandonment. Abandonment of a unit occurs when its owner loses any economic interest in the continued ownership of the property beyond the immediate future, and is willing to surrender title to it without compensation. Physical condition is a good, but not sufficient, indicator of abandonment: some units that appear physically abandoned may instead be on hold pending re-use ('warehousing"), and others that have actually been abandoned by their owners may still be maintained in tolerable condition by their tenants. The distinction between economic and physical abandonment is an important one for analytical purposes.[1]

Abandonment of an entire neighborhood occurs when public and/or private parties act on the assumption that long-term investment in the neighborhood, whether in maintenance and improvements or in new construction, is not warranted. It is only a matter of time before residents of an abandoned unit or an abandoned neighborhood are displaced.

Abandonment and gentrification are both reflections of a single long-term process, resulting from the changing economy of the central city. This process has two aspects: the shift from manufacturing to services, from reliance on mid-level skills to automation and de-skilling, on the one hand, which renders redundant large parts of the workforce and reduces lower-income rent-paying ability; and the increasing professionalization and concentration of management and technical functions, on the other, which creates additional higher-income demand for housing. These processes have spatial consequences: blue-collar workers (and potential blue-collar workers) are no longer needed in such numbers downtown; professional and technical workers are in ever-increasing demand there. Housing adjacent to central business districts reflects these changes. The pull exerted on one group by the changing economy of the central business district (CBD) fits in with the push against another. For the gentrifiers, all roads lead to downtown. For the poor, all roads lead to abandonment.

Thus the increasing polarization of the economy is reflected in the increasing polarization of neighborhoods: at the one end, abandonment, at the other end, gentrification.

The residential restructuring brought about by changing economic patterns is reinforced by the restructuring of business locations. The expansion of business and commercial uses in downtown requires changes in land use, both downtown and in its immediate environs. Residential must give way to business, and in the residential areas that remain (or are built) higher income is demanded and lower income is not. Property values downtown must be protected from discordant land uses and discordant elements of the population. The real-estate industry, particularly its more speculative members, both follows and accentuates these patterns.

The poor end up displaced by each of these developments. They are displaced where business wants to move in, because the land is too valuable to house them further. They are displaced where gentrification takes place, because the buildings and the neighborhoods are too good (read: too expensive) for them. They are displaced where abandonment takes place, because the buildings and the neighborhoods are not good enough to provide decent housing for them.

The next section of this chapter takes up, on a citywide scale, the extent of displacement from abandonment and from gentrification in New York City. Because data on gentrification are harder to come by than data on abandonment, and their interpretation is more controversial, the following section looks in some detail at three clearly gentrifying and two possibly gentrifying neighborhoods. The final section summarizes the major conclusions, considers the likely future course of events, and discusses some policy implications.

The city-wide extent of displacement from abandonment and gentrification

Conceptual issues and measurement

Displacement may be defined in terms either of households or of housing units, in individual or in neighborhood terms, and as a consequence of physical or economic changes. The most widely accepted definition is that of George and Eunice Grier (1978). The Griers' definition clearly covers physical causes, as when lack of heat forces tenants to move, as well as economic causes such as rent increases. Although these two sets of causes often overlap substantially, it is useful to distinguish between them analytically. Thus we refer to "economic displacement" and "physical displacement." In this study we are going to examine the displacement of individual households, and it is important to make another conceptual distinction here. If one looks simply at the housing units involved, and counts the last residents in that unit, then one gets a measure of "last-resident displacement." Yet it is possible that prior households occupying the same building were also displaced, and so it is necessary to make a count of what might be called "chain displacement." Both must be considered in an attempt to estimate displacement, and would be covered by the Griers' definition.

Further, however, there is a normal movement of households in any housing market, within any neighborhood. When a particular housing unit is voluntarily vacated by one household and then gentrified (or abandoned), so that another similar household cannot move in, and the total number of units available to such a household has thereby been reduced, we may also speak of displacement: "exclusionary displacement."

Exclusionary displacement is not included within the Griers' definition. A formal definition would run as follows:

Exclusionary displacement from gentrification occurs when any household is not permitted to move into a dwelling, by a change in conditions which affects that dwelling or its immediate surroundings, which

(a) is beyond the household's reasonable ability to control or prevent;
(b) occurs despite the household's being able to meet all previously imposed conditions of occupancy;
(c) differs significantly and in a spatially concentrated fashion from changes in the housing market as a whole; and
(d) makes occupancy by that household impossible, hazardous, or unaffordable.

The before-and-after measure often used in estimating displacement, the difference in housing availability over a given time period, implicitly includes exclusionary displacement. Such a before-and-after measure is generally based on a count of housing units in a given neighborhood, their occupants, and their characteristics, in

156

comparison to the larger area of which the neighborhood is a part. It includes exclusionary displacement, but it does not include chain displacement, since it is based on a count of units, not households.[3]

Finally, displacement affects many more than those actually displaced at any given moment. When a family sees its neighborhood changing dramatically, when all their friends are leaving, when stores are going out of business and new stores for other clientele are taking their places (or none at all are replacing them), when changes in public facilities, transportation patterns, support services, are all clearly making the area less and less livable, then the pressure of displacement is already severe, and its actuality only a matter of time. Families under such circumstances may even move as soon as they can, rather than wait for the inevitable; they are displaced nonetheless. This can be true for displacement from both gentrification and abandonment. We thus speak of the "pressure of displacement" as affecting households beyond those actually currently displaced. It is certainly a significant part of the displacement problem. Pressure of displacement can be distinguished from subjective fear of a remote possibility of displacement by looking not only at the perception but also the reality of what is happening in a neighborhood: subjective concern plus prices rising over the city average, for instance, might be taken as a crude benchmark.

The full impact of displacement must include consideration of all four factors: direct last-resident displacement, direct chain displacement, exclusionary displacement, and displacment pressure. No one set of figures will provide a measure of all four. The first two are best approached through demographic or mobility figures, the third through housing-unit figures, the fourth through a combination of these. Adding figures from the two different sources can produce double counting; excluding any source can produce undercounting. The following discussion tries to steer a middle course between these twin dangers, attempting to err on the conservative side; the resulting counts, however, are often, at this stage, unsatisfactory. But it is worth having conceptual clarity on definitions and concepts, and orders of magnitude as to figures, even if precise measurement is as yet unattainable.

Displacement from abandonment

The best evidence on the extent of abandonment (and thus the displacement arising from it) comes from New York City's triennial Housing and Vacancy Surveys, conducted for the City by the US Bureau of the Census.[3] It provides the basis for a housing-unit-based estimate of the extent of direct last-resident displacement (but

Table 8.1 Losses from the housing inventory, 1970–81.

demolished	154 722
condemned	21 186
burned-out, boarded-up, exposed to the elements	99 189
Abandonment losses	275 097
conversions to non residential use	22 149
mergers with another residential unit	23 754
Other losses	45 903
Total losses	321 000

not of chain or exclusionary displacement). The key figures are shown in Table 8.1.

"Losses" include all units that were in the housing inventory in 1970 but subsequently (up to 1981) removed from it. "Abandonment losses" (our term) include all units likely, from the Census survey, to have been abandoned in the period covered. Some minor adjustments must be made to take into account "losses" that appear to be abandonment but are really preparatory to re-use, and to add other real losses that do not appear in the Census survey. The resultant average figure for the 11 years covered is 31 000 units abandoned per year, or a total of 341 000 units. However, as a result of chain displacement and pressure of displacement, more households are displaced from abandonment than the number of housing units that are abandoned. Households whose individual unit may still be in a minimally adequate state of repair, and whose landlord is even still attempting to maintain the building on the market, may nevertheless be forced to move because of the external consequences of neighborhood abandonment. The danger of fire may be increased from empty buildings next door, the level of street crime, drug traffic, and vandalism may increase to an intolerable level, community facilities and support networks may be eroded, public services neglected, beyond the point where a decent life can be maintained.

The importance of these neighborhood abandonment factors in causing displacement can be gauged by looking at the extent to which abandonment is spatially concentrated. To give just one example: the Bronx had, in 1970, 17.5 percent of the City's households, Queens 24 percent. Yet the Bronx had 44 percent of the City's demolished buildings over the following 11 years, Queens only 3.6 percent (US Bureau of the Census 1970: Vol. 34, Table 33).

Thus an analysis of reasons given by "recent movers" for leaving their existing accommodations (presented in Ch. 9) shows "neighborhood condition" as a strong motivation for moving.

The pattern in areas of neighborhood abandonment is of rapid turnover of units throughout the neighborhood, both among units currently being abandoned and among those that have not yet reached this stage. Generally, the greater the choice of housing available to a household, the more likely it is to leave before being physically forced out by lack of heat or some other crisis condition. Thus there will be displacement of slightly higher-income households from units not yet abandoned, simultaneous with displacement of lower-income households from units at the very last stage of abandonment. Figure 8.1 shows the effects vividly. Of the five boroughs in New York City, the Bronx was most affected by abandonment. There, households at the top as well as at the bottom of the income distribution left the borough in substantial numbers during the three-year period shown. This is not explicable by population change in general: the number of renter households in the city as a whole actually went up slightly, from 1 930 000 to 1 933 887 (Stegman 1982: 73).

Although all these figures suggest that chain displacement, either from neighborhood abandonment or from earlier stages of individual abandonment, is likely to be very substantial, there is no way, with presently available data, to measure it authoritatively. It may not be unreasonable to estimate that the figure would be at least equal to that resulting from direct abandonment.

Thus the best estimate of total displacement from abandonment for New York City might well be a minimum of 31 000 but a more likely figure is 60 000 households, or 150 000 persons per year.[4]

Displacement from gentrification

Displacement from gentrification is harder to measure. Changes in absolute numbers of high- or low-income households in the city are inadequate because gentrification results more from movement *within* the city than from outside it. Mobility figures provide too little information on the cause of moves. Other figures are limited to physical displacement, and do not reflect economic displacement, or vice versa. Exclusionary displacement can be deduced from demographic figures, but must rely on rather broad assumptions about what would have happened without gentrification. Also, quantification of the pressure of displacement must be able to distinguish between the various causes of price increases more precisely than available data now permit. Nevertheless, a preliminary estimate can be made.

159

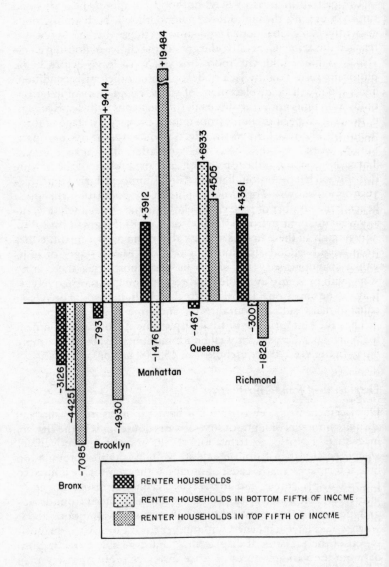

Figure 8.1 Gain or loss of renter households in bottom and top income quintiles, by borough, New York City, 1977 and 1980 (after Stegman 1982).

As to direct physical displacement, some indicators are available. Since before 1970, substantial tax benefits (both an exemption of tax on the increased value and an abatement equal to the allowable cost of the rehabilitation itself) are available to those who rehabilitate multi-family buildings under the J-51 program. Virtually all qualifying rehabilitation actually uses the program. There are no controls on the initial rent charged after rehabilitation; thus there is generally a significant turn from lower- to higher-income occupancy. The number of units affected in the 10-year period before 1980 was 376 940, or about 38 000 units a year. Analysis of their location bears out the assumption that most such units are generally part of the gentrification process: over one-third were in Manhattan, and the concentration in areas of known gentrification is great: one-third of the units between 70th and 86th Streets on the West Side, for instance, used J-51 during this period (City of New York Department of City Planning 1983:25). But some J-51-assisted units do not result in direct displacement: many subsidized units, for instance, are included in the count of those assisted by J-51. A modification downward of the 38 000 figure should thus be made. On the other hand, some rehabilitated units are not eligible for J-51; these would have to be added to the 38 000 figure.

The loss of SRO units (units in Single Room Occupancy buildings) provides a floor for the estimate of displacement, since it is generally conceded that the upgrading of SRO units results in displacement of their former residents, however displacement is defined. The number of such units has gone from 127 000 in 1970 to 20 309 in 1981, or an average of 9700 units lost each year. Those displaced from them were generally poor (85 percent with incomes under $3000 in 1979),[5] and the rehabilitation was overwhelmingly undertaken with J-51 benefits. The results were in almost every case housing for higher-income groups. A minimum of 9700 units, and perhaps as high as 38 000 households, may be estimated to have been directly displaced by the physical change in housing units in New York City each year.

As to economic displacement from gentrification, it is virtually impossible to distinguish between direct displacement, exclusionary displacement and the pressure of displacement. Economic displacement is perhaps best measured by the figures dealing with changes in gross rents. Between 1978 and 1981, at a time when the number of units renting for less than $200 decreased by 110 363, 24 096 units increased their rent from below $400 to $400–499, and a further 18 704 increased their rent from below to above $500. Clearly not all of these 42 800 units experienced rent increases as a result of gentrification or even household moves, and so this figure is on the high side for direct and exclusionary displacement. It may be less inflated once we include pressure of displacement.

Looking beyond units that remain in rental occupancy, economic displacement also results from cooperative and condominium conversions. The number of conversions in 1983 under non-eviction plans alone was 18 967 of which 6168 ended up priced at $100 000 or more. Conversions under eviction plans run at about 70 percent of the level of those under non-eviction plans (City of New York Department of City Planning 1983: 27); these are even more likely to result in direct displacement. Some of these units continue to be occupied by their former tenants, but the typical pattern is of a substantial increase in real occupancy costs after conversion. Thus there is exclusionary as well as direct displacement. Limiting ourselves to conversions resulting in units selling for over $100 000, probably 10 485 households, i.e. 6168+70% of 6168, are subject to direct or exclusionary displacement each year. This figure is in addition to the number of those economically displaced from units remaining rentals, but it does overlap with the number of those physically displaced.

Forced displacement is the most extreme form of displacement. Much of the displacement caused by gentrification appears impersonal; "market trends" cause increased prices, and an individual landlord only seems to be doing what all other landlords are doing when he raises rents, rehabilitates for a higher-income clientele, and watches as one tenant leaves and another (better able to afford the new rent) comes in. The tenant is forced to leave, just as much as if the landlord had personally visited him or her and said "Leave, or else!", with a club in his hand. But the force is of the market, not of the club. In some instances, however, the club or its equivalent is used directly. Harassment of undesired (lower-income) tenants is hardly rare in New York. Cutting off heat or utilities, failing to make repairs, letting garbage accumulate till the stench is overpowering, leaving lights out in the hall, leaving front doors open or broken, and window-glass broken and unrepaired, steps splintered, hallways cluttered – even setting fires – are all techniques for which cases are documented in court hearings and administrative records. Over 1300 charges of harassment a year were officially reported in New York, according to the recent study by Elliott et al. (1983). This no doubt understates the figure for actual harassment.

The available figures that may provide the basis for estimating household displacement from gentrification, then, include the following (all figures are annual averages):

physical	
upgrading under J-51	38 000
elimination of SRO units	9 700
economic	
rent increases to ‹$400	42 800
co-op conversions ‹$100 000	10 485
harassment charges	1 300

These figures overlap, so they may not simply be summed. It seems safe to conclude that displacement from gentrification (including direct and exclusionary displacement) is probably somewhere between 10 000 and 40 000 households a year. Without including those subject to the pressure of displacement, it is probably closer to the lower figure; if they are included, the number is probably closer to the higher figure.

These figures need to be increased by another factor. All indications are that the pace of gentrification has accelerated in the last three years, that is, since the time of the 1980 Census on which the foregoing estimates are based. At the same time, it is relatively clear that the pace of gentrification slowed during the middle years of the 1970s, as economic conditions worsened (see DeGiovanni 1983: 35). Thus any figures based only on changes from 1970 to 1980 will tend to understate the problem, as will any projections into the future based on 1980 figures only.

Thus total displacement, according to our estimates, includes between 31 000 and 60 000 households displaced from abandonment, plus between 10 000 and 40 000 households displaced from gentrification, or between 41 000 and 100 000 households displaced from the two causes together, in New York City, on the average, over the last decade. Assuming an average household size of 2.5 persons, this would mean between 102 500 and 250 000 persons not living in neighborhoods that would otherwise be home to them each year, because of the consequences of the spatial restructuring of the city.[6]

Neighborhood aspects of gentrification and displacement

Gentrification is not a process that works uniformly throughout the city: quite the contrary. It is the essence of gentrification that gentrifying areas and declining areas (abandoning areas, in cities such as New York) are spatially linked to a process of urban restructuring. This is one of the reasons why it is so difficult to measure the resulting displacement from aggregate figures for the city as a whole. If the scale of the analysis is too large, changes cancel each other out. But they can be seen, and more accurately measured, at the neighborhood level. As an introduction to the neighborhood analysis that follows, however, one important point must be made about the larger picture.

The reason for gentrification in New York City is not that there is a net increase in high-rent-paying ability in the city as a whole. On a number of key indicators, there is in fact a decline: the total population has shrunk from 7 894 862 to 7 071 639 (all figures compare 1970 with 1980); the proportion of white non-Hispanics has fallen from 61.6 percent to 51 percent; the proportion of high-income families (over $25 000 in 1970, over $50 000 in 1980, almost exactly the adjustment for inflation) has gone down from 6 percent to 5.4 percent; the number of those having a college education has declined from 813 563 to 776 557. The gentrification that is taking place results not from a massive influx of additional well-to-do to the city, but rather from a spatial reshuffling of a relatively constant or even declining number. Detailed analysis will show the pattern.

The pattern at the neighborhood level

This section examines five neighborhoods in New York City in which gentrification has been of major concern: the Upper West Side near Lincoln Center, Manhattan Valley to the north on the West Side, Clinton just to the south of 59th Street on the West Side, the Lower East Side, and Lower East Harlem (see Fig. 8.2). All of these areas are in Manhattan; they thus do not include any areas of "family gentrification."[7]

The five areas are very different, both from each other and even internally; one of the suprising findings from the study is the fine level at which change needs to be examined to obtain a clear picture of what is going on. To understand the internal dynamics, each neighborhood was divided, for purposes of analysis, into two areas: the one more "abandoned" and less gentrified (the "A" area), the other more gentrified and less abandoned (the "B" area).

Tables 8.2 and 8.3 present key indicators of change for the most significant census tracts in each neighborhood. In each table, the most important figures are the percentages in the two right-hand columns. These represent the percentage change in each indicator, for a given census tract, over and above the citywide average.[8] Table 8.2 shows changes in the percentage of those with a college education. One can identify tracts undergoing gentrification by the

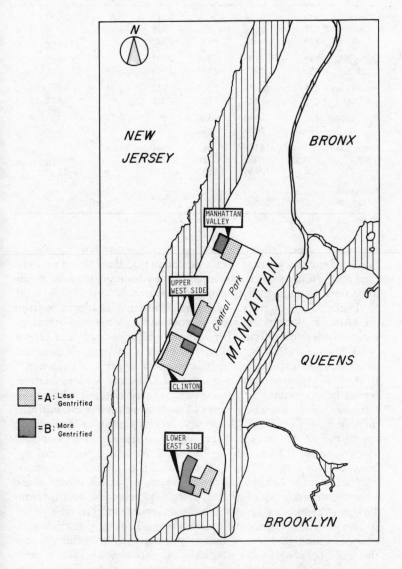

Figure 8.2 Neighborhood study areas in Manhattan.

Table 8.2 Index of population change: college graduates.

Area	Census tract	1970 total population	1970 college graduates	1980 college graduates	Percentage change compared with New York City "A" areas	"B" areas
Clinton	121	5790	455	2079		+28.52
	127	8622	352	916	+7.01	
	139	9617	1632	2822		+12.84
Upper West	149	2102	728	2593		+89.20
Side	153	8177	2198	3545	+16.94	
Manhattan	189	16021	913	824	+1.03	
Valley	195	8823	1731	2495		+9.13
East Harlem	170	9840	321	252	−0.23	
	160.02	3239	655	945		+9.42
Lower East	22.01	8147	512	341	−1.63	
Side	36.02	3437	327	385		+2.06
	38	10456	1137	2271		+11.32
New York City, all		7894862	813563	776557	−0.0047	

extent to which their increase in college-educated population exceeded the city average for the period in question. Based on all of the work done in the study, changes in education level seem the most reliable single indicator of gentrification.[9]

"Pockets" and "borders" of gentrification may be identified from the analysis. Pockets are areas surrounded by dissimilar development; borders those lying between dissimilar areas. In the Upper West Side, formerly a pocket, the process of gentrification has proceeded the furthest, and abandonment is nowhere in evidence.[10] In the "B" portions of Clinton and Manhattan Valley, both of which have evolved as pockets with the growth of Mid-town, Lincoln Center, the Convention Center, and to the north with the influence of Columbia University, gentrification is proceeding apace; their "A" areas are not yet as gentrified. In Lower East Harlem and the Lower East Side, both of which are "borders" between very disparate areas, there are signs of gentrification in the "B" areas (very little in Lower East Harlem, much more on the Lower East Side), but none at all in the "A" areas (the data are from 1980, and recent developments have accentuated the trends).

The pattern becomes even clearer from Table 8.3. It shows the change in high-rent-paying households between 1970 and 1980 for the same census tracts. Rents have caught up with and are now increasing more quickly than the increase in educational level in the

Table 8.3 Index of housing change: tenants paying higher rents.

Area	Census tract	1970 total household	1970 tenants paying $250+	1980 tenants paying $500+	Percentage change compared with New York City	
					"A" areas	"B" areas
Clinton	121	3 327	142	291		+4,43
	127	3 998	37	8	−0.78	
	139	5 963	765	1 109		+5.72
Upper West	149	1 125	261	2 319		+182.98
Side	153	4 900	311	2 281	+30.77	
Manhattan	189	5 236	128	47	−1.60	
Valley	195	3 993	106	287		+4.58
East Harlem	170	3 735	17	0	−0.51	
	160.02	1 345	99	268		+12.52
Lower East	22.01	2 882	0	0	−0.05	
Side	36.02	1 120	0	12		+1.02
	38	5 356	22	58		+0.62
New York City, all		2 836 872	113 776	115 083	−0.0005	

most gentrified area, the Upper West Side. In Clinton, rent increases lagged behind increases in educational levels; there were still some bargains to be had in 1980, but the shape of the future is clear from the change in educational level. The same is true, to a lesser degree, in Manhattan Valley, where the development is not as far along. But the process is underway throughout all three of these pockets of gentrification.

The pattern is different for the two border areas, East Harlem and the Lower East Side. Here we still see a sharp division *within* the area, in which gentrification is clear in the "A" areas, but *both* the education *and* the rent indicators are still below the citywide average change. Here the extent of future gentrification must remain (at least as of the time of the 1980 Census) an open question.

The overall pattern extrapolated from these tables, then, has three components: a substantially unchanged total demand for high-rent units (see "New York City, all" figures in both tables); stronger and clearer movement toward gentrification in "pocket" areas than in "border" areas; and inmigration of population with higher education preceding rent increases, which follow and rise sharply as gentrification reaches maturity.

A limited analysis of changes in market prices was undertaken in each of our neighborhoods,[11] and it supports the expectations derived from the rental data. There are sharp price increases in

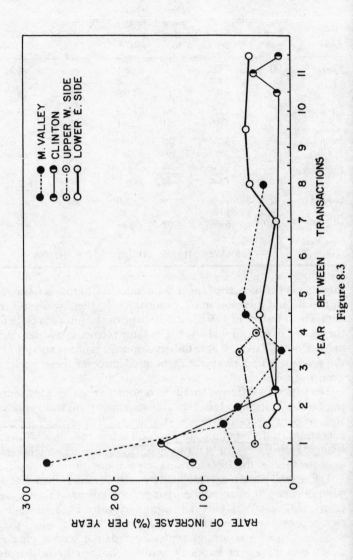

Figure 8.3

gentrifying areas, virtually no activity in abandoning ones. Figure 8.3 summarizes the data. The annualized (uncompounded) rate of increase in price is shown on the vertical axis; the length of time between sales on the horizontal. Although the correlation is not absolute, and the sample is very small indeed, the findings are suggestive as to the role of speculation in the gentrification process.

Real-estate speculation is a strong accompaniment of gentrification. The behavior of speculators, and of the real-estate market generally, is perhaps the single most sensitive indicator of what type of change is or is not going on in a neighborhood. Buyers and sellers in the real-estate market try to guess what will happen in the future; their actions reflect their predictions. When their interest is only short term, housing is purchased for profitable resale rather than to provide dwelling units, their actions are generally referred to as speculation. There is no reason to believe that a restraint on speculation would do more than to slow the rate of gentrification, but that slowing effect might be significant.

The consequences of neighborhood-level changes

Conclusions can be drawn from neighborhood-level data about three aspects of gentrification: its relation to social and economic polarization, to displacement, and to abandonment.

Gentrification contributes to the increasing residential polarization of the city by income, by education, by household composition, and by race. We have already seen the striking variation even within gentrifying neighborhoods classified as "border" areas. The extent of the increasing polarization can be seen even more dramatically at the borough level. Manhattan is of course the most gentrifying borough, the Bronx the least gentrifying and the most abandoned. Between 1970 and 1980, Manhattan increased its number of college-educated residents by 22.9 percent; in the city as a whole it went down 4.5 percent, and in the Bronx it went down 36.1 percent. Per capita income went up 105.2 percent in Manhattan, compared with an increase of 96.5 percent for the city and only 81.5 percent for the Bronx. Median contract rent went up 139 percent, compared with 113.6 percent for the city and 124.1 percent for the Bronx.

The same polarization can be seen graphically in Figure 8.1, discussed earlier. Manhattan gained rich and lost poor households between 1969 and 1981; the Bronx lost both rich and poor households, and lost many more rich than poor (rich and poor being defined as top and bottom income quintiles). The rich are concentrating in Manhattan, and they are leaving all the other boroughs

Table 8.4 Gentrification and racial change.

	1970 per-centage white	1980 per-centage white	per-centage change	Percentage change, white, in comparison with New York City
New York City	77.6	60.8	−15.8	—
Lower East Side				
gentrified tract 38	88.1	76.0	−12.1	+3.7
adjacent tract 36.02	77.4	51.0	−26.4	−10.6
tract 36.01	77.7	42.1	−35.6	−19.8
Clinton				
gentrified tract 139	78.4	72.7	− 5.7	+10.1
tract 135	72.1	47.0	−25.1	−9.3
adjacent tract 127	67.8	47.5	−20.3	−4.5

except Queens, where higher-income families can find better access to larger units. The same process of restructuring is also happening to a lesser extent within each borough.

The direct measurement of displacement from these changes is difficult from census data. The calculations for sample tracts are, however, suggestive. In tract 152, for instance, on the Upper West Side, with a high level of gentrification according to any indicator, the high-income population increased by 4.7 percent (5.3 percent more than the citywide figure), and the low-income population went down by 1.9 percent (10.7 percent lower than the citywide figure). That the increase in high-income residents *caused* the decrease in low-income residents of course cannot be conclusively established from such a simple correlation, nor can the question of whether the departure of the former residents was involuntary, but it defies common sense and daily experience to believe otherwise.

The same type of analysis can be performed for displacement using race rather than income as the indicator. Here we tested a slightly more complex hypothesis (derived from Spain 1981) that gentrification would cause not only a replacement of blacks by whites in tracts of high gentrification, but also a relocation of those displaced blacks into adjacent tracts. Table 8.4 presents the results from three tracts on the Lower East side and three tracts in Clinton. Using citywide change as the benchmark, the percentage change of whites in the tract of higher gentrification increased, and in the adjacent tracts it decreased. The Spain hypothesis seems to be borne out.

Where there is the most substantial abandonment in certain "border" areas, the figures do not show evidence of gentrification, as of 1980. This is true for the "B" parts of the Lower East Side and of East Harlem, for example. The indicators of non-gentrification are shown in Tables 8.2 and 8.3, and are corroborated by figures on race and ethnic change, income and population change, tax arrears, market prices, and losses from the stock. Where the border between gentrification and abandonment actually lies may indeed change; that there is a border is hard to deny.

Gentrification can thus exist side by side with abandonment; each contributes to the other, as their populations move (or are forced to move) in reverse directions, and both contribute to displacement. The process of gentrification operates intensively within very sharply defined boundaries, and can affect negatively the population on both sides of that boundary.

Evidence from other scattered sources supports the conclusions. If not by its newer name, gentrification has nevertheless been anticipated for the Lower East Side since after World War I (Grebler 1952), yet each prediction of imminent change proved wrong. The same is true, if only for more recent periods and to a lesser extent, of East Harlem and Manhattan Valley. Predictions of a turnaround date back 50 years, but have yet to be fulfilled in the terms in which they were cast.

These conclusions are relevant to the question of gentrification as a private market "cure" for abandonment. Leaving apart the point that gentrification benefits an entirely different category of persons than those injured by abandonment, the question is this: how likely is it that gentrification will reverse the trend toward abandonment in affected areas in the immediate future? The data presented here suggest, at least for the areas considered, that the answer is "Not very likely." When and if gentrification comes to areas previously abandoned, it either comes far too late to have any impact on those earlier affected by the abandonment, or it in fact aggravates the displacement caused by abandonment by stimulating a new source of displacement.

Thus the high levels of concern by many residents and housing groups about gentrification in or close to areas of abandonment are justified on three grounds. First, gentrification itself causes displacement. Second, given the lack of city policy dealing with gentrification, there is no certainty where it will occur. The extent of gentrification is of course limited, but no one knows with certainty where it will take place, and therefore many more areas fear it than will face it. Third, gentrification is being put forward, however erroneously, as the answer to abandonment and blight, as a rationale for public inaction. The rejection of gentrification in these nighborhoods is thus an integral part of a program calling for public action to combat abandonment.

We have, in this section, looked at a substantial amount of neighborhood-level data; in the preceding section, the dimensions of the problem at the citywide level were examined. It is now time to return to the more general level, summarize our findings, and examine some of the policy implications.

Present and future housing patterns in New York City

A summary picture of changes in housing in New York City would include the following components:

(a) *There is very substantial abandonment in New York City, displacing (directly, indirectly, or through chain effects) between 77 500 and 150 000 persons a year.* It has a clear spatial pattern: it takes place primarily in a secondary ring between the primary ring of increasingly upper-income housing around the central business district and the outlying suburban-type housing ring at the city's outskirts. These are the major areas of abandonment. Abandonment also takes place in individual areas close to the central business district, where, for historical reasons (working-class occupancy and building stock), the primary ring of upper-income housing did not develop.

(b) *There is very substantial gentrification in New York City, displacing (directly, indirectly, or through chain effects) between 25 000 and 100 000 persons a year in the current period.* Gentrification takes place primarily in areas immediately adjacent to the central business district and the primary ring of upper-income housing around it, radiating to the "border areas" of gentrification. Gentrification also takes place in pockets of housing occupied by poorer households within or on the fringes of the central business district, or in pockets of mixed use (loft areas, for instance) in similar locations. Although not considered here, gentrification may also take place in areas of particular environmental or housing quality convenient to the central business district (such as Brooklyn Heights or Park Slope in New York), and such areas may be more suitable for families than border or pocket areas.

(c) *Gentrification and abandonment are intimately related and mutually reinforcing.* Each directly contributes to displacement, and each aggravates the other. Abandonment aggravates gentrification by pushing out households, some of whom move and gentrify. Gentrification aggravates abandonment by

172

siphoning off people and resources, public and private, and by inflationary pressures in the remaining intermediate areas where higher prices and declining incomes in turn produce abandonment. Each aggravates the problems of finding substitute housing for those displaced, by removing whole areas of the city from realistic consideration and inflating prices even further in others.

(d) *Gentrification and abandonment have a strong spatial relationship to each other.* Gentrification may, after some time, follow abandonment, either at borders between the two or in pockets of abandonment. Generally, however, gentrification and abandonment take place in different parts of the city: in areas of major abandonment, there will not be gentrification, and in areas of major gentrification (or where it is realistically anticipated) there will be no abandonment.

What of the future? All of the factors involved in the restructuring of the city are continuing ones: the shift of the economy from manufacturing to services, the concentration of control and management, the multiplying international linkages of business, the proportionately increasing need for managerial, professional, and technical personnel, and the decreasing need for unskilled manufacturing and service workers, the increasing polarization of the population economically, the expanded needs of business for downtown commercial and office space, the tendency of government and of the real-estate industry to follow and aggravate the results of these processes at the residential and neighborhood level. If these are the factors that produce both gentrification and abandonment, then there is no reason to expect a change of direction in the housing market.

The pace of gentrification and abandonment will, however, vary. Frank DeGiovanni, in his careful study of gentrification in multiple cities, found that "nationwide macroeconomic changes" (DeGiovanni 1983: 33) seemed decisive in determining the extent of activity at any given point. If our theoretical explanation of gentrification/ abandonment is correct, then "macroeconomic changes" would *not* be synonymous with "prosperity" or "recession".[12] Rather, prosperity at the upper end of the economic spectrum and depression at the lower end are the key factors. These are only ambiguously captured by measures of national economic growth, which implicitly assume that both ends of the economic spectrum will prosper or suffer together. The historical facts are to the contrary. Indeed, we are witnessing today a period of high corporate profits and high unemployment: exactly the combination that theory would lead us to believe would most exacerbate displacement.

At the same time, the willingness of the government to comply with the wishes and preferences of those most decisive in the private market has never been greater. Public expenditures in major areas of abandonment are being reduced, and such expenditures in major areas of gentrification are being increased. The closing of hospitals, fire stations, schools, and police stations, and the generally and rapidly declining conditions of public services such as garbage pickup, accelerate abandonment. The use of Urban Development Action Grant funds for midtown hotel development, the financing of the Convention Center, and the various tax incentive programs, are all typical of actions fostering gentrification.[13] Public abandonment of some neighborhoods, following private disinvestment (redlining), and public investment in other neighborhoods, following strong private interest, both serve substantially to aggravate displacement.

By exactly the same token, however, public policy could reduce, indeed eliminate, displacement. Government plays a major role in land-use questions, and the courts have increasingly come to recognize the power (and indeed the obligation) to regulate land use for the public welfare.[14] If the objective is to improve the conditions of those with the most serious housing problems, the basic concepts are not difficult to lay out. They would run as follows.

The polarization, both of the economy and of the housing and neighborhood conditions that flow from it, must be reduced. The economic policies required for this purpose are beyond the scope of this chapter. The housing policies required are, however, relatively clear. Neighborhoods in danger of either abandonment or gentrification must be given control of their own destinies. Resources must be made available to them adequate for that purpose. Public policies dealing with housing (including the control of private actions, particularly speculative ones) must have as their clear objective the elimination of displacement in all its forms, whether by abandonment or by gentrification. Such policies have citywide implications and must be implemented citywide. The specific programs by which this could be accomplished have been presented in detail elsewhere.[15] The problem is not the lack of these ideas.

At the same time, some approaches that will *not* reduce displacement or improve housing for those most in need can be identified. Most importantly, gentrification does *not* provide the "cure" for abandonment. In the first place, gentrification will in fact only succeed abandonment in a limited number of neighborhoods (only pockets and perhaps some borders, but certainly not in centres of abandonment) by any operation of the private market. And, if it did, the cure would be as bad as the disease, because gentrification is as inherently linked with the displacement of lower-income house-holds as is abandonment itself. Public resources invested in such fashion as to "upgrade" a neighborhood (gentrify it), by introduc-ing higher-income or status groups into an area, will not help those of "lower" status already there; on the contrary.[16]

The large question is not *whether* abandonment can be avoided, gentrification controlled, displacement eliminated, or even *how* these things can be done, but rather whether there is the desire to do them. That is a question that can only be answered in the political arena.

Notes

1 For a fuller formal definition, see Marcuse (1981).
2 The adjustment procedure to include chain displacement is too complex to lay out here, but essentially it involves starting with Stegman's (1982) estimate, which covers apparent physical aban-donment, and adjusting to include economic abandonment.
3 It differs from other census results in its unusual attention to vacant units, and the detail of its data on the nature of such vacancies. The purpose of the triennial surveys is to determine the "vacancy rate" for rental units, needed under state enabling legislation to determine whether or not there is a "housing emergency," defined as a situation in which the "vacancy rate" is less than 5 percent. The most recent survey (for 1981) is contained in the report by Michael Stegman (1982); the preceding one, for 1978, is by this writer (Marcuse 1979). Both contain detailed discussions of reliability and interpretation. The 1978 report also contains a general discussion of the process of housing decline and its relation to vacancies and abandonment (Marcuse 1979: 128–34).
4 This is based on the city average of 2.5 persons per household, but probably a conservative assumption here, since abandonment tends to displace poorer, and thus normally larger, households (Stegman 1982: 2, 241).
5 Mayor's Office on SRO Housing; New York State Department of Social Services.
6 These figures are generally consistent with the few other detailed local studies that exist, which generally cover only direct displacement. In Seattle, a study estimated the figure at 1.4 percent of the population; in Denver, another study estimated 1.1 percent; in Portland, a study estimated 1.4 percent, with 40 percent of these from gentrification (see Ch. 9). If comparable percentages were applied to New York City, the

estimate would be 39 200 displaced, 15 680 from gentrification. This is not far from the figures in the text above. The figures might be expected to be somewhat higher in New York City, an extreme example of most urban phenomena.

7   Patterns of gentrification vary significantly by household type, even though they have a common etiology. The conventional pattern involves young couples or singles as the first gentrifying agents, households with young children moving in only later. This is plausible, given the difference in community facilities needed by the two groups, and particularly the importance of schools for young children. There are, however, a few neighborhoods where venturesome parents move in and gentrify, because prices are more favorable for their larger space needs and schools seem tolerable. In New York City such areas of "family gentrification" exist primarily in Brooklyn and perhaps Queens, but not, to this writer's knowledge, in Manhattan, with the possible exception of Hamilton Heights.

8   This methodology is similar to that used by Daphne Spain, of the Bureau of the Census's Center for Demographic Studies, and by Karl Taeuber in his studies of residential segregation (e.g. Taeuber 1982).

9   The study examined a substantial number of other potential indicators of gentrification. Two other indicators seem reasonably reliable (as well as theoretically plausible): changes in income, and race or ethnic origin. They are included in Figure 8.2.

10 Tract 149, near Lincoln Center, had major new construction; all other tracts were substantially built up in 1970. The changes they have experienced in the past decade meet the formal definition of gentrification.

11 The full data are reported in Marcuse (1984). See also Porras (1983).

12 At least not to the extent that these terms are defined using indicators of gross national product, growth rates, personal income, or other measures undifferentiated by group or class.

13 See the regular accounts in *City Limits: Community Housing News*, published monthly in New York City.

14 See the landmark Mt. Laurel II decision of the New Jersey Supreme Court (Southern Burlington County NAACP, 1983).

15 Major suggestions include the proposals for inclusionary zoning and a housing trust fund put forward by the Center for Metropolitan Action at Queens College, CUNY, and the Pratt Institute for Community and Environmental Development in Brooklyn; the proposals put forward by the present author in a report to the Community Service Society of New York; the initiatives of the Association for Neighborhood and Housing Development; and the plans of a number of thoughtful community groups in East Harlem, the Lower East Side, Brooklyn, the South Bronx, Clinton, and elsewhere. See Pratt Institute (1983).

16 The recent effort to use city-owned buildings in the Lower East Side for "artists' housing," heavily subsidized by the City, is an apparent example of such a policy; artists were certainly perceived by the

community, and perhaps intended by many in city government, to be the opening wedge in introducing a new higher-status demographic group into a community suffering for years from abandonment, but potentially well located for gentrification.

9

The anatomy of displacement in the United States

RICHARD T. LeGATES and CHESTER HARTMAN

With the exception of five pioneering studies (Black 1975, Gale 1976, National Urban Coalition 1977, Grier & Grier 1978, Clay 1979), the early literature on gentrification-related displacement was not grounded in empirical research. As late as 1979, the United States Department of Housing and Urban Development's major report on displacement cited only two empirical studies on what happens to displacees (US Department of Housing and Urban Development 1979).

In the late 1970s, there appeared a great outpouring of empirical studies of gentrification displacement in individual neighborhoods. These studies had the virtue of providing the grist from which theory could be built, but stopped short of attempting to explain the phenomena they described.

Today, attention is turning toward these explanations as researchers attempt to place what is now known about gentrification and displacement in the wider context of theories of urban change in capitalist societies.

This chapter is based upon research undertaken by the authors between 1979 and 1981 (LeGates & Hartman 1981). It draws upon 16 recent displacement studies as the basis for a description of the gentrification-caused displacement in the United States. It provides some of the data documenting one of the most trenchant social consequences of gentrification. The studies include research by a federal government agency (Hu 1979), city offices of planning and policy analysis (City of Portland Office of Planning and Development 1978, City of Seattle Office of Policy Planning 1978, Callan 1979, Flahive & Gordon 1979), a consulting firm (Development Economics Group 1977), professors of economics, sociology and geography (Collier *et al.* 1979, Goodman & Weissbrod 1979, Laska

& Spain 1979, Munski & O'Loughlin 1979) and student theses (Pattison 1977, Rosenberg 1977, Leach 1979, Park 1979, Sands 1979, Seifel 1979, Sieverding 1979). All were completed in the late 1970s. The studies were remarkably consistent in the thrust of their questions. The researchers sought to obtain demographic profiles of the inmovers to gentrifying neighborhoods, to profile outmovers and to determine the location, cost and adequacy of outmovers' post-move shelter. Because the studies were independently conducted, the format for presenting information was not uniform. This chapter preserves the format and the phraseology of the original studies. The pieces of this jigsaw puzzle are a bit ragged, but the picture of gentrification-caused displacement that emerges is quite clear and certainly more serviceable than any image previously available. Collectively, the 16 recent city and neighborhood studies of gentrification displacement provide a reasonable picture of who inmovers are, who outmovers are and what happens to them, and what the nature of the displacement process is. They also permit a focused image of the conflicts inherent in that process.

We have not tried to develop a comprehensive explanation of gentrification displacement in comparative perspective. Rather, we hope this summary of empirical research on gentrification displacement in the United States will encourage others to replicate our work in other countries, and make use of our findings to develop policies that address what is clearly a massive global, structural phenomenon with many damaging effects for displacees.

Characteristics of inmovers

Who are the persons moving into gentrifying neighborhoods, and how is their movement related to global changes in the world economy? If selected world cities are becoming centers of global corporate management and information processing, we would expect to see related demographic shifts worldwide. Managers – young, affluent, well-educated members of dominant elites – should be moving into prime urban neighborhoods close to emerging headquarters areas. Further investigation might uncover a global patterning in which such a change is well advanced in a small number of world cities, but echoed to a lesser degree in others.

Because they move into a defined geographical area, inmovers are by definition relatively easy to track down. Accordingly, the recent studies contain substantial evidence concerning inmovers' characteristics. Although the studies were designed and carried out independently, many sought the same information: age, family structure, income, race and occupation. Very strong patterns emerge from the studies and make it possible to construct a profile of the typical inmover.

Prior location

Most inmovers to gentrifying neighborhoods have moved from within the city itself and not from surrounding suburbs or other jurisdictions. Evidence from the recent studies corroborates the view that the "back-to-the-city movement" is a misnomer (Gale 1976). Eight studies surveying inmovers to nine different gentrifying neighborhoods asked their samples to report the location from which they had moved (Development Economics Group 1977, Pattison 1977, Hu 1979, Laska & Spain 1979, Park 1979, Sands 1979, Seifel 1979, Sieverding 1979). An average of 64 percent of the inmovers in these studies moved from within the same city. The figures ranged from 48 percent to 100 percent (LeGates & Hartman 1981). A study of San Francisco's Duboce Triangle (Park 1979) found that 50 percent of the inmovers had not been living in San Francisco five years earlier. The studies even suggest that the term "inmover" may be a misnomer. Two studies sought to determine the proportion of "inmovers" who moved *from within the neighborhood itself*. Both found substantial numbers: 33 percent in West Cambridge (Pattison 1977) and 40 percent in a sample of New Orleans neighborhoods (Laska & Spain 1979).

The number of inmovers to gentrifying neighborhoods decreases as one moves away from the city. Suburbs adjacent to the city in which the gentrifying neighborhood under study is located accounted for a range of 0 percent (Sieverding 1979) to 38 percent (Hu 1979) of all inmovers and averaged 9 percent. For cities like St. Paul, San Francisco and Boston, located near one or more other large cities, movement from other *cities* within the Standard Metropolitan Statistical Area (SMSA) was substantial (Pattison 1977, Park 1979, Sands 1979). Movement to gentrifying neighborhoods from elsewhere in the state and from out of state accounted for a very small percentage of immigration.

Available information suggests that the degree to which inmovers are essentially suburban or urban in their origins, as opposed to their immediate past residential location, varies. It has been hypothesized that even though inmovers may have been living within the city just prior to their move into the gentrifying neighborhood, they are essentially suburban in origin (Weiler 1978). The study of gentrifying neighborhoods in New Orleans contributes the most direct evidence and shows that 50 percent of the inmovers had grown up within the city of New Orleans itself (Laska & Spain 1979).

Age

Inmovers tend to be relatively homogeneous in age and are principally young adults. Although some elderly inmovers are reported in certain gentrifying neighborhoods, few children are. Of the inmovers to St. Paul's Ramsey Hill neighborhood, 45 percent were in the 30 to 39 age range, and 23 percent were in the 19 to 29 age group (Sands 1979). In West Cambridge, 46 percent of the buyers and 45 percent of the renters were in the 25 to 45 age group (Pattison 1977), and in Boston's Bay Village, 42 percent of the buyers and 43 percent of the renters were between 25 and 45 (Pattison, 1977). The dominance of young adults among inmovers was also documented for gentrifying neighborhoods in the District of Columbia (Development Economics Group 1977), St. Louis (Hu 1979), Cincinnati (Sieverding 1979), Boston's South End (Seifel 1979), and San Francisco (Park 1979).

Although the proportion of elderly inmovers varied considerably, most gentrifying neighborhoods for which age data were reported showed some elderly people moving in. The St. Paul neighborhood was an exception, with no inmovers over 60 years of age reported (Sands 1979). On the other hand, the second and third largest groups of purchasers of District of Columbia condominiums were reported to be elderly (over 65) and near elderly (from the mid-50s to 65) (Development Economics Group 1977). Other studies reported a proportion of elderly between these extremes.

Only two studies, the West Cambridge study (Pattison 1977) and the sample of gentrifying neighborhoods throughout New Orleans (Laska & Spain 1979), reported significant numbers of children among inmovers. One hypothesis sees the quality of neighborhood schools as the most important independent variable explaining the locational decisions of young adults with children. Because inner-city school systems are seldom good, few young parents will choose to settle in inner-city neighborhoods if they have another choice. The same two studies indicate the importance of the entire metropolitan school system, both public and private, in parents' decisions. The West Cambridge neighborhood was reported to have excellent public schools. New Orleans, however, was reported to have a poor public school system. The apparent paradox is explained by the fact that in West Cambridge many inmovers were attracted to the neighborhoods because the schools appeared to be the best available to them, but in New Orleans many inmovers with children apparently judged the entire New Orleans metropolitan public school system inferior and assumed that their children would go to private or parochial schools. Accordingly, location within a bad inner-city school system did not constitute an important disincentive to them.

Race

Inmovers are primarily white. Of the inmovers in St. Louis, 90 percent (Hu 1979), of those in New Orleans, 92 percent (Laska & Spain 1979) and of those in St. Paul, 97 percent (Sands 1979) were white. Inmovers to District of Columbia condominiums were described as "virtually all white" (Development Economics Group 1977). No study reported significant numbers of racial minorities moving into gentrifying neighborhoods.

Income

Inmover income is concentrated in the middle to upper end of the income range, well above city and SMSA medians and much higher than the income of the residents of gentrifying neighborhoods. Substantial numbers of high-income, but very few lower-income, inmovers were reported.

Condominium purchasers in the District of Columbia surveyed in 1976 had median incomes of $22 700 in 1975 (Development Economics Group 1977). The median 1978 income of inmovers to Cincinnati's Over-the-Rhine neighborhood was $14 213 (Sieverding 1979). San Francisco's Duboce Triangle had an average 1978 income (expressed in 1969 dollars) of $12 041 (Park 1979). The clustering of high-income inmovers and the absence of low-income ones is illustrated by the three studies which provided the following precise income ranges for inmover samples (Development Economics Group 1977, Laska & Spain 1979, Sand 1979):

| New Orleans | | Washington, DC | | St. Paul | |
$	%	$	%	$	%
0–20 000	33	0–10 000	6	0– 5 000	2
20 000–30 000	27	10 000–14 999	16	5 000– 9 999	4
30 000+	41	15 000–19 999	20	10 000–14 999	10
		20 000–24 999	15	15 000–19 999	24
		25 000+	42	20 000–24 999	18
				25 000–24 999	12
				30 000+	31

Family structure

Small households, consisting of a single individual or a couple, typify inmovers. Only two neighborhoods, West Cambridge (Pattison 1977) and New Orleans (Laska & Spain 1979), had significant numbers of conventional nuclear families with children. In another neighborhood, a substantial gay population and large numbers of unrelated individuals living together were reported (Park 1979). Most of the city- and neighborhood-level gentrification studies found a substantial number of single individuals among inmovers. Single individuals constituted 31 percent of Seattle's inmovers (City of Seattle Office of Policy Planning 1978), 37 percent of St. Paul's (Sands 1979), 52 percent in Boston's Bay Village (Pattison 1977) and 72 percent in Cincinatti's Over-the-Rhine neighborhood (Sieverding 1979). With the exception of the two studies reporting children, the other studies found very small average household sizes.

Occupation

The head of most inmover households is employed in a professional or managerial capacity. Some lower status, white-collar sales and clerical workers are also among the inmovers. Members of other occupational groups, or persons not in the workforce, are rare. In St. Paul and in the New Orleans neighborhoods surveyed, 75 percent of the inmovers were employed in professional or managerial work (Laska & Spain 1979, Sands 1979). In Boston's Bay Village 55 percent of the buyers and 57 percent in West Cambridge were professionals (Pattison 1977). Of the St. Louis sample, 50 percent consisted of persons in professional and technical occupations (Hu 1979), and 37 percent of inmovers to San Francisco's Duboce Triangle were professionals (Park 1979).

Clerical and sales workers are the next most frequently found categories. They accounted for 12 percent of the St. Paul inmovers (Sands 1979), 15 percent of the West Cambridge inmovers (Pattison 1977) and 30 percent of Boston's Bay Village buyers (Pattison 1977). Smaller numbers of sales and clerical workers were reported moving into other gentrifying neighborhoods. Virtually no craftspersons, operatives or laborers, either skilled or unskilled, were reported among inmovers. Only the District of Columbia condominium study noted a significant number of persons either not in the labor force or unemployed. More than one-third of those surveyed, the large group of elderly purchasers, were not in the workforce (Development Economics Group 1977).

Several studies noted an influx of persons with occupational skills related to housing rehabilitation. An astonishing one-fourth of all inmovers to the West Cambridge area were architects (Pattison 1977).

San Francisco affords the best example of how alternative life-style groups are making conventional occupational and class analysis difficult in some gentrifying neighborhoods. During the ten-year gentrification period, the number of self-employed craftspersons in the neighborhood increased dramatically (Park 1979). Most members of this group were white, educated children from middle- or upper-income families who had chosen housing-related blue-collar work. Those employed part-time had low incomes; those who worked full-time often had incomes comparable to or in excess of white-collar workers in the area.

The patterns that emerge from the above studies are so strong and consistent that it is possible to construct a profile of the typical inmover household. The household moving into a gentrifying neighborhood during the 1970s was white and moved from within the same city. It was composed of one or two young adults, either married or unmarried, but without children. Typically, one or more members were employed in a professional or managerial occupation and earned a substantial income well above the SMSA median.

Characteristics of outmovers

Just who is displaced from gentrifying neighborhoods? Are blue-collar, low-income, racial-minority, elderly, and other specific types of households always displaced to make way for a new managerial elite? Analysis of gentrifying neighborhoods in American cities shows that the patterns are complex, and some intuitive explanations are not correct. To what degree these findings hold true in other countries bears investigation.

Outmovers are more difficult to locate than inmovers. By definition they have moved away from a concentrated area and may, therefore, be difficult to track. Outmovers who are found are likely to represent a sample skewed toward higher-income and higher-status households unless surveys are carefully designed to account for the greater difficulty of tracking lower-income and more-marginal households. Fewer studies have attempted to track outmovers than inmovers, and their findings are less authoritative. Nonetheless, recent city- and neighborhood-level studies of the characteristics of outmovers contribute to an understanding of who they are. The studies show that there is a wider range in the age, race, income, family structure and occupations among outmovers than among inmovers.

Age

The range of ages among outmovers is suggested by the St. Paul neighborhood-level study which had the finest age breakdown. The following age range was reported: 1 to 18, 29 percent; 19 to 29, 14 percent; 30 to 39, 24 percent; 40 to 49, 11 percent; 50 to 59, 9 percent; 60 to 69, 6 percent; and 70 and over, 5 percent (Sands 1979). Of the displacees tracked from three South Baltimore neighborhoods, 29 percent were under 35, 43 percent were over 35 but under 60, and 27 percent were over 60 (Goodman & Weissbrod 1979). Other city and neighborhood studies also found a range of outmover ages.

Elderly persons comprise a significant proportion of the outmover populations, a particularly important finding in light of the difficult psychological and other life adjustments which elderly displacees face (Myers 1978). The primary group of persons displaced from District of Columbia units being turned into condominiums was elderly, and the second largest group was the near elderly (Development Economics Group 1977). In Seattle 30 percent of the outmovers were reported to be over 61 (City of Seattle Office of Policy Planning 1978). In St. Paul, 20 percent of the outmovers were over 50, and 11 percent were over 60 (Sands 1979). Other studies also show a significant number of elderly outmovers.

Children were reported among displacees in some neighborhoods. Of the outmovers from the St. Paul neighborhood, 29 percent were between the ages of 1 and 18 (Sands 1979). A marked decrease in the number of children in San Francisco's Duboce Triangle neighborhood was reported as gentrification progressed (Park 1979). Residents estimated at only six the total number of children living in Boston's Bay Village after gentrification (Pattison 1977).

Race

At the present time, most outmovers are white. A substantial and growing number are nonwhite, however, because gentrification is beginning to touch some predominantly minority neighborhoods and because the large minority subpopulations in some gentrifying neighborhoods tend to be disproportionately displaced. Most gentrification at the present time is occurring in white neighborhoods. One recent review of Polk data on the characteristics of 967 gentrifying tracts in nine cities concluded:

> By and large gentrification of central city neighborhoods is *not* occurring in the neighborhoods in which the existing literature would lead us to expect it. Net gains in professional households, rather than occurring in the core, predominantly poor and minority neighborhoods are more likely to occur in neighborhoods with fewer vacant units, with more owner-occupied units and with more professional households already. (Henig 1979)

Because the neighborhoods in which gentrification is occurring are white, it is not surprising that most outmovers are also white. White outmovers made up 96 percent of all outmovers in the District of Columbia (Collier *et al.* 1979), 90 percent in St. Louis (Hu 1979), 92 percent in Seattle (City of Seattle Office of Policy Planning 1978) and 93 percent in St. Paul (Sands 1979). Most displacees from West Cambridge and from Boston's Bay Village neighborhoods were also white (Pattison 1977).

Gentrification displacement is, however, already touching significant numbers of minorities. This is occurring for two reasons. First, in some cities in which gentrification has already progressed through the most desirable white neighborhoods, it is reaching into more deteriorated, primarily minority neighborhoods. Second, minorities constitute a significant subpopulation in many predominantly white gentrifying neighborhoods, and, in a number of cities, minorities have been disproportionately displaced from racially mixed neighborhoods.

The District of Columbia and San Francisco are the two cities nationwide in which gentrification has progressed furthest. In both cities, neighborhoods that are predominantly minority are undergoing gentrification. One long-term longitudinal study documents the process by which virtually all previous residents were displaced from four formerly black District of Columbia neighborhoods during a process the author terms "reinvasion" (Zietz 1979). Gentrification is reaching other District of Columbia neighborhoods, including Adams-Morgan and Capitol Hill. In San Francisco, gentrification is occurring in such predominantly black neighborhoods as the Western Addition, Hayes Valley and the substantially Hispanic Mission District. Displacement has also been reported in Cincinnati's substantially black Over-the-Rhine neighborhood (Sieverding 1979).

A number of gentrifying neighborhoods, which were predominantly white before gentrification began, had large black subpopulations, e.g. 34 percent in the New Orleans neighborhoods studied[1] (Laska & Spain 1979) and 31 percent in one District of Columbia census tract examined (Collier *et al.* 1979). Three neighborhood studies reported that blacks have been disproportionately displaced

186

from former racially mixed neighborhoods as gentrification proceeded. Those studies are from Boston's South End (Seifel 1979), San Francisco's Duboce Triangle (Park 1979) and Seattle (Leach 1979).

Income

In the neighborhoods studied, average outmover income was in the lower middle range, typically between $8000 and $14 000 in 1980 dollars. Substantial ranges from very low incomes to quite high incomes among outmovers have also been documented. All city and neighborhood gentrification displacement studies which reported median income data for outmovers found median income to be in the lower middle range. In Baltimore, more than four-fifths of the households in the sample had incomes below $19 000, and a majority, 54 percent, earned under $9000 (Goodman & Weissbrod 1979). Outmovers from District of Columbia condominiums had an average 1975 household income of $11 875 (Development Economics Group 1977). In St. Louis, 75 percent of the outmovers were reported to have incomes below the 1976 St. Louis SMSA average (Hu 1979). Forty-two percent of Seattle's outmovers had incomes in the $7600 to $17 500 range (City of Seattle Office of Policy Planning 1978). Boston's Bay Village outmovers were characterized as lower-middle income (Pattison 1977), and Cincinnati's Over-the-Rhine outmovers were below average income (Sieverding 1979).

Studies that recorded specific levels of outmover income showed quite a range. Generally, they displayed substantial numbers of low- and very low-income persons and a smaller, though significant, number of high-income persons among the outmovers. The most precise range of outmover incomes reported (Sands 1979) was:

St. Paul $	%
0– 5 000	19
5 000– 9 999	23
10 000–14 999	16
15 000–19 999	14
20 000–24 999	9
25 000–29 999	7
Over 30 000	12

District of Columbia condominium outmovers were reportedly trimodal, showing a group of lower-middle-income, young renters with an average income of $12 000, a group of nearly poor, elderly renters with an average income of $8500, and a group of relatively well-off, near elderly with an average income of $25 000 (Development Economics Group 1977). Seattle's outmover income clustered in the lower-middle range, but 26 percent of the outmovers had household incomes of under $7600, and 32 percent had incomes over $17 000 (City of Seattle Office of Policy Planning 1978). Seventeen percent of an outmover sample from New Orleans' Irish Channel and Lower Garden neighborhoods were reportedly on welfare (Rosenberg 1977).

Several studies ascribe the variation in income to the existence of distinct subpopulations among the outmovers. For example, within Boston's Bay Village neighborhood of predominantly lower-middle-income renters and homeowners was a distinct group of poor, rooming-house tenants (Pattison 1977). Among District of Columbia condominium buyers, income clearly broke along the age lines described above (Development Economics Group 1977). In another District of Columbia study of a single census tract, outmovers' income was sharply divided along racial lines, with the average household income of white renters ($15 289) being almost double the average household income of black renters ($8700) (Collier *et al.* 1979).

Family structure

A range of family structures is reported among outmovers, and includes single individuals, both male and female, families with and without children, and alternative household structures. Three studies indicate a substantial proportion of families with children among the outmovers. Forty-three percent of the outmover households in Portland had children (City of Portland Office of Planning and Development 1978), and Seattle reportedly had children in 32 percent of its outmover households (City of Seattle Office of Policy Planning 1978), with the figure rising to 55 percent in Seattle's gentrifying Madronna neighborhood (Leach 1979). Other studies reported substantial numbers of single individuals. Of the outmovers in the St. Paul sample 41 percent were single and another 29 percent were divorced, widowed or separated (Sands 1979). Forty-four percent of the sample from New Orleans' Irish Channel and Lower Garden neighborhoods were single (Rosenberg 1977). Several studies noted substantial numbers of "empty nesters" (elderly or near elderly households with grown children no longer at home) among the displacees. Fifty percent of the outmovers in the St. Louis sample were over 50 with no children living at home (Hu 1979). Some studies reported persons in various kinds of alternative living arrangements. For example, outmovers in New Orleans neighborhoods included a number of extended families and households composed of unrelated persons (Rosenberg 1977). In summary, outmover households represented a broad spectrum of family types and were much more diverse than the inmovers.

Occupation

Most displacee household heads are employed in either blue-collar or low-status white-collar (clerical and sales) work. There are substantial numbers of unemployed and welfare-dependent households as well as surprisingly large numbers of higher-status professional households among the displacees.

Both blue-collar and low-status white-collar workers were present in significant numbers in all outmover samples. The principal occupations prior to gentrification in Boston's Bay Village (Pattison 1977), West Cambridge (Pattison 1977), and Cincinnati (Sieverding 1979) were blue-collar workers. Lower-status white-collar workers were reported to be the numerical majority in San Francisco (Park 1979), St. Louis (Hu 1979) and St. Paul (Sands 1979).

Individuals engaged in high-status occupations and welfare-dependent individuals were also reported among the outmovers. In St. Paul, a surprisingly high 29 percent of the outmovers were professionals (Sands 1979). The neighborhoods also contained low-income persons, frequently in rooming houses, residential hotels and the less desirable rental stock. Seventeen percent of the outmovers in New Orleans' Irish Channel and Lower Garden neighborhoods were on welfare (Rosenberg 1977).

In summary, outmovers are a much more heterogeneous group than inmovers. It is not possible to profile a typical outmover household because of the range of characteristics involved. The range of outmover ages is quite broad, including children, young and middle-aged adults, and elderly. The majority of outmovers are white, but the number of minorities is substantial and growing. Most outmovers are lower-middle income. There are, however, significant numbers of low- and very low-income households as well as some high-income households among the outmovers. The range of family structure is substantial, including single individuals, childless couples, families with children and other groupings. The occupational characteristics of outmovers are also diverse. The bulk

189

of outmovers are either blue-collar or low-status white-collar (sales and clerical) workers. Outmovers also include substantial numbers of unemployed and welfare-dependent households and a surprising number of persons employed in professional and other high-status work.

What happens to displacees?

What happens to displacees from gentrifying neighborhoods? Do they disperse throughout the metropolitan region, cluster in inner-city ghettos, double up, make successive moves as gentrification proceeds, or what? Do they find affordable alternative housing or do they end up paying more and/or accepting less? Are impacts on displacees widely different depending upon who they are? These are important policy questions.

Until the late 1970s there was much conjecture, but little evi-dence, about what happened to outmovers. The 1979 HUD *Displacement Report* cited only two case studies which discussed the fate of outmovers, noting that the outmovers in these studies quickly found alternative shelter which was apparently adequate and affordable (US Department of Housing and Urban Development 1979). Popular accounts of gentrification displacement frequently assert that outmovers are geographically dispersed into less desirable dwelling units and neighborhoods at higher costs. The recent neighborhood- and city-level gentrification displacement studies provide some empirical evidence regarding these and other issues.

Location

Clustering is the most striking aspect of outmovers' post-move location. All studies found that outmovers tended to resettle close to, or indeed within, the neighborhoods from which they moved. Just as the word *inmover* was found to be something of a mis-nomer, the word *outmover* is misleading when applied uniformly to households within a gentrifying neighborhood which move somewhere else. It often appears that the "somewhere else" is within the same neighborhood. Three studies document the high incidence of outmovers resettling within the same neighborhood: 29 percent in one District of Columbia census tract (Collier *et al.* 1979), 46 percent of a sample of outmovers on welfare in one Baltimore neighborhood (Callan 1979), and a large number of the outmovers from Boston's South End (Seifel 1979). Most studies were not designed in such a way that intra-neighborhood moves of so-called outmovers are clearly identified.

Those outmovers who leave a gentrifying neighborhood tend to cluster near it. Thirty-three percent of two District of Columbia outmover samples in two separate studies relocated adjacent to the gentrifying neighborhood (Development Economics Group 1977, Collier *et al.* 1979). A study of gentrifying New Orleans neighborhoods found 43 percent of the outmovers relocating either in or near their old neighborhoods (Laska & Spain 1979). Clustering was also reported in Baltimore (Callan 1979, Goodman & Weissbrod 1979), San Francisco (Park 1979) and St. Paul (Sands 1979). The overwhelming majority of outmovers who do not resettle within or adjacent to the same neighborhood resettle within the same city. The studies reported that, to the extent that some outmovers left the cities in question, they tended to cluster in adjoining suburbs. Presently, there is little empirical evidence to support the assertion that significant numbers of black displacees are relocating in the suburbs. As indicated, most displacees are white. Available evidence further suggests that black displacees are equally as likely to cluster close to the neighborhoods from which they move.

The clustering effect documented in the recent studies raises the important issue of multiple displacements. That some households were repeatedly displaced as the boundaries of urban renewal projects were expanded has been well documented in the urban renewal displacement studies by Litchfield (1961) and Hartman (1964, 1971). Recent gentrification–displacement studies have noted instances of double or more displacements in the District of Columbia (Development Economics Group 1977), Cincinnati (Sieverding 1979), St. Paul (Sands 1979), and Boston's South End (Seifel 1979). It is likely that this phenomenon is occurring elsewhere as well.

Shelter costs

Recent gentrification–displacement studies report that outmovers' shelter costs almost always rise, sometimes modestly and sometimes dramatically. Lower-income residents bear particularly heavy shelter cost increase burdens in relation to their ability to pay. In three cities, post-move shelter costs were reported to have increased only slightly. In Seattle, 87 percent of the displacees were reported to be paying approximately 6 percent more than their former rent, with only 12 percent paying over 8 percent more (City of Seattle Office of Policy Planning 1978). The overall increase in median monthly shelter payments for displacees from District of Columbia units converted to condominiums was reported to be 2 percent

(Development Economics Group 1977). This figure is hard to square with other data in the report showing 13 percent increases in the average rent paid by displacees for one- and two-bedroom apartments. The Portland study concluded that outmover rents increased only slightly (City of Portland Office of Planning and Development 1978).

Two studies found substantial post-move rent increases. In St. Paul, post-move costs increased 33 percent[2] (Sands 1979). A sample of outmovers from South Baltimore was found to be paying an average of 53 percent more for new dwelling units (Goodman & Weissbrod 1979). No study reported that average shelter costs remained the same or declined.

The best evidence that lower-income residents bear particularly heavy rent increase burdens came from the St. Paul study. It analyzed previous and present rents of households which were and remained renters. Of 26 respondents, 3 were paying less rent, 3 were paying the same, and 20 were paying more rent. The absolute rent increases for some of the lowest-income renters were as great as or greater than the absolute rent increases of more affluent renters. Proportional shelter costs of renters almost always were more severe for lower-income renters than for more-affluent ones. A citywide sample of displacees in the Seattle study revealed that between moderate- and upper-income households, the percentage experiencing substantial housing cost increases was reasonably uniform. Among the households which had experienced increases, the percentage experiencing resultant budgetary strain was much higher for the lower-income households earning $7500 or less, for 37 percent of the households in the $7600 to $17500 range and for only 17 percent of the households with incomes over $17000 (City of Seattle Office of Policy Planning 1978). A study of District of Columbia outmovers made a somewhat related point about moving costs. The study concluded that black outmovers, whose income was only a little over half that of white outmovers, paid slightly lower absolute moving expenses, but, as a percentage of income, their moving expenses were 40 percent higher (Collier *et al*. 1979).

Satisfaction with new dwelling units and neighborhoods

Outmovers' evaluations of the comparative quality of their pre- and post-move dwelling units and neighborhood show a considerable range of subjective feelings. Outmover satisfaction is inversely correlated with income. The lower the household income, the more likely the household is to feel that the new dwelling unit and/or neighborhood is less satisfactory than the former one.

Table 9.1 Outmovers' post-move satisfaction with their new dwelling units (expressed in percentage terms).

	Better	Worse	Same	Unreported
District of Columbia	59	41	—	—
District of Columbia condominiums	38	28	26	10
Seattle	51	29	20	–
St. Louis		Generally better		
St. Paul	60	10	29	4

Existing gentrification-displacement studies have not attempted to obtain and analyze objective measures of dwelling-unit quality such as size, condition or site characteristics. Such objective measurement of housing quality is notoriously difficult. Some studies have instead surveyed outmovers to determine their subjective evaluation of how their new dwelling units and neighborhoods compare with their former ones.

Five studies from four cities reported on outmovers' post-move satisfaction with their new dwelling units (Development Economics Group 1977, City of Seattle Office of Policy Planning 1978, Collier *et al.* 1979, Hu 1979, Sand 1979). The results are summarized in Table 9.1. It is apparent that outmover satisfaction with post-move dwelling units was quite varied. These studies paralleled the previous section's documentation of the heterogeneity of outmovers.

Outmovers' subjective evaluations of the comparative quality of the neighborhoods to which they move also showed substantial variation. In St. Paul, the outmovers were reported to be "decidedly more positive" about their new neighborhoods (Sands 1979). In St. Louis, 60 percent of the outmovers considered their new neighborhoods better, and only 8 percent found the neighborhoods to be worse (Hu 1979). On the other hand, 27 percent of Seattle's outmovers considered their new neighborhoods worse, 38 percent the same and only 35 percent better (City of Seattle Office of Policy Planning 1978). A majority (58 percent) of the outmovers from one District of Columbia census tract studied judged their new neighborhoods worse (Collier *et al.* 1979).

None of the existing gentrification displacement studies was designed with a large enough sample to permit statistically reliable conclusions about the correlation between outmover satisfaction and a full array of demographic variables. Two important studies, however, did control for income. Lower-income outmovers were found to be least satisfied with their post-move dwelling units and neighborhoods. Compared with 29 percent of all Seattle's outmovers, 41 percent of the outmovers with incomes of $7500 or less judged their post-move dwelling worse than their former ones (Hu 1979). Thirty-eight percent of the lower-income Seattle outmovers considered their new neighborhoods worse, as compared with 27 percent of all outmovers (City of Seattle Office of Policy Planning 1978). Similarly, in Baltimore, 21 percent of the outmovers with incomes under $10 000 judged their new units to be worse than the old, as opposed to 8 percent for outmover incomes in the $10 000 to $20 000 range[3] (Goodman & Weissbrod 1979).

In summary, evidence of what happens to outmovers paints a picture of mixed hardship. Some outmovers appear to find satisfactory, even superior, housing without harm. Many others judge their units to be the same, and a substantial number judge them to be worse. Costs almost always rise, sometimes severely. Both objectively and subjectively, those with the lowest incomes tend to fare the worst in the process.

Displacement, integration and social conflict

Perhaps the most important of all are questions related to the political–economic–social changes that gentrification displacement is bringing about. Most theories of global economic and spatial change develop models of class conflict in which some occupational, racial, age, or life-style groups are pitted against others in the struggle for desirable land and buildings. What does a careful look at the facts contribute to an understanding of class conflict? Will a global restructuring of the economy create new forms of class and spatial conflict, or does it offer opportunities for social integration? The experience of American neighborhoods offers some important insights into these questions.

Two diametrically opposed scenarios dominate discussion of the connection between integration and gentrification displacement in the United States. In the optimistic view, gentrification will not cause social conflict and will produce neighborhoods which are an exciting mix of different races, classes and life-style groups living together. The HUD *Displacement Report* takes the position that revitalization offers a "unique opportunity" for integration (US Department of Housing and Urban Development 1979). A more pessimistic view holds that gentrification will force low-income minority groups out of desirable inner-city neighborhoods to less desirable areas, thus reducing their quality of life and diffusing and defusing their political power.

Longitudinal (time-series) studies with microlevel analysis are needed for analyzing integration in gentrifying neighborhoods. Segregation in a gentrifying neighborhood may take place at an extreme microlevel. For example, in Boston's South End, analysis at the neighborhood level would appear to show a well integrated community of white, black, Asian and Hispanic groups of a range of classes and life-styles living within the same neighborhood. However, analysis at the census tract, block and building level (Seifel 1979) shows the area to be quite segregated into clearly defined racial and class enclaves. Similarly, static studies, which look at the racial or class composition of a changing neighborhood at one point in time, may mistakenly conclude that a neighborhood which is really in transition has achieved stable integration. Georgetown, in the District of Columbia, would have appeared an integrated neighborhood midway in its transition from an all-black to a virtually all-white neighborhood.

Five recent empirical studies provide longitudinal and microlevel empirical evidence on the racial dynamics of gentrifying neighborhoods (Cybriwsky 1978, Auger 1979, Munski & O'Loughlin 1979, Seifel 1979, Zietz 1979). All five suggest that gentrification produces racial conflict and will not necessarily promote integration. A study of white "reinvasion" pushing black populations out of four District of Columbia neighborhoods was conducted by sociologist Eileen Zietz (Zietz 1979). Zietz found that virtually all the original resident blacks were ultimately pushed out. In two studies, racial minorities who remained after gentrification were also found to be segregated. In Boston's South End, black tenants, who once lived throughout a large number of both racially segregated and integrated census tracts, had been largely relocated to assisted-housing projects at the fringes of the neighborhood, particularly that part bordering the low-income black Roxbury section of Boston (Seifel 1979). Similarly, in two New Orleans neighborhoods, Lower Marginy and Algiers Point, remaining blacks in the predominantly white post-gentrification neighborhoods were clustered in discrete enclaves (Munski & O'Loughlin 1979). Three other studies document racial conflict and opposition by middle- and upper-class white inmovers to lower-income and black households entering, or even remaining in, the neighborhoods (Cybriwsky 1976, Auger 1979).

A survey of inmover attitudes in gentrifying New Orleans neighborhoods provides information on inmover expectations and values (Laska & Spain 1979). Approximately half of the respondents expected their neighborhoods to be all or mostly white within five years. The expectation of living in all- or nearly all-white neighborhoods was strongly and positively correlated with increasing income. This survey also found that generally the inmovers were opposed to housing policies which would encourage or even help maintain an income mix, and by implication racial mix, in the neighborhoods. Only 17 percent favored additional housing for the elderly in their neighborhoods, 9 percent favored scattered public housing, 7 percent desired more private apartments and 0 percent wanted more housing projects.

In Boston's South End, more overt conflict was reported between long-term residents, who represented a mix of races and classes, and higher-status, primarily white inmovers (Auger 1979). The Ad Hoc Committee for a South End for South Enders launched a scathing attack on the newcomers, who responded in kind. An observer reported raucous shouting matches, litigation, picketing and inflammatory press releases and exposés in the continuous skirmishing between racial and class factions in this neighborhood.

The most detailed and most disturbing study of race and gentrification is by Ukrainian–American geographer Roman Cybriwsky, who purchased a home in Philadelphia's gentrifying Fairmount area (Cybriwsky 1978). Cybriwsky documented an alliance between long-term, white ethnic residents and white, higher-status newcomers mutually committed to keeping out lower-income, black encroachment from the North Philadelphia ghetto. The Fairmounters were described as firm in their resolve to exclude blacks, and the newcomers were described as fearing blacks, black crime and the declining property values as much as the Fairmounters. Fairmount street gangs scrawled racist graffiti on walls, broke the windows of one black household who had moved into the neighborhood, and attacked, with rocks and bottles, blacks who strayed into the area. Cybriwsky found that the newcomers tacitly supported the goals, if not the tactics, of the long-term residents.

In summary, gentrification has frequently been found to produce racial and class conflict. There is no evidence that it will necessarily lead to integration.

Rethinking gentrification displacement in the United States

The empirical studies of gentrification displacement described in this chapter fundamentally alter in important respects the conventional image of the gentrification displacement phenomenon.

First, they indicate a great deal of gentrification-caused displacement. As late as 1978, the most authoritative reconnaissance of displacement conducted for HUD had reported "no more than one to two hundred households" displaced annually as a result of reinvestment in any of 18 cities reconnoitered (Grier & Grier 1978), a finding restated in HUD's 1979 *Displacement Report* to Congress (US Department of Housing and Urban Development 1979). In contrast the four city-level studies, either estimating annual displacement or containing data from which such an estimate could be advanced, reported annual gentrification-caused displacement to be in the 2000- to 7000-person range for Denver (Flahive & Gordon 1979), New Orleans (Laska *et al.* 1980), Portland City (City of Portland Office of Planning and Development 1978) and Seattle (City of Seattle Office of Policy Planning 1978). Elsewhere, based on these studies and other data, the present authors have estimated that total annual displacement in the United States is approximately, and conservatively, 2.5 million persons (LeGates & Hartman 1981).

It is significant to note that HUD (and the Census Bureau HUD Annual Housing Survey), doubtless responding to the widespread criticism of its cavalier and denigrating attitude toward the displacement problem, has more recently adopted a more realistic and comprehensive view of the phenomenon. Unlike in its earlier statistical surveys and reports, it now acknowledges that moves induced by rent increases are for the most part to be regarded as displacement. HUD's 1981 report to Congress on displacement (US Department of Housing and Urban Development 1981) acknowledges that in 1979 as many as 2.4 million Americans were displaced by private activity alone, a figure that does not include the various forms of public displacement (local housing code enforcement, construction of roads and public facilities, government urban renewal and community development activities, etc.), and does not take into account "indirect" or "secondary" displacement effects.

Second, displacement imposes substantial hardships on some classes of displacees, particularly lower-income households and the elderly. Although some displacees report finding similar or improved dwelling units and neighborhoods, a substantial number report a deterioration in post-move dwelling units and/or neighborhood quality. Rents almost always increase, modestly for some households, substantially for others. Lower-income outmovers are particularly hit, finding the least satisfactory alternative units and neighborhoods and facing the highest proportional shelter-cost increases. For elderly displacees, the neighborhood studies show particular hardships.

The picture of inmovers that emerges from the recent gentrification-displacement studies corroborates the conventional profile of inmovers as white, young adult, high status, white collar, and relatively affluent. It contravenes the popular image that they move directly to the gentrifying neighborhoods from the suburbs. Indeed, a substantial number of inmovers originate within the neighborhood itself.

The picture of outmovers departs from conventional stereotypes of poor or blue-collar, minority households. The ranges of outmover races, ages, family structures, occupations and incomes are wide, much wider than among inmovers. It appears, however, that first-generation gentrification affects primarily white, lower-middle-class, socially heterogeneous neighborhoods. It does not primarily reach low- or very low-income minority neighborhoods. Surprisingly, white-collar workers, perhaps a numerical majority in the cities studied, are prevalent. The studies do confirm that significant numbers of low- and very low-income outmovers, including welfare-dependent individuals, are among outmovers from most gentrifying neighborhoods. Surprisingly, some quite high-status, high-income households are also among the outmovers. Their departures are probably motivated by a lack of desire or ability to pay higher rent; conversion of apartments into condominiums; remodeling, which requires their moving; or eviction as a result of a new owner's desire to occupy the unit. There is a wide range of ages and family structure types among outmovers. Many children and elderly individuals are counted among the outmoving group.

The studies show that outmovers consistently cluster close to their prior residences and that they almost always experience some rent increase. Different segments of the outmover population experience quite different outcomes with respect to dwelling-unit and neighborhood satisfaction.

The recent gentrification-caused displacement studies document substantial racial, class and life-style conflicts in gentrifying neighborhoods. Although gentrification in most cities has not yet reached primarily black or other minority neighborhoods, there are documented instances in which entire black neighborhoods have been replaced by a process of white reinvasion. In other neighborhoods, which were primarily minority or racially mixed, blacks have been disproportionately displaced or sifted into enclaves within the neighborhood. Recent studies have also documented opposition of white inmovers to continued racial and class mix in the neighborhoods to which they have moved. The studies also confirm political sparring and some violence.

Gentrification and displacement: a comparative research agenda

The development of studies of gentrification and displacement in the United States suggests how comparative research is likely to proceed during the 1980s. Three broad areas of inquiry emerge: (a) How similar are patterns in one country to those in others? (b) What is the overall global pattern? and (c) How can the observed phenomena be explained and understood?

During the 1980s, scholars in different countries will undoubtedly continue the empirical research begun in the late 1970s. Hopefully the findings reported here will encourage replication to see in what ways the pattern of gentrification and displacement in other countries is similar to or different from that in the United States. Similarly, empirical work in other countries will surely raise new questions for American empirical resarch. At this level the essential questions are the ones addressed by empirical research in the United States: how much gentrification and displacement is there, and where is it occurring? Who is moving into gentrifying neighborhoods, and who is moving out? What happens to displacees? The new comparative question is, how do patterns of gentrification and displacement differ from one country to another?

As existing studies of gentrification and displacement in different countries are shared and new ones completed, a higher level of integration will become possible. Is the gentrification phenomenon linked to key world cities or is it broadly diffused? Is there a global hierarchy in which top managers are the inmovers in some cities; middle managers in others; clerical and sales workers in yet others? Are there sharp differences among countries based on an evolving specialization of functions in the world economy? Are there important differences in spatial structure and conflict based on the different class and ethnic patterns of different countries?

The 1980s should see a great advance in the important work of comparative theory-building attempted in this book. As the gentrification and displacement situation in different countries is fully explored, and as comparative analysis maps the global pattern, urban political economists and others will be in a position to incorporate the empirical findings into evolving theory about economic trends and metropolitan spatial structure, and to test the power of existing theory to explain or predict gentrification and displacement patterns.

Much is already known about gentrification and displacement throughout the world, and explicit road maps are being developed for further research and theory-building. But events have a way of overtaking even the most agile and diligent researchers. Despite these gaps in our knowledge, it is necessary now to use what is presently known in order to protect displacees and mitigate the effects of displacement, even as the research agenda unfolds.

Notes

1   Historically, New Orleans has long had an unusual pattern of whites and blacks living in the same neighborhoods. In many of the older New Orleans neighborhoods, whites live in the principal residential structures facing on the streets and blacks in smaller structures along a back alley which once were slave quarters.
2   The author hypothesizes that if inflation had been considered, it is possible that there was little or no increase for most households.
3   The report concludes somewhat surprisingly, however, that 33 percent of outmovers with incomes over $20000 reported their new dwelling units to be worse than their former ones.

Gentrification of the City

CONCLUSION

10

From "renaissance" to restructuring: the dynamics of contemporary urban development

PETER WILLIAMS and NEIL SMITH

The notion that gentrification represents some sort of urban renaissance or revival is widespread, particularly in the United States (Gruen 1964, Alpern 1979, Sumka 1979, DeVito 1980, Demarest 1981). This perspective would imply some kind of prior secular decline and now a reversal of established trends. That is really the meaning of renaissance and it was the explicit symbolism behind the naming of Detroit's Ford-inspired Renaissance Center; the spiritual renewal after the fall. The popularity of the renaissance/revival theme lies in its inherent optimism and the belief that squalor is being expunged and the city is being reclaimed for the respectable classes. As such it is a sharply partisan view of contemporary urban change and one which negates the real history of urban development and change. There was no such simple fall and there is no such simple rebirth.

The history of urban development is a story of the constant patterning and transformation of the city landscape. More rapid and more institutionalized with the advent of capitalism, this transformation process can be seen as a constant structuring and restructuring of urban space with nothing remaining untouched for very long. Although such changes in urban form and structure are always taking place, they do not occur at a constant pace, nor proceed in a uniform direction. Rather, like the larger patterns of change in capitalist society itself, this tends to be a cyclical process. There are periods in which new spatial patterns are set in a relatively rapid restructuring, and other periods in which established patterns become more entrenched, rather than new ones set. Of course, there is no clean historical break between these different kinds of process, since to a considerable extent they occur simultaneously. Thus if we examine the period from 1945 to 1973 in most advanced capitalist societies, it is evident that the most profound transformation in urban structure revolved around the suburbanization process. This represented a dramatic consummation of processes that had originated much earlier in the 20th century and even in the late 19th century. At the same time, the suburbanization of the postwar period was laying the foundation for the restructuring that would come to dominate in the 1970s. The important question is this: if the history of cities is one of constant structuring and restructuring, why is gentrification and the contemporary restructuring or urban space so significant, if indeed it is?

In the first place, it cannot be claimed that the process is without precedent. Even if most urban restructuring has involved an outward expansion of the capitalist city, there are more than a few historical examples of the "redevelopment" of central-city areas. The most obvious example, albeit an unintentional predicament, is the rebuilding of cities, from London to San Francisco, after their devastation by fire. More important is the kind of transformation accomplished largely by the private market in most 19th-century cities. In London, for example,

> the City was transformed from a residential–industrial area into a depopulated conglomeration of banks, offices, warehouses, and railway stations. Its poorer inhabitants were unceremoniously evicted to make way for this glittering symbol of late Victorian capitalism. (Stedman Jones 1971: 151–3)

Engels (1973 edn.) observed the same process in Manchester, documenting its effect on the working class, and in a now-famous passage, Marx (1967 edn, vol. I, 657) observed the general effect of so-called improvements, as they were known at the time in Britain:

> "Improvements" of towns, accompanying the increase of wealth, by the demolition of badly built quarters, the erection of palaces for banks, warehouses, etc., the widening of streets for business traffic, for the carriages of luxury, and for the introduction of tramways, etc., drive away the poor into even worse and more crowded hiding places.

If Haussmann's rebuilding of Paris in the 1850s and 1860s was more planned, with military and political purposes playing a considerable role, the results were virtually the same for the working class (Pinkney 1958).

The prior occurrence of "improvements" and renewal in the central city is sometimes construed to minimize the importance of the contemporary gentrification process. It is viewed by some as a periodic feature in the "natural" life cycle of cities. We do not accept this naturalistic interpretation of the market or of urban social processes. The major problem with this approach is its ahistorical treatment of urban growth and urban processes (see, for example, Jacobs 1969, 1984), contending that the earliest cities and the most modern are governed by the same laws and generalizations. We hold, on the contrary, that urban processes are quite specific to different societies, different periods, and especially different modes of production, and that the contemporary process of gentrification is quintessentially a feature of the advanced capitalist city. Gentrification would be impossible in cities where there was no well-developed geographical division of residential location by class. Previous societies certainly incorporated class divisions, but these were not expressed in a systematic differentiation of urban residential space. Medieval cities, as is well known, were divided by horizontal distance in individual buildings, not by geographical location.[1] In reality, gentrification as we know it could only appear on the agenda after the industrial revolution had led to the dramatic expansion of cities, and the suburbanization process accomplished an increasingly acute geographical differentiation as part of this expansion. As society expanded and restructured, so its spatial manifestations changed. The creation of exclusive domains, such as the suburbs, meant that gentrification became feasible.

What we are arguing here is that although 19th-century clearances had a very similar effect on working-class housing, namely a reduction in available units and even an increase in prices (Allan 1965, Rodger 1982), these "improvements" were not responsible for such a significant restructuring as we seem to be experiencing today. We are not arguing that the contemporary rebuilding and restructuring of the central and inner urban areas represents an end to suburbanization; nor are we arguing that it represents such a profound change in urban structure as occurred with the advent of suburbanization. Rather, we *are* arguing that just as suburbanization was the spatial expression of a larger social and economic process (Harvey 1978, Aglietta 1979), so too gentrification is a highly visible spatial process deeply rooted in current patterns of social and economic differentiation. The task for us here is to attempt to assess the immediate direction and consequences of this urban restructuring. How substantial will the changes be? What kind of urban areas will be fashioned in the immediate future? What will be the effects of the process on today's city residents and on urban politics and conflict? These are our concerns in this concluding essay.

Throughout the book different authors have sought to penetrate the imagery of gentrification and expose the essential processes at work. Thus we have exposed the inadequacies of much current commentary on this process and have attempted a more deep-seated and rounded understanding of its form, causes, and immediate consequences. What we seek to do here is to look ahead and project this understanding onto our knowledge of the unfolding of capitalist societies so that we can begin to grasp the contemporary and future significance of gentrification.

The future of the central city

In the heady days following World War II, it became increasingly fashionable, given seemingly unlimited economic and technological expansion, to study and anticipate the urban future. It was an optimistic era; the future not only looked bright, but, more than that, it seemed almost controllable. We anticipated the end of business cycles, the end of poverty (at least in the developed world) and the end of ideology. This passion for futurism was especially intense in the United States, which then still represented the most forward pioneer in many social, economic and cultural trends. Today, this kind of futurism has virtually disappeared (but see Gappert & Knight 1982). Its demise was not simply the result of changing academic fashions, but was very closely related to specific social, political and economic changes that emerged between the late 1960s and 1973 and which rendered futurism a difficult and increasingly utopian pursuit. Even economic forecasters now acknowledge that it is no longer possible to predict with any accuracy the course of events.

The fundamental problem with these kinds of attempts to forecast (and sometimes even predict) the future lay in their methodology. So constant were the upward trends at the time (or so it appeared) that there seemed to be no major objection to forecasting the future through what we might call speculative extrapolation. Current trends were plotted, the trajectory extrapolated, and the results were interpreted, with a modicum of respectable speculation, for given futures: 1990, 2000 and 2025 (see, for example, Berry 1970). Already losing its appeal with the political uprisings of the late 1960s and the beginnings of financial crisis in the world money markets, this methodology was quickly rendered obsolete with the full onslaught of world economic crisis in 1973. Speculative extrapolation provides no tools for comprehending widespread and rapid reversals of established trends. More than that, the emergence of a complex and interlinked world economy means there are no longer any sheltered national systems.

Discussions today of the future of the city are more cautious, less speculative, and suffer less from the naive linearity of extrapolative futurism (Davies & Champion 1983). It remains vital to understand the direction and pace of social trends, but these are increasingly treated in the context of multiple tendencies that are often contradictory; the future is treated as more and more contingent. A certain amount of speculation is inevitable in considering the future of the central city, but today that speculation tends to be based on a more sophisticated understanding of the substantive forces involved. Much effort has therefore been devoted to explaining the different facets of physical decay and social deprivation in the urban center (see, for example, Anderson *et al.* 1983), and it is upon this kind of explanatory analysis that discussion of the future must be based. We isolate here four sets of forces, or agents of change, which will be among the most crucial in determining the future landscape of the central city. These are as follows: the new international division of labor, the changing function of cities, the economic crisis, and the role of the state. These should be seen not as separate "factors" determining urban development, but as elements of a larger, integrated whole. Nor should they be viewed as exclusive; separating out these four agents of change, we have also omitted others that will help substantially to shape the future. For example we have set aside questions of demographic change, the sexual division of labor, and the rise of new technology, either because we feel their effects are largely covered in the above headings, or because their effect is likely to be secondary.

What we are arguing is that we can only discuss the future of gentrification within a broader understanding of what is happening to cities and societies. We begin by briefly discussing the new international division of labor which now dominates the world economy.

The new international division of labor

We would argue that the continuing development of a new international division of labor will be the major determinant, at the regional scale, of urban restructuring. Cities in so-called declining regions, from Glasgow and Gary to Newcastle, Australia, can expect relatively low investments of capital in the built environment, whereas others, such as Boston, Bristol and Toronto, are likely to experience increases, or at least no relative decrease, in capital investments. The reasons for this are in part complex, in part intuitively obvious. The major impetus behind the new international division of labor (Fröebel *et al.* 1980) comes from the internationalization of capital: not commodity capital, which has been internationalized for centuries in the form of trading companies, nor finance capital which has been internationalized for decades in the form of multinational corporations, but *productive* capital in the form of capital invested directly in the production process.

Whereas previous production processes tended to be organized at the subnational regional level (thus the old regional geography distinguished regions on the basis of the production of specialized commodities) industrial production today is increasingly organized across international boundaries and more on the basis of differential wage rates. The "world car" is only the most obvious illustration; from textiles to electronic games, steel products to computer systems, the final product is assembled from components produced in several or more countries. The insularity of regions within national economies is no more, and this has led to a restructuring of geographical space at the regional level which impresses certain patterns on urban centers (Massey, 1979, Carney *et al.* 1980, Smith 1985). New international regions are being created; Clydeside, Merseyside, and the Ruhr share an experience at odds with that of south-east England, Queensland, and California. Certainly all of the latter have themselves experienced downturns, and some major centers within them have lost jobs and population, but the regions as a whole remain prosperous and vibrant.

In many cities that were the old industrial core of advanced capitalism, the new international division of labor has brought a dramatic deindustrialization of the productive base. Capital has been withdrawn in part or in whole from the basic manufacturing infrastructure of these cities, and as a result it is also withdrawn from other land uses, residential, commercial, retail, and so on. This pattern of economic decline, broadly related to industrial decline in older centers, is resulting in a cruel dialectic of decay and opportunity. In cities such as Liverpool, England, and Gary, Indiana, it is decay that dominates the present and immediate future, whereas in Baltimore and perhaps Pittsburgh the drastic cheapening of central locations brought on by this decay has been capitalized (quite literally) as a means of reconstructing and restructuring the urban center.

The new international division of labor has also resulted in the concentration of modern industrial and nonindustrial activities, leading to strong economic growth in certain cities, from the American sunbelt and the Japanese industrial centers to the "European arc" stretching from the East Midlands of England, through the Netherlands, to Frankfurt. Although many of the cities in these areas are also experiencing economic and physical decline in the center, this is generally less intense than in the deindustrialized regions, and the consequent restructuring at the center is often masked by the general prosperity. Much of the growth in these cities is in peripheral areas and beyond, in the small towns surrounding the metropolitan area.

In summary, then, we can expect that as the new international division of labor develops further, many predominantly older cities will continue to experience an outflow of capital and a consequent decline in economic and physical conditions. This need not be universal; rather it will be highly uneven. Decline, however, engenders profitable opportunity in so far as central locations are available at low prices. The extent to which these opportunities will be capitalized upon is much more difficult to estimate since it immediately involves a consideration of alternative competitive investment opportunities, and this in turn leads us to the question of economic crisis and the pattern of economic growth and depression in the next decade. Before broaching this question, however, let us examine the changing function of the city.

Urban hierarchy and city function

In the wake of deindustrialization and the disproportionate increase in "service" jobs, it has become conventional wisdom that cities have been transformed from industrial centers into service centers. This is correct, but far too general to provide an understanding of the complex hierarchy of cities and city functions that is evolving. In the last few years, several authors have suggested that we are witnessing, for the first time, the emergence of truly global cities and a closely articulated hierarchy of urban areas in the world economy. This is part of the process of regional transformation and the development of the new international division of labor discussed earlier. Cohen (1981) suggests that in the last few decades we have witnessed the decline of the "metropolis and region" structure which dominated the United States, and other advanced capitalist nations, in the first part of the 20th century. As national economies were increasingly wrenched into the international economy, the urban areas that operated as national-level centers in these economies were increasingly bifurcated into international and simply national centers. A further layer of regional centers was also expanded. He argues that New York, London and Tokyo have already emerged as global cities in the sense that their largest financial and corporate enterprises are involved more in international than in national transactions (Cohen 1981: 308; see also *Business Week* 1984: 100).

Many of the other large cities have suffered a relative demise, losing some of their international functions but retaining considerable corporate administrative activity. Even such large metropolises as Chicago, Amsterdam–Rotterdam, Manchester, and Melbourne seem to fall into this category. Other smaller urban areas have been separated out as merely regional centers. This pattern, of course, is not static, and Cohen suggests that cities like Frankfurt and San Francisco (and Sydney and Toronto, we would add) may well be vying for international status. Noyelle (1983) and Noyelle and Stanback (1981) come to similar conclusions about a new urban hierarchy, but since their analysis has a narrower, more national focus, they provide a different categorization of cities.

The point here is not the argument over which cities fit where in the hierarchy. Rather, it is to recognize that the development of this new urban hierarchy is simultaneously creating a new hierarchy of urban functions. If the late feudal city was defined by the concentration of commercial capital (in market "towns"), and the early capitalist city by the concentration of productive capital in industry, the late capitalist city is defined differently again. For the international and most of the national cities, it is the concentration of money capital and the gamut of financial, administrative and professional services that lubricate the money flow; it is this function that defines the late capitalist cities at the top of the new urban hierarchy. The situation of the regional centers and smaller cities is more ambiguous. Although their economies are also changing toward certain kinds of services, many of them are likely to remain local manufacturing centers, producing goods for which there is no effective international or national market.

Now it is reasonable to expect that central urban areas will be differentially affected according to their place in this emerging hierarchy and their changing function. Cohen (1981: 307) argues that the difference between international- and national-level urban centers is reflected in "higher prices for rents and services which result from the pronounced agglomeration of corporate and corporate-related activities" in the global cities. Indeed, if one looks at the housing market in the centers of these global cities, it seems likely that this market would remain buoyant even in the face of any further economic recession which adversely affects housing. The Manhattan real-estate market, for example, as transacted by brokers or in the pages of *The Times* or the *New York Times*, is geared not to local or even national but to international trends and demands.

Thus it would seem that we can expect a Manhattanization of the international city. By this we mean not simply an architectural Manhattanization with the clustering of skyscrapers in the center;

that is already largely accomplished. Rather, we can expect a *social Manhattanization* whereby the agglomeration of corporate and corporate-related activities at the center leads to a further agglomeration of upper-income residential neighborhoods and of lavish recreation and entertainment facilities. The main question here is the extent to which this type of gentrification will permeate down the urban hierarchy. Since they too harbor considerable concentrations of corporate and related activities, many national centers are likely to experience a continued Manhattanization, if more selective *vis-à-vis* geographical neighborhoods. Regional centers (such as Dublin and Baltimore, Vancouver and Adelaide) have already experienced gentrification, but the continutation of this process in the face of economic crisis will be more contingent upon local conditions and policies.

Certainly we are not suggesting that the extreme wealth and indulgence of New York's Manhattan, or of Mayfair or Belgravia in London will reach out into all the presently gentrified inner areas. However, we would suggest that there are important connections between this process of social Manhattanization and the more mundane restratification process which is taking place in the inner suburbs. The creation of corporate financial and service economies is achieved not simply by the establishment of global headquarters buildings in one selected center, but also by the creation of a network of activities across the globe. That network reaches down into a large number of urban centers. Alongside this new administrative economy come all the elements necessary to maintain it: advanced education centers, cultural facilities, science parks, and the whole panoply of recreational and life-style accompaniments.

Just as the new urban hierarchy is interconnected, so the new social hierarchy that derives from the emergence of administrative economies is both connected and dispersed across space. Manhattan and Mayfair provide homes for the elite in accessible and relatively safe environments. The executives, professionals and public servants who service the economy cannot live in such close proximity, but they can easily displace an increasingly residualized working class from the inner areas of those cities where this new economy concentrates. Indeed, in conjunction with the demand for office space, such groups are able to transform the old working hearts of such cities into office, home and leisure centers, e.g. the transformation of the dock areas of Bristol, Vancouver and London. Thus, when we talk of Manhattanization, it is essential to think of the spread effects. Manhattan symbolizes the transformation of economies, but the impact of that transformation does not simply remain there.

Economic crisis

The continued economic crisis is likely to have the most profound effect on the immediate future of the central city. The reason for this, quite simply, is that changes in urban form are brought about by investments of capital in the built environment, and investment patterns are dramatically different in periods of crisis than in periods of expansion. In quantitative terms, there is no simple equation between economic crisis and levels of investment in the built environment. A number of authors have discussed the tendency for massive quantities of capital to move into construction on the eve of crisis (Ambrose & Colenutt, 1975, Harvey 1978). Thus the office boom in London in the early 1970s preceded an economic slump beginning in 1973, and reinvestment in 1978 preceded the slump of the late 1970s and early 1980s. Housing starts in the US have varied wildly in the late 1970s and early 1980s (from 1.07 million in 1982 to over 2 million in 1983) with the end of one "recession," then a hiatus, the beginning of another recession, and then a short but dramatic recovery. The astonishing rise in new office construction in 1983 and 1984 in most US cities undoubtedly presages another sharp economic decline.

The temporality of investment has therefore been cyclical and highly uneven in spatial terms. The sharp oscillations typical of the American economy in recent years have not been experienced in the United Kingdom, where the economy has been depressed throughout since 1979, with only small and occasional periods of growth. Even more important, there have been significant spatial changes in the pattern of investment at the urban scale. Whereas, in previous decades, the suburbs and the outer city have claimed the vast majority of new investment in the built environment, these outer areas no longer dominate so thoroughly. According to Data Resources Inc., an estimated 42 percent of total construction capital in the United States in 1983 ($54 billion) was committed to renovation and remodeling, much of it located in the central city (*Business Week* 1983). Rehabilitation is much less sensitive to changes in the interest rate. This suggests a significant spatial countercyclical trend. Although in general the volume of construction declines considerably during crisis, within this decline we appear to be seeing a considerable transfer of capital from suburban new starts to central and inner–city rehabilitation efforts.[2]

Of course the latter still lags behind the former in absolute terms, and although central area investment increased in relative terms, as a result of the most recent recession, it is not clear how vital a countercyclical tendency gentrification actually is. Indeed the impressionistic evidence suggests that in most US cities, central city rehabilitation stayed "up" through the first 12 months of recession until the first half of 1982, but declined in late 1982, only to increase again rapidly in 1983. In conclusion it is not clear how representative the American experience actually is. We would expect that in Britain, mainland Europe, even Australia, where to different degrees the state is more involved in the land and housing markets, gentrification will be less susceptible to the booms and troughs of the private market.

Obviously, then, there is no simple way to forecast the effect of economic crisis on gentrification and urban restructuring. The most immediate influences on the level of activity are the mortgage and interest rates, and to the extent that there is a sustained rise in these rates, or that they remain high, as part of the recurrence of economic crisis, then central urban restructuring is likely to be adversely affected; capital will be invested elsewhere, if at all, and would-be buyers will delay their purchase of residential and commercial space. More broadly, relationships between gentrification and the administrative economy are relatively clear. Any factors that restrict the expansion of that economy, in total and in specific locations (for example high interest rates, which inhibit new office construction, or a fall in market rents, which leads to the postponement of new schemes), can reduce the pressures that are ultimately expressed through gentrification. The residential choices of the people who occupy the professional and managerial posts arising from the development of this economy are in turn heavily conditioned by those forces. Thus, in that it affects the production as well as the consumption of the gentrified landscape, the advent of deeper economic crisis is probably the most salient potential barrier to the present momentum of urban restructuring.

The role of the state

Thus far, the state's involvement in urban restructuring has been essentially reactive. This is not to diminish the importance of the state's role but to place it in context. The mid-century slum clearance and urban renewal programs initiated by many governments represent the most direct and far-reaching attempts at intervention by the state in this sector. These were attempts to reverse the decay of centrally located residential, industrial and commercial areas where property had become obsolete. The conventional lament that these programs were often social failures, rehousing fewer people than they displaced, mistakes the proclaimed justification of slum clearance for its real goal. These programs were more

214

economic in motivation than social, and in that respect were successful. State intervention both provided new opportunities for private investment and reduced the risk involved.

In the 1970s and 1980s, the state has been less involved in the process. In Britain, the 1977 Inner City White Paper marked the attempt to codify an urban policy and continue the state's centrality (Home 1982), but even before the election of Thatcher it was clear that little would come of the White Paper. Since then, the major urban initiatives have been the Enterprise Zones and privatization campaigns, both of which attempt to reduce the role of the state in urban reconstruction. In the United States there has been a similar pattern of the state extricating itself from direct responsibility for redevelopment. From 1949 to 1974 the Federal Government had become increasingly involved in redevelopment efforts, but with the Nixon moratorium on new public housing (1971) and the installation of the Community Development Block Grant (CDBG) program (1974), the Federal Government pulled back from direct involvement. Carter's UDAG programme (Urban Development Action Grant), implemented in late 1977, and his ill-fated National Urban Plan of 1979, represented a temporary and only partly effective attempt to reinstigate federally planned urban redevelopment. In the 1980s, the Reagan administration has pulled back dramatically, declaring that urban redevelopment is a job for the private market. Some federal funding remains and there are limited local sources, but these are increasingly divided between tax incentives for large corporate projects and small-scale ancillary projects such as street lighting, neighborhood spruce-up projects, and sidewalk herringbone paving.

The reduction in state funds has affected different cities differently. In the United Kingdom it has led to a considerable slowdown in rehabilitation and redevelopment, although this is less noticeable in London, as one might expect. In the United States, so far, the process has been more vulnerable to the vagaries of the economy. However, the full impact of federal cuts may not yet have been felt. Only since 1982 have local governments begun to reorganize their plans for gentrification, citing the Reagan cuts. To take one prominent but not necessarily representative example, the New York City plan to redevelop Harlem (City of New York 1982) explicitly cites federal cutbacks and emphasize the need to reorient plans for the gentrification of Harlem (Schaffer & Smith 1984) toward the private sector. The role of the public sector here will essentially involve the supply of seed money and seed projects, as well as the packaging of larger private undertakings. Nonetheless, because of the perceived risk of trying to gentrify Harlem, and because the City owns over 35 percent of housing stock in the area, it is likely that the success or failure of the city government's plans will be central to the future of the area.

Although the present trend toward privatization suggests a diminished role for the state, the latter's plans will remain important determinants of change. But there is also no guarantee that the state will maintain its selective involvement in the restructuring process. It is possible, indeed likely, that, in response to economic crisis and its effects on urban areas, the state will be forced to revert to a heavily interventionist role. This is already the direction of British Labour Party policy, and the intent of the Democrats' "New New Deal." To the extent that these "Public Works" programs lead to increased public investment in construction, the central urban areas are the most likely focus, especially in the United States where physical and economic decay at the centre is much more advanced than in other countries, and much greater than at the time of the original New Deal.

Thus, although the direct role of the state in the restructuring process is presently secondary to private capital, this might not be so with the recurrence of economic downturn. If the state becomes more directly involved, the issues of urban restructuring will become much more highly politicized. At local as well as national levels, the state will be forced to defend and legitimate its active role in gentrification. In Britain and to a lesser extent Australia this is already occurring, but in the United States it has been possible for the state to come out unabashedly in support of gentrification. Further, with greater state involvement, the forward momentum and the limitations of the process are made more contingent. Large fiscal deficits notwithstanding, the state's freedom from constraints of short-term profitability will provide a wide arena of action in which the outcomes are dominated by political struggles rather than economic investment decisions.

Although direct involvement in the restructuring of urban space is presently limited (grand plans are no longer fashionable or feasible), there are also many indirect routes by which the state assists both reconstruction in general and gentrification in particular. The structure of the taxation and subsidy systems, joint initiatives, and the creation of an investment climate favorable to restructuring are all part of the ways in which the state assists such changes. Gentrification poses a particularly interesting example. Although it is recognized to have negative effects on what is viewed as a residual population, governments of all complexions are viewing its effects in an increasingly favorable light because of the extent of private capital involved. In Britain the state provided improvement grants that were seen to have contributed to gentrification, but these may now be more restricted to low-income groups. This is a reflection of budgetary restrictions rather than any opposition to gentrification. Indeed there are many other ways in which the state in Britain, in the form of central and local government, is creating a favorable investment climate: maintenance of a buoyant home-ownership market, conservation policies, the sale of public housing, mortgage-interest relief, and a sheltered circuit of housing finance.

Gentrification contributes substantially to the imagery of success. The very act of renewal, recovery and rehabilitation in which individuals engage has enormous appeal to governments at all levels, and particularly to those taking the view that it is the suppression of the individual by the state that brought about economic decline. Others who place faith in the efforts of communities are often equally receptive to gentrification because they see the steady infusion of middle-class people into an area as one way of ensuring that the community will exercise its rights; it will break the cycle of deprivation and bring about general renewal. Of course, the originators and supporters of such policies either do not comprehend that "success" and "social balance" generally lead to the replacement of one population by another, or else they comprehend it and support this displacement.

Social Manhattanization: the polarization of the city?

The trends we have identified suggest a continued momentum toward a gentrified central and inner city. The direction of this change is toward a new central city dominated by middle-class residential areas, a concentration of professional, administrative and managerial employment, and the upmarket recreational and entertainment facilities that cater to this population (as well as to tourists). Though relatively central enclaves of working-class residents will surely remain, the momentum of the present restructuring points to a more peripheralized working class, in geographical terms. Of course, as we have stressed, this remains a tendency. The "bourgeois playground" at the centre is as yet partial and selective; it is not happening in all cities, nor are all affected cities already a replica of Manhattan. This is why we have tried to emphasize the possible limits and obstacles to the process.

This apparent geographical polarization of the city is not simply an isolated "spatial process," but rather the spatial result of a deeper social restructuring. In fact, there is remarkable agreement across

217

the political spectrum that this polarization is taking place. On the left, we saw in the mid-1970s the emergence of labor-market segmentation theory (Edwards *et al.* 1975). According to this body of theory, which has become almost conventional wisdom among radical economists, the capitalist economy creates a "dual labor market" with primary and secondary sectors. The primary sector is dominated by white males who enjoy reasonable wages, job security, and union representation. The secondary sector is dominated by "women and minorities," where pay scales are calibrated to the minimum wage, conditions are bad, work hours are erratic and union representation is rare.

On the right, the discussion in this period was of structural unemployment and its effect on the so-called middle class, by which was generally meant white workers and professionals with stable and relatively well-paying employment. In the wake of ten years either in or between recessions, the reality of polarization has penetrated right-wing visions of the city. Implicitly recognized in the Enterprise Zone proposals, this polarization is given explicit formulation in the American context by George Sternlieb:

> Thus the vision of the city becomes strikingly bipolar: on the one hand the city of the poor, with anywhere from a quarter (Boston) to a seventh (New York) of the population on welfare; with crime rates that stagger the imagination even when appropriate allowance is made for their vagaries; and with truancy levels vastly understated by the official reporting techniques, which make a mockery of the traditional role of public education as a homogenizing influence and ladder upward for the urban proletariat.
>
> Separate and distinct from this – though frequently in physical proximity, it is psychologically and fiscally at a vast distance – is the city of the elite. Varying in scale from a very few select blocks in some municipalities to substantial and growing population thresholds in others is the city in which inhabitants are matched to the new postmanufacturing job base, peopled by groups who do not require or utilize the local service base. (Sternlieb & Hughes 1983: 463)

This polarization has probably been sharpest in the United States, where economic fluctuations have been sharper, workers are less organized against the employers' offensive, and the welfare system is so meager in its coverage. At the national level, 1983 was a year of rapid economic growth and declining unemployment, yet the rate of poverty actually increased to over 15 percent of the total population; 6 million have been added to the ranks of the official poor since 1980. The poverty rate for blacks increased to 35.7 percent, the highest level since such figures were first collected in 1966; for households headed by women the figure rose to 36 percent

(Pear 1984). The selectivity of the so-called economic recovery is even clearer at the urban scale. Although New York City is again gaining jobs, the level of unemployment is up, since a large proportion of the new jobs has gone to commuters. The city budget is again registering a surplus after the default of 1975, yet poverty is up: "More people than at any time since the Depression are ... hungry and homeless, and about one of every four New Yorkers is below the poverty level." The "recovery" is making New York a "city of haves and have-nots" (Goodwin 1984).

This social polarization is matched spatially with the expansion of elite enclaves near the center, and the development of a siege mentality at the "frontier" of gentrification. Census data reveal that Manhattan was the 14th richest county in the United States in 1979 with a per capita income of $10 889, whereas the Bronx, just across the Harlem river, was 2280th out of 3132, with a per capita income of only $2943. At the census tract level, the polarization is even more dramatic; by some measures the richest and poorest census tracts in the entire country are less than five miles apart (in Manhattan and the Bronx, respectively). The polarization of New York City is probably more extreme than in many other cities in the advanced capitalist world, but the same general pattern is repeated from Washington, DC to Edinburgh. The Manhattanization of central areas into elite enclaves is matched by a sharper ghettoization of minorities, the poor, and parts of the working class.

In light of the rapid changes that have ensued since 1973, the dual-economy thesis appears too static to capture the kind of restructuring that is taking place. The reduction of living standards has affected not only the secondary sector, but also workers in the primary sector; deindustrialization and employers' demands for productivity increases along with wage reduction have cut sharply into the power and "privileges" of primary-sector workers. Even in the midst of a strong recovery in the United States and a lackluster one elsewhere, the polarization of society is eroding any duality of the labor market and placing more and more workers in low-paying, insecure jobs. In the depression following recovery, we can expect this trend to be accelerated and the social and spatial polarization accentuated. This is the immediate prospect.

Policies and strategies

The conservative approach to these questions is essentially to support the restructuring process as one of renaissance while lamenting the polarization. "From this point of view," according to

Sternlieb and Hughes (1983: 467), gentrification is a "triumph" since it leads to higher property-tax returns and greater "economic vigor" in the city. They issue an appeal for class cooperation, arguing that this is the only realistic approach: "If cities are to be reconstructed, a reconciliation between the two warring parties is going to be required. *The poor need the rich.*" We are arguing the exact opposite. First, the restructuring process is already established, and required no social reconciliation of the kind sought. Secondly, the restructuring process itself is partly responsible for the polarization of rich and poor, and simply to appeal for reconciliation in the face of that reality is utterly utopian. As polarization proceeds, conflict is almost inevitable (Hargreaves, undated).[3] When and where are the only questions. Thirdly, the poor only need the rich so long as the society's resources are owned and controlled by "the rich," and access to these resources for the poor depends on selling one's labor power for a wage (assuming the availability of jobs), presumably to "the rich." Yet it is precisely their control of society's resources and the outflux of capital in search of higher profits that has contributed to the dilapidated urban landscapes of the central city. That is how much "the poor need the rich." We can hardly be satisfied with formulaic apologies for the status quo in place of serious analysis.

Is is often further argued that the benefits of gentrification are far greater than the costs (Schill & Nathan 1983). Whether this is true is doubtful, but more important it is beside the point. The benefits and costs are so unevenly distributed that one has to look not at some overall equation but at different segments of the population. There are distinct losers as well as winners, and the consistent losers are the poor and working class who will be displaced as gentrification proceeds, and who will confront higher housing costs in tight markets (Hartman 1983). In New York City the vacancy rate is below 2 percent, and a housing emergency is generally considered to exist when vacancies fall below 5 percent. It is against this background that the city has launched its plan to gentrify Harlem. Mayor Edward Koch is on record as having said that he sees no problem with Manhattan becoming a place where only those earning $40 000 or more can live.

Many residents of targeted neighborhoods feel the threat acutely. Others, especially homeowners (some of whom will be working class) or small business owners, anticipate substantial economic gains, but many of these end up disappointed. There is considerable conflict over gentrification, but, in the English-speaking world at least, these have usually been small-scale, isolated and fragmented struggles. Further, the results have not been encouraging. There have been fights against state-subsidized hotel projects, new roads destroying old communities, the influx of speculators into working-class neighborhoods, the building of luxury flats, and so on. But none of these has sparked a movement or reaction comparable to the situation in Amsterdam or Berlin, where hundreds of thousands of people have rioted in the late 1970s and early 1980s over both the shortage and expense of housing.

Indeed it may not be possible to prevent gentrification. In so far as it is mainly a private-market phenomenon, its occurrence is unplanned and only partly predictable at the neighborhood level. Fighting it is like fighting a brush fire, and takes considerable organization. If it is difficult to stop head-on, can the process somehow be deflected in such a way as to benefit or at least minimize the costs for working-class residents? This has been the effect of state involvement in the United Kingdom, where some local authorities have rehabilitated dwellings and reinstalled the old tenants. This was only achieved as the result of pressure put on local councils, and does not in any case apply to a large proportion of renovated properties. Moreover, the cutback in spending means few local authorities now do this while all are required to sell their properties to tenants. Ultimately this will enhance the gentrification process. In the United States, there has been little interest yet in this approach. Gentrification is still seen by most city governments, as well as the Federal Government, not as the cause but as the solution to the city's "housing problem", a "triumph", in the words of Sternlieb and Hughes (1983).

This is precisely the kind of triumph that Frederick Engels (1975 edn: 71) had in mind when he criticized the cynical attempt of the ruling class to "turn the city into a luxury city pure and simple:"

In reality the bourgeoisie has only one method of settling the housing question after *its* fashion – that is to say, of settling it in such a way that the solution continually poses the question anew. This method is called "*Haussmann*" . . . By "Haussmann" I mean the practice, which has now become general, of making breaches in the working-class quarters of our big cities, particularly in those which are centrally situated, irrespective of whether this practice is occasioned by considerations of public health and beautification or by the demand for big centrally located business premises or by traffic requirements, such as the laying down of railways, streets, etc. No matter how different the reasons may be, the result is everywhere the same: the most scandalous alleys and lanes disappear to the accompaniment of lavish self-glorification by the bourgeoisie on account of this tremendous success, but – they appear again at once somewhere else, and often in the immediate neighbourhood.

The style and form of restructuring is different today but the process is just as intense. What remains is the Catch-22 character of the problem for working-class residents of decayed inner-city neighborhoods (Schaffer & Smith 1984). These residents are ghettoized in areas of economic deprivation and social malaise as well as physical decay, and the influx of capital and social resources is the first prerequisite for improving the quality of life. Without an influx of capital, the decay will continue. Yet *with* a large-scale investment of capital in these neighborhoods, and the fashioning of attractive communities, present residents are pushed out to housing that is not appreciably better than that which they left. Either way they lose; if the city manages to solve part of its housing problem, it is at the expense of surrounding municipalities. The poor remain poor wherever they are moved.

The conservative argument traditionally plays down the extent of gentrification and the effects of restructuring, claiming no reversal of suburbanization trends at the national level. For residents of targeted neighborhoods, however, national statistical trends are rather abstract in the face of rising rents and landlord harassment. Once the process begins in a neighborhood, and rents begin to increase more rapidly, the gentrification develops a momentum of its own on the private market. It is in recognition of this that many residents anticipate the process with fear. From their point of view it is necessary to fight for control of their community (Hartman *et al.* 1981). It is always a difficult fight, but there are two main victories that can be gained. In the short term, fighting against gentrification can force the state to ameliorate some of the hardest costs. More important, however, in the longer term, gentrification struggles can lead to the building of organizations throughout the city which can demand both local community control as well as the dominant voice in how the city is to be restructured. It is at this point that we can clearly see human agents beginning to triumph over the structures within which they live.

In the long run, the only defense against gentrification is the "decommodification of housing" (Achtenberg & Marcuse 1983). Decent housing and decent neighborhoods ought to be a right, not a privilege. That of course is unlikely to be achieved through a series of reforms; rather, it will take a political restructuring even more dramatic than the social and geographical restructuring we now see. Only then will it be appropriate to talk about social renaissance.

What then is the likely future? There are clearly a variety of forces at work. The gentrifying middle classes are themselves becoming politically important. The emergence of so-called "Yuppies" (young, upwardly mobile, urban professionals), and the seriousness with which they are being taken by politicans, demonstrate the capacities of that group. It is unclear whether they will attempt to

222

form alliances with the people they are potentially displacing. Certainly we can cite examples where this has occurred, but it is not apparent that this has slowed displacement. Indeed there is a certain irony that their attempts to promote the provision of social services in gentrifying areas have resulted in higher tax bills, which have in turn helped force out industries employing the people they were seeking to defend. The working-class populations in these areas are under attack with respect to both jobs and homes, and it is not at all clear that they will survive the onslaught except in much reduced numbers.

It might also be that the seeds of disruption lie in the instability of home-ownership and the service economy, as well as in the worn-out infrastructure in the areas being gentrified. These areas will require increasingly large investments to redevelop and maintain them adequately. Can the economy deliver such funds via government grants and wage packets? It is uncertain to say the least, particularly in Britain, where peripheralization in the world economy is most advanced.

Although it is possible to forecast a collapse in the office market, and a change in the administrative economy through the use of high technology leading to the residualization of all but a few urban centers, it would seem that, for the next 25 years, we are likely to witness an intensification of the gentrification process. But nothing is certain and the exercise of political power by different classes and groups could lead to a very different outcome. One of the most salient checks may well be the increase in violence and crime as well as political organization that will come about as more and more of the urban population in centers throughout the world are marginalized and pushed outside the mainstream of social and economic life. Although gentrifiers may collectively mobilize the police in their support, and successfully so, the very threat of uprisings is highly inimical to continued gentrification.

We have already entered the realm of speculation. What is apparent, however, is that the answer to whether gentrification will continue to spread and intensify will not be found in an analysis of the process itself. Whether the future brings an extension of the present market-led process and the displacement of the poor will depend on economic changes in that market and political interventions that push the market one way or another. This in turn depends on the success of different classes and groups organizing in defence of their own interests.

Notes

1   Horizontal differentiation still occurs in some European cities as a relic, but the pattern has changed substantially.

2   It is notoriously difficult to identify the incidence of gentrification –
    central and inner-city rehabilitation and rebuilding by middle- and
    upper-class inmovers – from physical and economic housing data at the
    national level. The figures used here are necessarily rough indicators,
    with very obvious limitations. See Gale (1984) for some thoughts on
    this.
3   This prediction has already gained a horrifying credibility in the riots in
    Britain in 1985. There is evidence that in one area, Brixton, the pressure
    created by gentrification was *one* of the elements at work.

Bibliography

Abrams, C. 1965. *The city is the frontier.* New York: Harper & Row.

Abu-Lughod, J. 1982. *The myth of demetropolitanization.* Paper presented at the Symposium on Social Change, University of Cincinnati.

Achtenberg, E. and P. Marcuse 1983. Towards the decommodification of housing: a political analysis and a progressive program. In *America's housing crisis – what is to be done?,* C. Hartman (ed.), 202–31. London: Routledge & Kegan Paul.

Advisory Council on Historic Preservation 1980. *Report to the President and the Congress of the United States.* Washington, DC: Government Printing Office.

Aglietta, M. 1979. *A theory of capitalist regulation: the U.S. experience.* London: New Left Books.

Albrandt, R. S. 1977. Explanatory research on the redlining phenomenon. *American Real Estate and Urban Economics Association Journal* **5** (4), 473–81.

Alexander, C., S. Ishikawa and M. Silverstein, with M. Jacobson, I. Fiksdahl-King and S. Angel 1977. *A pattern language: towns, buildings, construction.* New York: Oxford University Press.

Allan, C. M. 1965. The genesis of British urban redevelopment with regard to Glasgow. *Papers and Proceedings of the Regional Science Association* **6**, 149–57.

Allen, J. 1983. Property relations and landlordism, a realist approach. *Society and Space* **1**, 191–203.

Allman, T. D. 1978. The urban crisis leaves town and moves to the suburbs. *Harper's* (December), 41–56.

Alonso, W. 1960. A theory of the urban land market. *Papers and Proceedings of the Regional Science Association* **6**, 149–57.

Alpern, D. M. 1979. A city revival? *Newsweek* **97** (3) (January 15), 28–35.

Althusser, L. 1977. *For Marx.* London: Verso.

Ambrose, P. and B. Colenutt 1975. *The property machine.* Harmondsworth: Penguin.

Anderson, J. 1983. Geography as ideology and the politics of crisis: the Enterprise Zones experiment. In *Redundant spaces in cities and regions?,* J. Anderson and R. Hudson (eds.), 313–50. London: Academic Press.

Anderson, J., S. Duncan and R. Hudson (eds.) 1983. *Redundant spaces in cities and regions? Studies in industrial decline and social change.* London: Academic Press.

Aristedes 1975. Boutique America. *American Scholar* **44** (Autumn), 533–9.

Auger, D. A. 1979. The politics of revitalization in gentrifying neighborhoods: the case of Boston's South End. *Journal of the American Planning Association* **45** (October), 515–22.

225

Bacon, E. 1976. *Design of cities*, revised edition. New York: Penguin.

Ball, M. 1983. *Housing policy and economic power: the political economy of owner occupation*. London: Methuen.

Baltimore Department of Housing and Community 1975. *Home Mortgage Disclosure Act of 1975*, Hearings of the Senate. Washington, DC: Government Printing Office.

Baltzell, E. D. 1958. *Philadelphia gentlemen: the making of a national upper class*. New York: Free Press.

Banfield, E. C. 1968. *The unheavenly city; the nature and future of our urban crisis*. Boston: Little & Brown.

Bartholomew, H. and Associates 1929. *A plan for the city of Vancouver*. Vancouver: City of Vancouver.

Bartley, J. 1982. Urban change and politics – responses and non-responses in Islington between 1945 and 1979. Paper presented at the annual conference of the Political Studies Association, Canterbury: University of Kent.

Baudrillard, J. 1968. *Le système des objets*. Paris: Gallimard.

Baudrillard, J. 1981. *For a critique of the political economy of the sign*. St. Louis: Telos Press.

Baumann, Z. 1982. *Memories of class: the pre-history and after-life of class*. London: Routledge & Kegan Paul.

Beale, C. 1977. The recent shift of the United States population to non-metropolitan areas, 1970–75. *International Regional Science Review* 2 (2), 113–22.

Beauregard, R. A. 1984. Structure, agency and urban redevelopment. In *Capital, class and urban structure*, M. Smith (ed.), 51–72. Beverly Hills: Sage Publications.

Bell, D. 1973. *The coming of post-industrial society; a venture in social forecasting*. New York: Basic Books.

Bell, D. 1976. *The cultural contradictions of capitalism*. London: Heinemann.

Berry, B. J. L. 1970. The geography of the United States in the year 2000. *Transactions of the Institute of British Geographers* **51**, 21–54.

Berry, B. J. L. 1974. *The human consequence of urbanization*. London: Macmillan.

Berry, B. J. L. 1976. The counterurbanization process: urban America since 1970. In *Urbanization and counterurbanization*, B. Berry (ed.), 17–30. *Urban Affairs Annual Review*, Vol. II. Beverly Hills: Sage Publications.

Berry, B. J. L. 1980a. Inner city futures: an American dilemma revisited. *Transactions of the Institute of British Geographers*, N.S. **5** (1), 1–28.

Berry, B. J. L. 1980b. Forces reshaping the settlement system. In *Cities and firms*, H. Bryce (ed.), 59–79. Lexington, Mass.: Lexington Books.

Black, G. undated. *Study of the inner city of Adelaide public housing market*. Adelaide: South Australian Council of Social Service.

Black, J. T. 1975. Private market housing in central cities: a survey. *Urban Land* (November).

Black, J. T. 1980a. Private-market housing renovation in central cities: an urban land institute survey. In *Back to the city*, S. Laska and D. Spain (eds.), 3–12. New York: Pergamon Press.

226

Black, J. T. 1980b. The changing economic role of central cities and suburbs. In *The prospective city: economic, population, energy and environmental developments*, A. Solomon (ed.), 80–123. Cambridge, Mass.: MIT Press.

Blackaby, F. (ed.) 1978. *De-industrialization*. London: Heinemann.

Blowers, A., C. Brook, P. Dunleavy and L. McDowell (eds.) 1981. *Urban change and conflict: an interdisciplinary reader*. London: Harper & Row.

Bluestone, B. and B. Harrison 1982. *The deindustrialization of America: plant closing, community abandonment, and the dismantling of basic industry*. New York: Basic Books.

Blum, D. 1983. The evils of gentrification. *Newsweek* (January 3), 7.

Boddy, M. 1976a. The structure of mortgage finance: building societies and the British social formation. *Transactions of the Institute of British Geographers* N.S. **1** (1), 58–71.

Boddy, M. 1976b. Political economy of housing: mortgage finance and owner-occupation in Britain. *Antipode* **8** (1), 15–24.

Boddy, M. 1980. *The building societies*. London: Macmillan.

Boddy, M. 1981. The property sector in late capitalism: the case of Britain. In *Urbanization and urban planning in capitalist society*, M. Dear and A. J. Scott (eds.), 267–86. London: Methuen.

Bourdieu, P. 1979. *La distinction critique social du Jugement*. Paris: Minuit.

Bourne, L. S. 1981. *The geography of housing*. London: Edward Arnold.

Boyer, B. D. 1973. *Cities destroyed for cash*. Chicago: Follett.

Bradbury, K., A. Downs and K. Small 1982. *Urban decline and the future of American cities*. Washington, DC: The Brookings Institution.

Bradford, C. P. 1979. Financing home ownership: the federal role in neighbourhood decline. *Urban Affairs Quarterly* **14** (3).

Bradford, C. P. and L. S. Rubinowitz 1975. The urban–suburban invest-ment disinvestment process: consequences for older neighbourhoods. *Annals of the American Association of Political and Social Sciences* **422,** 77–86.

British Columbia Business Journal 1972. False Creek Basin offers opportunity of the decade. *British Columbia Business Journal* **4** (April), 38–9.

British Property Federation 1975. *Policy for housing*. London: British Property Federation.

Broadbent, W. 1973. *GIAs and gentrification (a case study in Brentford)*. BA thesis. School of Planning, Kingston Polytechnic, London.

Brown, K. 1981. Race, class and culture: towards a theorization of the 'choice/constraint' concept. In *Social interaction and ethnic segregation*, P. Jackson and S. Smith (eds.), 185–203. London: Academic Press.

Bryce, H. J. (ed.) 1979. *Revitalizing cities*. Lexington, Mass: Lexington Books.

Business Week 1984. The New York colossus. *Business Week* (July 23).

Business Week 1983. Remodeling: small builders hammer out a profitable niche. *Business Week* (November 7).

Butler, S. 1981. *Enterprise Zones: greenlining the inner cities*. New York: Universe Books.

Callan, P. 1979. *Impact of the proposed Eutaw Place/Madison Avenue historic districts in Reservoir Hill*. Baltimore: Department of Housing and Community Development.

Callinicos, A. 1983. The 'new middle class' and socialist politics. *International Socialism* **2** (20), 82–119.

Cameron, G. (ed.) 1980. *The future of the British conurbations*. London: Longman.

Cannadine, D. 1977. Victorian cities: how different. *Social History* **4**, 457–82.

Cannadine, D. 1980. *Lords and landlords: the aristocracy and the towns, 1774–1967*. Leicester: Leicester University Press.

Carney, J., R. Hudson and J. Lewis (eds.) 1980. *Regions in crisis: new perspectives in European regional theory*. London: Croom Helm.

Carroll, J. 1982. *Intruders in the bush: the Australian quest for identity*. Melbourne: Oxford University Press.

Castells, M. 1976a. The wild city. *Kapitalistate* **4–5** (Summer), 2–30.

Castells, M. 1976b. *The urban question*. London: Edward Arnold.

Castells, M. 1983. *The city and the grassroots*. London: Edward Arnold.

Castells, M. and K. Murphy 1982. Cultural identity and urban structure. In *Urban policy under capitalism*, N. I. Fainstein and S. S. Fainstein (eds.), 237–59. Beverly Hills: Sage Publications.

Centre for Urban Research and Action 1977. *The displaced: a study of housing conflict in Melbourne's inner city*. Melbourne: Centre for Urban Research and Action.

Chalkin, C. W. 1968. Urban housing estates in the eighteenth century. *Urban Studies* **5** (1), 67–85.

Chall, D. 1984. Neighborhood changes in New York City during the 1970s. *Quarterly Review of the Federal Reserve Bank of New York*, Winter 1983–84, 38–48.

Challen, M. G. 1973. *Causes and effects of gentrification on the existing housing stock of inner London*. M.Phil. thesis. School of Environment Studies, University College, London.

Chernoff, M. 1980. Social displacement in a renovating neighborhood's commercial district: Atlanta. In *Back to the city*, S. Laska and D. Spain (eds.), 204–19. New York: Pergamon Press.

Chown, J. 1967. Facing up to taxation. *Investors Chronicle, Property Supplement* (March 17).

Christiano, M. 1982. New life being pumped into hearts of European cities. *Washington Post* (September 18), E53.

Churchill, D. 1954. *False Creek development: a study of the actions and interactions of three levels of government as they affected public and private development of the waterway and its land basin*. MA Thesis. University of British Columbia.

City of New York 1982. *Redevelopment strategy for central Harlem*. Unpublished report by the Task Force for the Mayor, August.

City of New York Department of City Planning 1983. *City Fiscal Year 1984 Community Development Program*. New York: City of New York.

City of New York Department of City Planning 1984. *Private reinvestment and neighbourhood change*. New York: City of New York.

City of Philadelphia 1978. *An urban strategy*. Philadelphia: City of Philadelphia.

City of Portland Office of Planning and Development 1978. *Displacement of residents of Portland due to urban reinvestment*. Portland: Portland, Oregon, Office of Planning and Development.

City of Seattle Office of Policy Planning 1978. *Seattle displacement study*. Seattle: Seattle Office of Policy Planning.

Clay, P. L. 1979. *Neighborhood renewal: trends and strategies*. Lexington, Mass.: Lexington Books.

Clay, P. L. and R. M. Hollister 1983. *Neighbourhood policy and planning*. Lexington, Mass.: D. C. Heath.

Cocke, E. 1983. *Change, conflict and power: gentrification in Australia*. Unpublished seminar paper. Urban Research Unit, Research School of Social Sciences, Australian National University.

Cohen, R. B. 1981. The new international division of labor, multinational corporations and urban hierarchy. In *Urbanization and urban planning in capitalist society*, M. Dear and A. Scott (eds.), 289–315. London: Methuen.

Collier, B., A. Gabbin, C. Lawrence and M. White 1979. *From theory to praxis: an analysis of some aspects of the displacement process in the District of Columbia*. Working Paper No. 11. Washington, DC: Department of Economics, University of the District of Columbia, Mt. Vernon Square Campus.

Cox, K. 1984. Social change, turf politics and concepts of turf politics. In *Public service provision and urban development*, A. Kirby, P. Knox and S. Pinch (eds.), 283–315. London: Croom Helm.

Cybriwsky, R. A. 1978. Social aspects of neighborhood change. *Annals of the Association of American Geographers* **68** (March), 17–33.

Cybriwsky, R. A. and J. Western 1982. Revitalizing downtowns: by whom and for whom? In *Geography and the urban environment: progress in research and applications*, D. T. Herbert and R. J. Johnston (eds.), Vol. 5, 343–65. Chichester: Wiley.

Davies, R. L. and A. G. Champion (eds.) 1983. *The future for the city centre*. London: Academic Press.

Dear, M. and A. Scott (eds.) 1981. *Urbanization and urban planning in capitalist society*. London: Methuen.

DeGiovanni, F. 1983. Patterns of change in housing market activity in revitalizing neighborhoods. *Journal of the American Planning Association* **49** (Winter), 22–39.

Demarest, M. 1981. He digs downtown. *Time* **118** (8), 42–53.

Department of the Environment 1977. *Housing policy*. Cmnd 6851. London: HMSO.

Development Economics Group 1977. *Condominiums in the District of Columbia*. Washington, DC: Office of Housing and Community Development.

DeVito, M. J. 1980. Retailing plays key role in downtown renaissance. *Journal of Housing* **37** (4), 197–200.

Diggins, J. P. 1978. Barbarism and capitalism. The strange perspectives of Thorstein Veblen. *Marxist Perspectives* **1** (2), 138–55.

Dingemans, D. J. 1979. Redlining and mortgage lending in Sacramento, California. *Annals of the Association of American Geographers* **69** (2) (June), 225–39.

Douglas, M. 1978. *Natural symbols: explorations in cosmology*. Harmondsworth: Penguin.

Downs, A. 1981. *Neighborhoods and urban development*. Washington, DC: The Brookings Institution.

Duncan, J. and D. Ley 1982. Structural marxism and human geography: a critical assessment. *Annals of the Association of American Geographers* **72** (1), 30–59.

Dunn, P. 1982. Neighbours: a relationship that struggles to survive. *Sunday Times* (December 19), 29.

Dyos, H. J. 1961. *Victorian suburb: a study of the growth of Camberwell*. Leicester: University Press.

Dyos, H. J. 1968. The speculative builders and developers of Victorian London. *Victorian Studies* **11,** 641–90.

Edwards, R., M. Reich and D. Gordon (eds.) 1975. *Labor market segmentation*. Lexington, Mass.: Lexington Books.

Ehrenreich, B. and J. Ehrenreich 1979. The professional–managerial class. In *Between labor and capital*, P. Walker (ed.), 5–45. Boston: South End Press.

Elias, N. 1974. *Le société de cour*. Paris: Clamann-Levy.

Elligott, F. J. 1977. *The planning decision-making process of Vancouver's False Creek: a case study 1968–74*. MA thesis. University of British Columbia.

Elliott, M. *et al.* 1983. *An evaluation and redesign of New York City's anti-harassment programs*. New York: New School for Social Research.

Engels, F. 1973 edn. *The condition of the working-class in England*. Moscow: Progress Publishers.

Engels, F. 1975 edn. *The housing question*. Moscow: Progress Publishers.

Eversley, D. and L. Bonnerjea 1980. *Changes in the resident populations of inner areas. The inner city in context*, Paper No. 2, Social Science Research Council, London.

Fainstein, N. and S. Fainstein (eds.) 1982. *Urban policy under capitalism*. London: Sage Publications.

False Creek Development Group 1977. *False Creek: South Shore*. Vancouver: City Planning Department.

False Creek Study Group 1971. *False Creek proposals report 3*. Vancouver: Thompson, Berwick, Pratt and Partners, and City Planning Department.

Featherstone, M. 1982. The body in consumer culture. *Theory, Culture and Society* **1** (2), 18–33.

Flahive, M. and S. Gordon 1979. *Residential displacement in Denver: a research report*. Denver: Joint Administration Committee on Housing.

Fleetwood, B. 1979. The new elite and the urban renaissance. *New York Times* (January 14), 16–20, 22, 26, 34–5.

Form, W. 1954. The place of social structure in the determination of land use. *Social Forces* **32,** 317–23.

Friedmann, J. and G. Wolff 1982. World city formation: an agenda for research and action. *International Journal of Urban and Regional Research* **6** (3), 309–44.

Fröebel, F., J. Heenrichs and O. Kreye 1980. *The new international division of labour.* Cambridge: Cambridge University Press.

Fukui, J. 1968. *A background report of False Creek for the Vancouver Board of Trade.* Vancouver.

Gale, D. E. 1976. *The back-to-the-city movement . . . or is it?: a survey of recent homeowners in the Mount Pleasant Neighborhood of Washington, DC.* Washington, DC: Department of Urban and Regional Planning, George Washington University.

Gale, D. E. 1979. Middle class resettlement in older urban neighborhoods. *Journal of the American Planning Association* **45** (July), 293–304.

Gale, D. E. 1980. Neighborhood resettlement: Washington, DC. In *Back to the city,* S. Laska and D. Spain (eds.), 95–115. New York: Pergamon Press.

Gale, D. E. (1984). *Gentrification, condominium conversion and revitalization.* Lexington, Mass.: Lexington Books.

Gappert, G. and R. Knight (eds.) 1982. *Cities in the 21st century. Urban affairs annual review* vol. 23. Beverly Hills: Sage Publications.

Giddens, A. 1979. *Central problems in social theory, action, structure and contradiction in social analyses.* London: Macmillan.

Giddens, A. 1981. *A contemporary critique of historical materialism.* Berkeley: University of California Press.

Glassberg, A. 1979. *The politics of middle-class return to the city, Anglo-American perspectives.* Occasional paper 79–8, Center for International Studies. St. Louis: University of Missouri.

Goldberg, M. and J. Mercer 1980. Canadian and U.S. cities: basic differences, possible explanations, and their meaning for public policy. *Papers of the Regional Science Association* **45,** 159–83.

Goodman, A. and R. Weissbrod 1979. *Housing market activity in South Baltimore: immigration, speculation and displacement.* Baltimore: Johns Hopkins Center for Metropolitan Planning and Research.

Goodwin, M. 1984. Recovery making New York city of haves and have-nots. *New York Times* (July 28).

Gorz, A. 1982. *Farewell to the working class.* Boston: South End Press.

Gottlieb, M. 1982. Space invaders: land grab on the lower East Side. *Village Voice* **27** (50) (Decembere 14), 10–16, 50.

Gottmann, J. 1961. *Megalopolis. The urbanized northeastern seaboard of the United States.* New York: Twentieth Century Fund.

Grebler, L. and F. G. Mittelbach 1978. *The inflation of housing prices: its extent, causes and consequences.* Lexington, Mass: Lexington Books.

Grebler, L. 1952. *Housing market behavior in a declining area.* New York: Columbia University Press.

Gregory, D. 1984. Contours of crisis? Sketches for a geography of class struggle in the early industrial revolution. In *Explorations in historical geography: some interpretive essays*, A. Baker and D. Gregory (eds.). Cambridge: Cambridge University Press.

Greve, J. 1965. *Private landlords in England*. London: Bell.

Grier, G. and E. Grier 1978. *Urban displacement: a reconnaissance*. Washington, DC: US Department of Housing and Urban Development.

Gruen, V. 1964. *The heart of our cities*. New York: Simon & Schuster.

Gusfield, J. (ed.) 1963. *Symbolic crusade. Status politics and the American temperance movement*. Urbana: University of Illinois Press.

Habermas, J. 1981. New social movements. *Telos* **49**, 33–8.

Hall, P. 1981. *The inner city in context*. London: Heinemann.

Halpern, K. 1978. *Downtown U.S.A.: urban design in nine American cities*. New York: Whitney Library of Design.

Hamnett, C. 1973. Improvement grants as an indicator of gentrification in inner London. *Area* **5** (4), 252–61.

Hamnett, C. 1984a. Gentrification and residential location theory: a review and assessment. In *Geography and the urban environment, progress in research and applications*, D. Herbert and R. Johnston (eds.), 282–319. Chichester: Wiley.

Hamnett, C. 1984b. The lost gentrifiers. *New Society* (15 March), 415–16.

Hamnett, C. and W. Randolph 1982. How far will London's population fall? A commentary on the 1981 census. *The London Journal* **8** (1), 95–100.

Hamnett, C. and W. Randolph 1984. The flat break-up market in central London: a case study of residential area transformation. *Transactions of the Institute of British Geographers* **9** (3), 259–79.

Hamnett, C. and P. Williams 1980. Social change in London: a study of gentrification. *Urban Affairs Quarterly* **15** (4), 469–87.

Hargreaves, K. 1976. *Fitzroy preservation study – comments on the social and economic aspects of architectural preservation*. Melbourne: Centre for Urban Research and Action.

Hargreaves, K. (ed.) undated. *"This House Not for Sale": Conflicts between the housing commission and residents of slum reclamation areas*. Melbourne: Centre for Urban Research and Action.

Harloe, M. 1980. Decline and fall of private renting. *Centre for Environmental Studies Review* **9**, 30–4.

Harris, M. 1973. Some aspects of social polarization. In *London: urban patterns, problems and policies*, D. Donnison and D. Eversley (eds.), 156–89. London: Heinemann.

Harris, N. 1980. Deindustrialization. *International Socialism* **7**, 72–81.

Harris, N. 1983. *Of bread and guns: the world economy in crisis*. Harmondsworth: Penguin.

Hartman, C. 1964. The housing of relocated families. *Journal of the American Institute of Planners* **30** (November), 266–86.

Hartman, C. 1971. Relocation: illusory promises and no relief. *Virginia Law Review* **57**, 745–815.

Hartman, C. 1979. Comment on "neighbourhood revitalization and displacement: a review of the evidence." *Journal of the American Planning Association* **45** (4) (October), 488–94.

Hartman, C. (ed.) 1983. *America's housing crisis – what is to be done?* London: Routledge & Kegan Paul.

Hartman, C., D. Keating and R. LeGates 1981. *Displacement: how to fight it.* Berkeley: National Housing Law Project.

Harvey, D. 1973. *Social justice and the city.* Baltimore: Johns Hopkins University Press.

Harvey, D. 1975a. Class-monopoly rent, finance capital and the urban revolution. In *The manipulated city: perspectives on spatial structure and social issues in urban America,* S. Gale and E. Moore (eds.), 145–67. Chicago: Maaroufa Press.

Harvey, D. 1975b. Class structure in a capitalist society and the theory of residential differentiation. In *Processes in physical and human geography,* R. Peel, M. Chisholm and P. Haggett (eds.), 354–69. London: Heinemann.

Harvey, D. 1978. The urban process under capitalism: a framework for analysis. *International Journal of Urban and Regional Research* **2** (1), 100–31.

Harvey, D. 1982. *The limits to capital.* Oxford: Basil Blackwell.

Harvey, D. and L. Chatterjee 1974. Absolute rent and the structuring of space by governmental and financial institutions. *Antipode* **6** (1), 22–36.

Harvey, J. 1981. *The economics of real property.* London: Macmillan.

Havemann, E. 1962. The triumph of Philadelphia's angry men. *Reader's Digest* (December), 244–52.

Henig, J. 1979. *Gentrification and displacement in urban neighborhoods: a comparative analysis.* Washington, DC: George Washington University.

Henig, J. 1980. Gentrification and displacement within cities: a comparative analysis. *Social Science Quarterly* **61,** 638–52.

Henig, J. 1982. *Gentrification in Adams Morgan: political and commercial consequences of neighborhood change.* George Washington Studies No. 9. Washington, DC: Center for Washington Area Studies, George Washington University.

Holcomb, H. B. 1982. Urban publicity: remaking the image of a city. *Proceedings of the Applied Geography Conferences* **5,** 161–8.

Holcomb, B. 1984. Women in the rebuilt urban environment: the United States experience. *Built Environment* **10** (1), 18–24.

Holcomb, H. B. and R. A. Beauregard 1981. *Revitalizing cities.* Washington, DC: Association of American Geographers.

Home, R. 1982. *Inner city regeneration.* London: E. & F. N. Spon.

House of Commons 1982. *The private rental housing sector.* London: HMSO.

Hu, J. 1979. *A survey study of FNMA's pilot city lending program in St. Louis.* Paper presented at the Midwest Economics Association Annual Conference, Chicago, Illinois, April 5–7.

Isard, W. 1956. *Location and space-economy.* Cambridge, Mass.: MIT Press.

Jackson, P. and S. Smith (eds.) 1981. *Social interaction and ethnic segregation.* London: Academic Press.

Jacobs, J. 1961. *The death and life of great American cities.* New York: Vintage.

Jacobs, J. 1969. *The economy of cities.* New York: Vintage.

Jacobs, J. 1984. *Cities and the wealth of nations*. New York: Random House.

James, F. 1977. *Private reinvestment in older housing and older neighborhoods: recent trends and forces*. Committee on Banking, Housing and Urban Affairs, U.S. Senate, July 7 and 8, Washington, DC.

Joyner, L. 1982. Full scale restoration in Selma. *Southern Living* (September), 82–6.

Kain, J. 1962. The journey to work as a determinant of residential location. *Papers and Proceedings of the Regional Science Association* **9**, 137–60.

Kemble, R. 1980. False Creek: decline and rebirth. *Canadian Architect* **25** (July), 14–35.

Kemeny, J. 1981. *The myth of home ownership: private versus public choices in housing tenure*. London: Routledge & Kegan Paul.

Kemp, P. 1982. Housing landlordism in late nineteenth century Britain. *Environment and Planning A* **14**, 1437–47.

Kendig, H. 1979. *New life for old suburbs: post-war land use and housing in the Australian inner city*. Sydney: George Allen & Unwin.

Kendig, H. 1984. Gentrification in Australia. In *Gentrification, displacement and neighborhood revitalization*, B. London and J. Palen (eds.), 235–53. Albany: State University of New York Press.

Klausner, D. 1983. *Superseding the separation of the spheres: linking production with social consumption and reproduction*. Geography Discussion Papers, New Series, No. 7. Graduate School of Geography, London School of Economics.

Kleniewski, N. 1982. *Neighborhood decline and downtown renewal: the politics of redevelopment in Philadelphia, 1952–1962*. PhD thesis. Temple University.

König, R. 1973. *A la mode: on the social psychology of fashion*. New York: Seabury Press.

Lake, R. W. (ed.) 1983. *Readings in urban analysis: perspectives on urban form and structure*. New Brunswick, NJ: Center for Urban Policy Research, Rutgers University.

Lamarche, F. 1976. Property development and the economic foundations of the urban question. In *Urban sociology: critical essays*, C. G. Pickvance (ed.), 85–118. London: Tavistock.

Lang, M. 1982. *Gentrification amid urban decline*. Cambridge, Mass.: Ballinger.

Laska, S. and D. Spain 1979. Urban policy and planning in the wake of gentrification. *Journal of the American Planning Association* **45** (October), 523–31.

Laska, S. and D. Spain (eds.) 1980. *Back to the city: issues in neighborhood renovation*. Elmsford, NY: Pergamon Press.

Laska, S., J. Seaman and D. McSeveney 1980. *Inner city reinvestment: neighborhood characteristics and spatial patterns over time*. Paper presented at the Southern Sociological Society.

Leach, V. 1979. *Upfiltering and neighborhood change in the Madronna area of Seattle, Washington*. MA thesis. Department of Geography, University of Washington.

Lefebvre, H. 1978. *De l'état*. Vol. 4. *Les contradictions de l'état moderne*. Paris: Union Générale d'Editions.

LeGates, R. and C. Hartman 1981. Displacement. *Clearinghouse Review* **15** (July), 207–49.

LeGates, R. and K. Murphy 1981. Austerity, shelter and social conflict in the United States, *International Journal of Urban and Regional Research* **5** (2), 255–75.

Lenman, B. 1977. *An economic history of modern Scotland, 1660–1976*. Hamden, Conn.: Archon Books.

Lewis, J. P. 1965. *Building cycles and Britain's growth*. London: Macmillan.

Ley, D. 1980. Liberal ideology and the postindustrial city. *Annals of the Association of American Geographers* **70** (June), 238–58.

Ley, D. 1981. Inner city revitalization in Canada: Vancouver case study. *Canadian Geographer* **25** 124–48.

Ley, D. 1982a. Of tribes and idols: a reply to Greenberg and Walker. *Antipode* **14** (1), 38–43.

Ley, D. 1982b. *The politics of landscape in a post-industrial city*. Paper presented to the International Seminar, Centre of Canadian Studies, University of Edinburgh.

Lipton, S. G. 1980. Evidence of central city revival. In *Back to the city*, S. Laska and D. Spain (eds.), 42–60. New York: Pergamon Press.

Litchfield, N. 1961. Relocation: the impact on housing welfare. *Journal of the American Institute of Planners* **27** (August), 199–203.

Logan, W. S. 1980. *Gentrification in inner Melbourne: pattern, process and meaning*. PhD thesis. Department of Geography, Monash University, Melbourne.

Logan, W. S. 1982. Gentrification in inner Melbourne: problems of analysis. *Australian Geographical Studies* **20** (1), 65–95.

Lojkine, J. 1976. Contribution to a marxist theory of capitalist urbanisation. In *Urban sociology, critical essays*, C. Pickvance (ed.), 119–46. London: Tavistock.

London, B. 1980. Gentrification as urban reinvasion: some preliminary definitional and theoretical considerations. In *Back to the city*, S. Laska and D. Spain (eds.), 77–92. New York: Pergamon Press.

Long 1971. The city as reservation. *Public Interest* **25**, 22–38.

Lowe, J. R. 1967. *Cities in a race with time: progress and poverty in America's renewing cities*. New York: Random House.

McCullough, J. G. 1965. Philadelphia's movers and shakers. *Philadelphia Evening and Sunday Bulletin*.

McDowell, L. 1983. Towards an understanding of the gender division of urban space. *Society and Space* **1** (1), 59–72.

McKay, D. and A. Cox 1979. *The politics of urban change*. London: Croom Helm.

McNamara, P. F. 1979. Property development, financial institutions and the state. *Antipode* **11** (3), 56–66.

Marcuse, P. 1979. *Rental housing in the City of New York, Supply and*

Conditions, 1975–1978. New York: Department of Housing Preservation and Development.

Marcuse, P. 1981. *Housing abandonment: does rent control make a difference?* Washington, DC: Conference on Alternative State and Local Policies.

Marcuse, P. 1984. *Report on study of displacement in New York City, with conclusions and recommendations*. New York: Community Service Sector.

Markusen, A. 1980. City spatial structure, women's household work, and national urban policy. *Signs* **5** (Spring), 23–44.

Marx, K. 1967 edn. *Capital* (3 volumes). New York: International Publishers.

Massey, D. 1979. In what sense a regional problem? *Regional Studies* **13**, 233–43.

Massey, D. and R. Meegan 1980. Industrial restructuring versus the cities. In *The inner city, employment and industry*, A. Evans and D. Eversley (eds.), London: Heinemann.

Massey, D. and R. Meegan 1982. *The anatomy of job loss: the how, why and where of employment decline*. London: Methuen.

Merrett, S. 1976. *Gentrification*. Political economy of housing workshop, housing and class in Britain, Conference of Socialist Economists, London.

Merrett, S. 1979. *State housing in Britain*. London: Routledge & Kegan Paul.

Merrett, S. and F. Gray 1982. *Owner occupation in Britain*. London: Routledge & Kegan Paul.

Mills, C. W. 1972. *White collar. The American middle classes*. London: Oxford University Press.

Milner-Holland report 1965. *Report of the committee on housing in Greater London*. London: HMSO, Cmnd 2605.

Mollenkopf, J. H. 1978. The postwar politics of urban development. In *Marxism and the metropolis: new perspectives in urban political economy*, W. K. Tabb and L. Sawers (eds.), 117–52. New York: Oxford University Press.

Mollenkopf, J. H. 1983. *The politics of urban development*. Princeton: Princeton University Press.

Moulaert, F. and P. Salinas (eds.) 1983. *Regional analysis and the new international division of labor*. Boston: Kluwer Nijhoff.

Muller, P. 1976. *The outer city*. Resource Paper 75–2. Association of American Geographers, Washington, DC.

Mullins, P. 1982. The "middle-class" and the inner city. *Journal of Australian Political Economy* **11**, 44–58.

Munski, D. and J. O'Loughlin 1979. Housing rehabilitation in the inner city: a comparison of two neighborhoods in New Orleans. *Economic Geography* **55** (January), 52–70.

Muth, R. 1961. The spatial structure of the housing market. *Papers and Proceedings of the Regional Science Association* **7**, 207–20.

Myers, P. 1978. *Neighborhood conservation and the elderly*. Washington, DC: The Conservation Foundation.

National Urban Coalition 1977. *Displacement city neighborhoods in transition*. Washington, DC: National Urban Coalition.

Nevitt, A. 1966. *Housing, taxation and subsidies: a study of housing in the United Kingdom*. London: Nelson.

Norton, R. 1979. *City life-cycles and American urban policy*. New York: Academic Press.

Noyelle, T. 1983. The implications of industry restructuring for spatial organization in the United States. In *Regional analysis and the new international division of labor*, F. Moulaert and P. Salinas (eds.), 115–33. Boston: Kluwer Nijhoff.

Noyelle, T. and T. Stanback 1981. *The economic transformation of American cities*. New York: Conservation of Human Resources.

Pace, V. S. H. 1976. *Society Hill, Philadelphia: historic preservation and urban renewal in Washington Square East*. PhD thesis. University of Minnesota.

Packard, V. 1963. *The status seekers. An exploration of class behavior in America*. Harmondsworth: Penguin Books.

Palen J. and B. London (eds.) 1984. *Gentrification, displacement and neighbourhood revitalization*. Albany: State University of New York Press.

Paley, B. 1978. *Attitudes to letting in 1976*. London: OPCS Social Survey Division, HMSO.

Pappi, G. W. 1981. The petite bourgeoisie and the new middle class: differentiation or homogenisation of the middle strata in Germany. In *The petite bourgeoisie. Comparative studies of the uneasy stratum*, F. Bechhofer and B. Elliott (eds.), 105–20. London: Macmillan.

Park, R. 1936. Human ecology. *American Journal of Sociology* **42**, 1–15.

Park, W. 1979. *Displacement in San Francisco's Duboce Triangle neighborhood* (unpublished).

Parsons, D. J. 1980. *Rural gentrification: the influence of rural settlement planning policies*. Research Papers in Geography, University of Sussex.

Pattison, T. 1977. *The process of neighborhood upgrading and gentrification*. MA thesis. Department of Urban Studies and Planning, Massachusetts Institute of Technology.

Pawley, M. 1978. *Home ownership*. London: Architectural Press.

Pear, R. 1983. Sharp rise in childbearing found among U.S. women in early 30s. *New York Times* (June 10).

Pear, R. 1984. Rate of poverty found to persist in face of gains. *New York Times* (August 3).

Peet, R. 1975. Inequality and poverty: a marxist–geographic theory. *Annals of the Association of American Geographers* **65** (December), 564–71.

Perin, C. 1977. *Everything in its place: social order and land use in America*. Princeton: Princeton University Press.

Petshek, K. R. 1973. *The challenge of urban reform: policies and programs in Philadelphia*. Philadelphia: Temple University Press.

Philadelphia City Planning Commission 1963. *Plan for center city*. Philadelphia: Pennsylvania.

Phillips, W. M. undated. *The city policy committee*, mimeo. Urban Archives, Paley Library, Temple University.

Phillips, W. M. Interviews. Transcripts of interviews conducted with

Philadelphia's leaders of the 1940s to 1960s. Urban Archives, Paley Library, Temple University.

Pinkney, D. H. 1958. *Napoleon III and the rebuilding of Paris*. Princeton: Princeton University Press.

Porras, S. 1983. *Lower East Side housing market dynamics: policy implications*. MA thesis. Division of Urban Planning, Columbia University.

Power, A. 1972. *A battle lost, Barnsbury, 1972*. Islington, London: Friends House.

Pratt, G. 1982. Class analysis and urban domestic property. A critical examination. *International Journal of Urban and Regional Research* **6** (4), 481–501.

Pratt Institute Center for Metropolitan Action 1983. *Inclusionary zoning and housing trust fund: a proposal*. New York: Pratt Institute.

President's Commission for a National Agenda for the Eighties 1980. *Urban America in the eighties, perspectives and prospects*. Englewood Cliffs, NJ: Prentice-Hall.

Prior, P. F. 1980. *Disinvestment in privately rented housing: the concept of total returns*. (unpublished.)

Progressive Architecture 1980. Homemaking at Harborside, *Progressive Architecture* **61** (August), 78–82.

Rapkin, C. and W. G. Grigsby 1960. *Residential renewal in the downtown core*. Philadelphia: University of Pennsylvania Press.

Reeder, D. A. 1965. *Capital investment in the Victorian suburbs of western London*. PhD thesis. University of Leicester.

Richards, C. and J. Rowe 1977. Restoring a city: who pays the price? *Working Papers* **4** (Winter), 54–61.

Rodger, R. 1976. *Creating a livable inner city community*. Ottawa and Vancouver: Ministry of State for Urban Affairs and False Creek Development Group, City Planning Department.

Rodger, R. 1982. Rents and ground rents: housing and the land market in nineteenth-century Britain. In *The structure of nineteenth-century cities*, J. H. Johnson and C. G. Pooley (eds.), 39–74. London: Croom Helm.

Rose, D. 1984. Rethinking gentrification: beyond the uneven development of marxist urban theory. *Society and Space* **2** (1), 47–74.

Rosenberg, H. 1977. *Areas of relocation of displaced Lower Garden District and Irish Channel residents*. MA thesis. Urban Studies Institute, University of New Orleans.

Roseth, J. 1969. *The revival of an old residential area*. PhD thesis. Faculty of Architecture, University of Sydney.

Rouse, J. W. 1978. The lure of an urban life style. In *Conservation and new economic realities: some views of the future*. Washington, DC: The Conservation Foundation.

Sanders, H. T. 1980. Urban renewal and the revitalized city: a reconsideration of recent history. In *Urban revitalization*, D. B. Rosenthal (ed.), 103–126. *Urban Affairs Annual Reviews*, Vol. 18. Beverly Hills: Sage Publications.

Sands, S. 1979. *Population change due to housing renovation in St. Paul's Ramsey Hill area.* MA thesis. University of Minnesota.

Saunders, P. 1981. *Social theory and the urban question.* London: Hutchinson.

Saunders, P. 1982. *Beyond housing classes: the sociological significance of private property rights in means of consumption.* Urban and Regional Studies Working Paper No. 33, University of Sussex.

Sayer, A. 1982. Explanation in economic geography: abstraction versus generalization. *Progress in Human Geography* **6** (March), 68–88.

Scattergood, R. 1956. *The city policy committee: a Philadelphia story of a civic organization which "made good."* Mimeo.

Schaffer, R. and N. Smith 1984. *The gentrification of Harlem.* Paper presented at the annual conference of the American Association for the Advancement of Science, May 27.

Schill, M. H. and R. P. Nathan 1983. *Revitalizing America's cities: neighborhood reinvestment and displacement.* Albany: State University of New York Press.

Seifel, E. 1979. *Displacement: the negative environmental impact of urban renewal in the south end of Boston.* MA thesis. Department of Urban Studies and Planning, Massachusetts Institute of Technology.

Sieverding, H. 1979. *Displacement in reinvestment neighborhoods.* Senior Project, Department of Urban Planning, University of Cincinnati.

Smith, D. 1982. *Conflict and compromise: class formation in English society, 1830–1914.* London: Routledge & Kegan Paul.

Smith, N. 1979a. Toward a theory of gentrification: a back to the city movement by capital not people. *Journal of the American Planning Association* **45** (4) (October), 538–48.

Smith, N. 1979b. Gentrification and capital: theory, practice and ideology in Society Hill. *Antipode* **11** (3), 24–35.

Smith, N. 1982. Gentrification and uneven development. *Economic Geography* **58** (2) (April), 139–155.

Smith, N. 1984. *Uneven development.* Oxford: Basil Blackwell.

Smith, N. 1985. Deindustrialization and regionalization: class alliance and class struggle. *Journal of the Regional Science Association* **55**.

Smith, N. and M. LeFaivre 1984. A class analysis of gentrification. In *Gentrification, displacement and neighborhood revitalization*, J. Palen and B. London (eds.), Albany, NY: State University of New York Press.

Smith, R. 1976. Collingwood, Wren leftovers and political change: aspects of local level politics in the 1970s. *Labour History* **18**, 42–57.

Solomon, A. P. and K. D. Vandell 1982. Alternative perspectives on neighborhood decline. *Journal of the American Planning Association* **48** (Winter), 81–98.

Spain, D. 1980. Indicators of urban revitalization: racial and socioeconomic changes in central-city housing. In *Back to the city*, S. Laska and D. Spain (eds.), New York: Pergamon Press.

Spain, D. 1981. A gentrification scorecard. *American Demographics* **3**, 14–19.

Stanback, T. M. Jr. and T. Noyelle 1982. *Cities in transition: changing job structures in Atlanta, Denver, Buffalo, Phoenix, Columbus, Ohio, Nashville and Charlotte.* Totowa, NJ: Rowman and Allanheld.

Stedman Jones, G. 1971. *Outcast London. A study in the relationship between classes.* Oxford: Clarendon Press.

Stegman, M. 1982. *The dynamics of rental housing in New York City.* Piscataway, NJ: Center for Urban Policy Research, Rutgers University.

Stephen, A. 1984. The town hall follies. *Sunday Times* (May 13), 33, 34.

Sternlieb, G. 1971. The city as sandbox. *Public Interest* **25**, 14–21.

Sternlieb, G. and K. Ford 1979. The future of the return-to-the-city movement. In *Revitalizing cities*, H. Bryce (ed.), 77–104. Lexington, Mass.: D. C. Heath.

Sternlieb, G. and J. W. Hughes 1976. *Post industrial America: metropolitan decline and inter-regional job shifts.* New Brunswick: Center for Urban Policy Research, Rutgers University.

Sternlieb, G. and J. W. Hughes 1983. The uncertain future of the central city. *Urban Affairs Quarterly* **18** (4), 455–72.

Stetson, D. 1983. U.S. official sees New York City vulnerable as economy picks up. *New York Times* (May 10), B3.

Stevens, E. 1982. Baltimore renovates, rebuilds and revitalizes. *Art News* **81** (8), 94–7.

Stillwell, F. 1980. *Economic crisis, cities and regions.* Syndey: Pergamon Press.

Stone, M. E. 1978. Housing mortgage lending and the contradictions of capitalism. In *Marxism and the metropolis: new perspectives in urban political economy*, W. Tabb and L. Sawers (eds.), 179–207. New York: Oxford University Press.

Stratton, J. 1977. *Pioneering in the urban wilderness.* New York: Urizen Books.

Sumka, H. 1979. Neighborhood revitalization and displacement: a review of the evidence. *Journal of the American Planning Association* **45** (4) (October), 480–7.

Swierenga, R. P. 1968. *Pioneers and profits: land speculation on the Iowa frontier.* Ames, Iowa: Iowa State University Press.

Szelenyi, I. 1981. Structural changes of and alternatives to capitalist development in the contemporary urban and regional system. *International Journal of Urban and Regional Research* **5** (1), 1–14.

Taeuber, K. 1982. *Research issues concerning trends in residential segregation.* CDE Working Paper, 83–93. Madison: Center for Demography and Ecology, University of Wisconsin.

TEAM 1968. *TEAM policy adopted September 7, 1967 by vote of general membership.* Mimeo.

Thompson, F. M. L. 1974. *Hampstead: building a borough, 1650–1964.* Leicester: Leicester University Press.

Thrift, N. 1983. On the determination of social action in space and time. *Society and Space* **1** (1), 23–58.

Thrift, N. and P. Williams, in preparation. *Class and space.* London: Routledge & Kegan Paul.

Turner, F. J. 1958 edn. *The frontier in American history.* New York: Holt, Rinehart & Winston.

University of Amsterdam 1967. *Urban core and inner city. Proceedings of the International Study Week.* Amsterdam: E. J. Brill.

US Bureau of the Census 1970. *Census of housing.* Series HS(1). Washington, DC: Government Printing Office.

US Bureau of the Census 1981. *Statistical abstract of the United States: 1981* (102nd edition). Washington, DC: Government Printing Office.

US Bureau of the Census 1982. *Statistical abstract of the United States: 1982–83* (103rd edition). Washington, DC: Government Printing Office.

US Department of Housing and Urban Development 1979. *Displacement report.* Washington, DC: Government Printing Office.

US Department of Housing and Urban Development 1980. *The conversion of rental housing to condominiums and co-operatives. A national study of scope, causes and impacts.* Washington, DC: Government Printing Office.

US Department of Housing and Urban Development 1981. *Residential displacement: an update – report to Congress.* Washington, DC: Government Printing Office.

US House of Representatives, Subcommittee of the City 1977. *How cities can grow old gracefully.* Washington, DC: Government Printing Office.

Urry, J. 1981. *The anatomy of capitalist societies.* London: Macmillan.

Vancouver Planning Commission 1980. *Goals for Vancouver.* Vancouver: British Columbia.

Vancouver Planning Department 1970. *Report on submission to the False Creek brochure.* Vancouver: British Columbia.

Van Gelder, L. 1981. The New World discovers Columbus. *Village Voice* (September), 23–9.

Van Weesep, J. 1981a. Condomania: the proliferation and impact of condominiums in the USA. *Geografische en Plannologische Notities 6.* Amsterdam: Vrije Universiteit.

Van Weesep, J. 1981b. *The sponsors of condominiums in large U.S. cities.* Occasional Paper, Center for Metropolitan Planning and Research. Baltimore: Johns Hopkins University.

Veblen, T. 1953 edn. *The theory of the leisure class. An economic study of institutions.* New York: Mentor.

Vischer, Skaburskis, Planners 1980. *False Creek area 6 phase 1: post-occupancy evaluation.* Vancouver: Vischer, Skaburskis.

Wald, M. 1984. Back offices disperse from downtowns. *New York Times* (May 13).

Walker, P. (ed.) 1979. *Between labor and capital: the professional–managerial class.* Boston: South End Press.

Walker, R. A. 1978. The transformation of urban structure in the nineteenth century and the beginnings of suburbanization. In *Urbanization and conflict in market societies,* K. R. Cox (ed.), 165–211. London: Methuen.

Walker, R. A. 1981. A theory of suburbanization: capitalism and the construction of urban space in the United States. In *Urbanization and urban planning in capitalist society,* M. Dear and A. J. Scott (eds.), 383–429. London: Methuen.

Walker, R. and D. Greenberg 1982a. Post-industrialism and political reform: a critique. *Antipode* **14** (1), 17–32.

Walker, R. and D. Greenberg 1982b. A guide to the Ley reader of marxist criticism. *Antipode* **14** (1), 38–43.

Wallace, D. A. 1960. Renaissancemanship. *Journal of the American Institute of Planners* **26** (August), 157–76.

Wallerstein, I. 1974. *The modern world-system I. Capitalist agriculture and the origins of the European world economy in the sixteenth century*. New York: Academic Press.

Warner, S. B. 1972. *The urban wilderness: a history of the American city*. New York: Harper & Row.

Weber, M. 1978 ed. *Economy and society: an outline of interpretive sociology*. Berkeley: University of California Press.

Weiler, C. 1974. *Philadelphia: neighborhood, authority, and the urban crisis*. New York: Praeger.

Weiler, C. 1978. *Reinvestment displacement: HUD's role in a new housing issue*. Washington, DC: Government Printing Office.

Western, J. 1981. *Outcast Cape Town*. London: George Allen & Unwin.

Williams, M. 1982. The new Raj: the gentrifiers and the natives. *New Society* (January 14), 47–50.

Williams, P. 1976. The role of institutions in the inner London housing market: the case of Islington. *Transactions of the Institute of British Geographers* N.S. **1**, 72–82.

Williams, P. 1978. Building societies and the inner city. *Transactions of the Institute of British Geographers* N.S. **3**, 23–34.

Williams, P. 1984a. Economic processes and urban change: an analysis of contemporary patterns of residential restructuring. *Australian Geographical Studies* **22** (1), 39–57.

Williams, P. 1984b. Gentrification in Britain and Europe. In *Gentrification, displacement and neighborhood revitalization*, J. Palen and B. London (eds.), 205–34. Albany, NY: State University of New York Press.

Williams, R. 1977. *Marxism and literature*. New York: Oxford University Press.

Wolfe, J., G. Drover and I. Skelton 1980. Inner city real estate activity in Montreal: institutional characteristics of decline. *Canadian Geographer* **24**, 348–67.

Wright, E. O. 1979. *Class, crisis and the state*. London: New Left Books.

Wright, L. and P. Collymore (eds.) 1980. Vancouver. *Architectural Review* **167**, 321–4.

Zietz, E. 1979. *Private urban renewal: a different residential trend*. Lexington, Mass.: Lexington Books.

Zukin, S. 1982a. Loft living as "historic compromise" in the urban core: the New York experience. *International Journal of Urban and Regional Research* **6** (2), 256–67.

Zukin, S. 1982b. *Loft living: culture and capital in urban change*. Baltimore: Johns Hopkins University Press.

Author Index

Subject Index

247

uneven development
HD 82 . SSB125 1991

david ley [post-ind. city]

zukin

FLL